9/29/99
Ingram
50
Insy

Decade of Transition

*Eisenhower, Kennedy, and the Origins of
the American-Israeli Alliance*

ABRAHAM BEN-ZVI

COLUMBIA UNIVERSITY PRESS / NEW YORK

Columbia University Press
Publishers Since 1893
New York   Chichester, West Sussex
Copyright © 1998 Abraham Ben-Zvi

Library of Congress Cataloging-in-Publication Data
Ben-Zvi, Abraham.
    Decade of transition : Eisenhower, Kennedy, and the origins of the
American-Israeli alliance / Abraham Ben-Zvi.
        p.   cm.
    Includes bibliographical references (p. 193) and index.
    ISBN 0–231–11262–9 (acid-free paper). — ISBN 0–231–11263–7 (pbk.
: acid-free paper)
    1. United States—Foreign relations—Israel. 2. Israel—Foreign
relations—United States. 3. United States—Foreign
relations—1953–1961. 4. United States—Foreign
relations—1961–1963. 5. Kennedy, John F. (John Fitzgerald),
1917–1963. 6. Eisenhower, Dweight D. (Dwight David), 1890–1969.
I. Title.
E183.8.I7B45   1998
327.7305694—dc21   98–5232
                                                                        CIP

*This book is dedicated to the memory of
Ruth (Trude) Rosenbaum, my wife's cherished and
beloved mother, and a model of gracefulness, affection and
loving care, who witnessed it all.*

The Jaffee Center for Strategic Studies (JCSS)

The Center for Strategic Studies was established at Tel Aviv University at the end of 1977. In 1983 it was named the Jaffee Center for Strategic Studies in honor of Mr. and Mrs. Mel Jaffee. The objective of the Center is to contribute to the expansion of knowledge on strategic subjects and to promote public understanding of and pluralistic thought on matters of national and international security.

The Center relates to the concept of strategy in its broadest meaning, namely, the complex of processes involved in the identification, mobilization, and application of resources in peace and war, in order to solidify and strengthen national and international security.

Jaffee Center for Strategic Studies
TEL AVIV UNIVERSITY

Contents

Preface and Acknowledgments

In the process of researching the book: *The United States and Israel: The Limits of the Special Relationship*, which attempted to elucidate the role of coercive means and measures within the American-Israel framework, I was struck by the gap between the widespread perception of the Eisenhower Administration as invariably and irrevocably hostile to Israel, and the considerably more nuanced and dynamic set of attitudes and approaches evident in the numerous documents I reviewed. Since the book dealt with several crisis episodes, in which the United States exerted pressure upon Israel between 1953 and 1993, this recognition remained largely peripheral in that delimited and confined context. After all, the recurrent behavioral pattern of the Eisenhower Presidency in the two cases explored in the book: the Water Crisis of 1953, and the Suez Crisis of 1956–1957 was largely predicated upon the premises of utmost firmness and irreconcilability. My conviction that if one is to proceed beyond the narrow and constrained parameters of these crisis episodes he is bound to discover a considerably broader spectrum of American strategies and tactics *vis-à-vis* Israel, prompted me to return to the Eisenhower era but this time to review the entire Eisenhower White House years in terms of the basic policies pursued by his administration toward Israel. Years of extensive research in the Seeley G. Mudd Manuscript Library at Princeton University, the Dwight D. Eisenhower Library in Abilene, and the Israel State Archives, enabled me to identify the multifaceted and divergent layers incorporated into the administration's approach toward Israel. Combined with my work at the John F. Kennedy Presidential Library in Boston and my review of the recently published volumes (nos. 17 and 18) of the series *Foreign Relations of the United States, 1961–1963,* and of volume 8 of the series: *Documents on the Foreign Policy of Israel,* this wealth of documentary material provided the historical infrastructure for my interpretation of the Eisenhower era as the incubation period in which the groundwork of the American-Israeli alliance was laid, with the Kennedy

Administration consolidating and accelerating processes the Eisenhower foreign policy elite had set in motion.

The book covers the period between the inauguration of the Eisenhower Administration and the landmark decision of the Kennedy Administration, in August 1962, to sell to Israel the Hawk antiaircraft missile. However, certain developments that took place in 1963 and that were inextricably related to earlier policies and actions are also addressed.

I wish to thank most sincerely Yair Evron, Azar Gat, Moshe Grundman, Mark Heller, Efraim Kam, Aharon Klieman, Joseph Kostiner, Anat Kurz, Emily Landau, Ariel Levite, Nanette Loebenberg, Zeev Maoz, Gil Merom, Itamar Rabinovich, Dan Schueftan, Yossi Shain, Arie Shalev, Zaki Shalom, Yiftah Shapir, Ariel Sobelman, Nahman Tal, and all the research assistants in the Jaffee Center for Strategic Studies at Tel-Aviv University for their thoughtful suggestions on various aspects of this work. Part of the manuscript was completed while I was the Visiting Goldman Professor of Government at Georgetown University in Washington, D.C., in the academic year 1995–1996. The outline of the work and some of its findings were discussed in my Government 370 course: "American-Israeli Relations." All my students in this course, and particularly Natasha Basley, Pierre Baussard and Pierre Heilbron, made stimulating and insightful comments on several theoretical components of the project.

I am also indebted to Roslyn Langbart and Sylvia Weinberg for their dedicated and thoroughly professional work on all the technical aspects of the manuscript, and to Kate Wittenberg, Editor-in-Chief of Columbia University press, for combining, once again, the highest professional standards with a very thoughtful and encouraging attitude. I also wish to thank Leslie Bialler for the most careful and professional manner in which he edited my manuscript. The staff of the Bender-Moss Library at Tel-Aviv University, the Dwight D. Eisenhower Library in Abilene, the John F. Kennedy Presidential Library in Boston, and the Israeli State Archives in Jerusalem—all provided valuable technical and bibliographical assistance.

ABRAHAM BEN-ZVI
January 1998

Decade of Transition

I

A Theoretical Framework and Objectives

In recent years, various facets of American-Israeli relations have increasingly become the subject of a heated debate among scholars.[1] Notwithstanding the irreconcilable differences between some of the overall interpretations, as well as the specific lines of argumentation advanced in the context of certain delimited case studies, most works have remained fully and irrevocably committed to a fixed set of axioms and preconceptions, which constitute a prism through which all major developments within the American-Israeli dyad were continuously appraised and evaluated. In the context of the period 1953–1962, which will be the focus of the following analysis, two axioms have been particularly widespread and pervasive. The first depicts the entire Eisenhower era as one monolithic and homogeneous period, with the administration irreversibly committed to an immutable cluster of strategic beliefs, which portrayed Israel as a strategic liability and as a major obstacle "to improving [the] environment [of the] United States-Arab relations."[2] The second axiom, inextricably linked to the first and closely patterned on its logic and basic premises, maintains that Washington's apparent tilt toward Israel during the early 1960s was the direct outcome of John F. Kennedy's victory in the presidential elections of November 1960. As an integral part of the ethnic Democratic coalition forged by President Franklin Delano Roosevelt during the early 1930s, the American Jewish community fully shared many of President Kennedy's domestic priorities and concerns, and its leadership—in sharp contrast to the Eisenhower era—gained access to the White House and enjoyed a relatively broad margin of maneuverability in seeking to reshape and redirect American policy toward Israel. In this respect, Candidate Kennedy's remarks of August 8, 1960 (made in the course of his meeting with thirty Jewish leaders in New York), which were permeated with sympathy and empathy toward Israel, were the prelude to and the precipitant of the reaffirmation of the traditional, deeply rooted bonds of friendship and solidarity between the Democratic party and its leadership and broad segments of the Jewish community.[3]

According to this domestically oriented line of argumentation (which underscores not only that about 80 percent of the Jewish vote was for Kennedy, but also the significance of the Jewish vote in such critical states as Illinois and New York), this process of rapprochement was to culminate two years later when the President succumbed to the pressures exerted by the "powerful Jewish lobby" and thus decided, in August 1962, to cross the Rubicon and sell Israel Hawk antiaircraft, short-range missiles.

The recent declassification of a wealth of documentary material in the Dwight D. Eisenhower Library at Abilene, the Seeley G. Mudd Manuscript Library at Princeton University, and the John F. Kennedy Presidential Library at Boston has provided a new springboard for challenging these two axioms, and thus for replacing some of the crude dichotomies and simplistic generalizations that still abound in the literature, with a more nuanced and differentiated picture of American-Israeli relations as they actually unfolded between 1953 and 1962.

Although several events of great magnitude took place on the scene of American-Israeli relations during this decade, among them the Suez Crisis, which was initiated by Israel on October 29, 1956, or the American military intervention in Lebanon in July 1958, and became the focus of extensive research,[4] the period as a whole received little attention by scholars.[5] By virtue of its relative tranquillity, it was downgraded and outweighed by periods that appeared either permeated with tension and fraught with conflict (such as the period between the Six-Day War of June 1967 and the Yom Kippur War of 1973) or rich with diplomatic activity and pregnant with prospects of regional accommodation (such as the period between the Geneva Peace Conference of December 1973 and the Egyptian-Israeli Peace Treaty of March 1979). Largely overlooked in the existing literature was the possibility that, for all its apparent relative uneventfulness, the period 1953–1962 (and particularly the second term of the Eisenhower Administration), could still be viewed as a period of incubation—one in which, as early as 1958, the seeds of change in the very essence and intrinsic nature of American-Israeli relations had not only been planted, but also had begun to bear fruit.

Against this backdrop, the major objective of the following examination is to fill the vacuum while approaching the process by which the American-Israeli alliance was forged and consolidated as incremental and continuous. Thus, while President Kennedy's decision—of August 1962—to provide Israel with sophisticated (albeit purely defensive) weapons systems may at first glance appear fundamentally incompatible with some of the basic tenets of the traditional American Middle East posture (and particularly with the longstanding American refusal to become an arms supplier to Israel) and thus, as a drastic and sudden about-face in American strategic thinking and behavior in the region, the following reconstruction of the Eisenhower era in the Middle East as it was shaped, delineated, and progressively modified will seek to demonstrate, instead, that the decision to sell Israel the Hawk missiles constituted the culmination and formalization of an entire cluster of cognitive (and to a lesser extent, operational) processes. These processes had been ongoing since the very inception of President Eisenhower's second term in the White House, and were thus not a sharp deviation from the proclivities, preferences, and policies that characterized the latter years of the Eisenhower Administration. In other words, in approaching Israel, President Kennedy pursued a posture that was closely and inextricably patterned on at least some of the premises and tenets that had begun to surface during the years 1957–1960 (and particularly in the wake of the Iraqi revolution and the American military intervention in Lebanon in July 1958).

And while these premises were amplified, expanded, and incorporated into a broader complex of strategic understandings and agreements in the course of the Kennedy Presidency, their core had been established earlier, as the gap between some of President Eisenhower's initial beliefs

and policies and the actual dynamics of a recalcitrant and volatile regional environment became increasingly evident to the President during
his second term in office.

It is true that this emerging congruity did not entail a comprehensive
ideological or strategic convergence between Washington and Jerusalem,
nor were these premises instantly translated into a coherent body of
strategic agreements and understandings. Tentative and partial as they
were, these early perceptions of Israel as a strategic asset, which had surfaced in an explicit and clear form for the first time in the course of the
Lebanese and Jordanian crises of 1958, laid the conceptual foundation
and groundwork for a growing consensus within the American-Israeli
framework, and thus paved the way toward more assertive, explicit, and
formal patterns of collaboration.[6] Thus, unlike the pervasive and widespread propensity to explain this convergence, which became increasingly salient during the Kennedy era, exclusively in terms of the pressures exerted upon the President by the forces and organizations which
comprised—in the aggregate—the "Israeli lobby" in Washington,[7] the
following review of the decade 1953–1962 will focus on the perceived dynamics of the strategic regional environment as the central independent
variable, which profoundly affected American perceptions of and attitudes toward Israel during the years that preceded John F. Kennedy's victory in the presidential elections of 1960. It is precisely during this period
that the influence of the "Israeli lobby" upon the shaping of American
policy in the Middle East reached its nadir. Confronted with an administration that, from its very inception, was determined to ignore "the pressure exercised by Jewish groups,"[8] the forces constituting this lobby were
largely reduced to impotence. The changes that did take place during the
Eisenhower Presidency in the American approach toward Israel were,
therefore, derived exclusively from shifting strategic visions of the region
and did not reflect the influence of domestic factors and constraints.

In order to define more systematically the specific components which
are continuously integrated into these strategic visions and domestic factors, a distinction should be made between the "American national interest" paradigm (which comprises the traditional complex of geostrategic interests and objectives, which the architects of American diplomacy
continuously sought to promote in the Middle East during the decade
1953–1962), and the "special relationship" paradigm (which comprises
a broad cluster of predispositions, sentiments and attitudes toward Israel
in American public opinion, which are permeated with sympathy, support and affection).[9]

A more detailed juxtaposition of the national interest paradigm and the special relationship orientation as they were initially shaped and delineated in the context of American policy in the Middle East, portrays a picture of an irreconcilable gap in terms of their respective premises and derivative policy recommendations. The national interest orientation, which is closely patterned on a pure and unmitigated structural-realist view of the international environment, concerns a cluster of clearly defined vital security interests that American policymakers consistently believed the nation needed to maintain and defend in the region. The traditional realist objectives derived from these interests and strategic preferences included the desire to mitigate (or, at the very least, stabilize) the Arab-Israeli conflict; the wish to maintain political and economic access to Arab oil; and the quest to increase American influence in the area at the expense of the Soviet Union (but without risking a direct superpower confrontation).[10]

While these basic objectives, which American diplomacy sought to promote during the decade under consideration, have remained essentially unchanged, the specific policies delineated and shaped in accordance with their logic and basic premises have undergone significant modifications and revisions in view of the dynamics of the regional environment and the lessons drawn by American policymakers as a result of their initial inability to accomplish at least some of their core objectives.

Predicated upon a complex of quintessential constructivist, inner-directed beliefs and attitudes, the elements that merge into the special relationship paradigm reflect "a widespread fund of goodwill toward Israel [in American public opinion] that is not restricted to the Jewish community," and an equally strong and persistent commitment to Israel's continued national existence, integrity, and security. In the words of William Quandt:

> The bond between the United States and Israel is unquestionably strengthened because of the presumed congruence of values between the two nations. Americans can identify with Israel's national style—the commitment to western-style democracy, the ideals of individualism and freedom—in a way that has no parallel on the Arab side. Neither the ideal of well-ordered Muslim community nor that of a modernizing autocracy evokes much sympathy among Americans. Consequently, a predisposition no doubt exists in American political culture that works to the advantage of the Israelis.[11]

Indeed, comprising a cluster of broadly based attitudes that underscore the affinity and similarity between the two states in terms of their pioneering spirit, heterogeneous social composition, and commitment to democratic values and principles, this paradigm emerged as a legitimate and pervasive concept on the American domestic scene as soon as Israel was established in 1948 and remained essentially intact for more than three decades.[12] Its core was implicit in President Truman's decision (made despite the strong opposition of Secretary of State George Marshall, Undersecretary of State Robert Lovett, and the Head of the Near East Division in the Department of State, Loy Henderson) that the United States would be the first country to recognize Israel.[13]

There can be no doubt that Truman's actions were patterned on moral, cultural, and religious premises (such as the perception of Israel as fulfilling the biblical prophecy that the Jews would return to the promised land, which is particularly pervasive among Evangelicals and Christian Fundamentalists) rather than on strictly geostrategic, national security considerations. Further reinforced by Truman's perception of American public opinion, it was the logic of the special relationship paradigm that momentarily overshadowed and outweighed, in May 1948, the complex of calculations linked to a nonsentimental vision of the world and the Middle East.

Notwithstanding the pervasiveness and legitimacy of the images incorporated into the special relationship paradigm, and notwithstanding the broadly based vision of Israel as a "small, courageous and democratic nation which is trying to preserve its independence,"[14] and to promote objectives (such as the absorption of massive waves of immigration), which are seen as corresponding to "the American spirit"), the following analysis will attempt to demonstrate that, during the period under review, all major decisions pertaining to Israel taken by both the Eisenhower and the Kennedy Administrations were almost exclusively patterned on strategic, geopolitical considerations, rather than on the cluster of domestic attitudes, proclivities, and preferences integrated into the special relationship paradigm. In other words, the gradual shift of American policy from an initial vision of Israel as a strategic liability and an impediment to Washington's broad regional containment designs to one of Israel as a strategic asset and a power capable of assisting the U.S. in an effort to stop Soviet penetration and encroachment, reflected the learning experience of both presidents (and particularly of President Eisenhower) in view of the apparent inadequacy of their preliminary strategic posture, and did not originate in the pressures exerted by the proponents of the special relationship paradigm. Thus, while the groups and organizations associated with this orientation did attempt to soften certain punitive measures adopted by the Eisenhower Administration (which became particularly evident during the 1956 Suez Crisis), or to accelerate the process of growing collaboration between the U.S. and Israel during the second term of the Eisenhower Presidency as well as during the Kennedy era, their success was, on the whole, limited; and in none of these instances did they manage to achieve more than tactical—mostly marginal—accomplishments. And although considerations premised upon the special relationship paradigm occasionally reinforced considerations patterned on the national interest orientation, they never provided an alternative or substitute to Washington's perceptions of the regional strategic landscape, which were translated into compatible, derivative policies and courses of action. Repeatedly, whenever the two paradigms diverged, it was the national interest paradigm that downgraded and outweighed the special relationship orientation by dictating behavior, which reflected the official visions of the threats and opportunities inherent in the strategic circumstances while remaining largely oblivious to the proclivities, sentiments, and desires of the advocates and representatives of the special relationship paradigm.

In this context, the major distinction which should be drawn in terms of American strategic views of the regional environment is between the first and second terms of the Eisenhower Presidency rather than between the Eisenhower and the Kennedy periods. And while President Kennedy further expanded and accelerated an overall process that had been set in motion during the latter Eisenhower years, some of these initial policies—particularly those concerning Egypt—in no small measure constituted a return to the first Eisenhower period. In other words, the phased and gradual change in the American strategic perception of Israel unfolded in an era during which the Jewish community in the United States—the backbone of the special relationship paradigm—had not yet appeared on the national scene as a viable and well-organized political element and, as such, could not play any significant role in reorienting the American posture toward Israel. Thus, "although Jewish leaders would make the rounds of the State Department and at times would be received by the President [Eisenhower], they were listened to politely but failed to influence the decision makers." . . . The policy was pursued with consistency from the President down to the lower echelons of the State Department, part of a highly formal system.[15]

For all their legitimacy and broad public appeal, the emotional and sentimental components of the special relationship paradigm could not in themselves provide, during the entire Eisenhower period, a substitute for the more tangible and concrete considerations of national security.

In order to better elucidate the actual dynamics and fluctuations in American-Israeli relations as they unfolded during the period 1953–1962, we shall employ (and refine) several notions from crisis and bargaining theory to show that even in the absence of the military option, certain recurrent types of international interactions, which are patterned on the basic premises of crisis theory, can be identified in an essentially cooperative or consensual context.[16] These concepts, which will be largely applied to the period 1953–1956 as a distinct category of non-violent, intramural crisis determinants,[17] will be juxtaposed with a second set of concepts, patterned on some, albeit not all, of the premises of bargaining theory. These concepts will be applied to the more benign context of the period 1957–1962. More specifically, the main notions and concepts which will serve as our principal analytical tools (although in a revised form that takes into account the specific nature of the American-Israeli framework) are immediate and long-term (or basic) deterrence and coercive diplomacy (between 1953 and 1956), as juxtaposed with the "bargaining strategy" (of the cross-issue linkage type), and the "strategy of reciprocity," which is equivalent to the "tit-for-tat" strategy (between 1957 and 1962).[18]

In seeking to integrate into the analysis these concepts and notions from the fields of bargaining and crisis theory, it is assumed that if one proceeds beyond the standard use of the term crisis, which implies that "whatever is occurring might result in the outbreak of war,"[19] he is bound to discover a wide complex of situations permeated with tension, confusion, and misunderstanding, even though they do not meet the definitional criterion of high probability of involvement in military actions.

Unlike the strategy of deterrence, which seeks to convince an opponent not to initiate any harmful action, coercion deals with past or present action. Deterrence constitutes an effort to dissuade an adversary, through the use of threats, whether implicit or explicit, stated or demonstrated, from doing something it has not yet started to do by demonstrating that the costs of doing so will exceed the anticipated gain. This strategy is contemplated if a state feels that another state is dissatisfied with the existing status quo and is disposed to pursue its revisionist activity in a manner harmful to the focal actor. It therefore becomes appealing when decisionmakers feel that, unless they clearly commit themselves to the preservation of the status quo, there is a high probability that the opponent will alter it in a manner that runs contrary to the national interest.[20]

Whereas deterrence is designed to prevent an opponent from taking some action before it begins, coercion attempts either to persuade the adversary to stop something it is already doing that is distasteful or harmful, or to undo what it has already accomplished. On both occasions, it is "employed to deal with the efforts of an adversary to change a status quo situation in his own favor."[21] The more ambitious the demand on the opponent, the more difficult the task of coercive diplomacy becomes. In other words, although the purpose of both deterrence and coercion is "to establish influence on the intentions and behavior of an actor by threatening him with, or placing him under, some form of punishment,"[22] deterrence can be thought of as an essentially defensive strategy, while coercive diplomacy can be either defensive or offensive in nature. Furthermore, whereas defensive coercion is intended to induce the rival to halt an undesired action, offensive coercion (which sometimes takes the form of a blackmail strategy), is designed to compel a victim "to give up something of value without putting up resistance."[23]

In examining the American efforts, during the years 1953–1956, to predicate its posture toward Israel upon the premises of deterrence and coercion, two distinctive types of deterrence should be identified. The first, "immediate deterrence," refers to a situation in which the threat of an imminent specific action intended to disrupt the status quo is perceived, leading the defender of the status quo to issue threats designed to dissuade the potential challenger from undertaking this action.[24] The second type, "long-term (or basic) deterrence," which is patterned on the notion of "general deterrence," denotes a continuous effort by the defender of the status quo to deter the potential challenger from carrying out a broad cluster of moves and actions.[25] While the first variant deals with short-term, well-defined and specific crisis situations, the second variant refers to a multifaceted, comprehensive strategy implemented systematically over a long period of time in an effort to prevent the potential challenger from resorting to action on a broad spectrum of contingencies and options. For all these differences, both types are predicated upon the logic of "extended deterrence," which seeks to dissuade the challenger from committing an undesired action against a third party.[26]

While focusing on the U.S. as the power which exerted pressure upon Israel by resorting to the strategies of deterrence and coercion, attention should also be given to the exercise—by Israel—of counter extended deterrence vis-à-vis the Eisenhower Administration. This strategy of counter-deterrence consisted of reprisals and retaliatory raids against Egypt and Jordan during the period 1953–1956. Intended to signal defiance and recalcitrance in the face of continued American pressure (long-term deterrence), this posture culminated—in October 1956—in the Israeli decision to launch a preventive strike against Egypt in the Sinai Peninsula.[27]

Regardless of its particular nature, successful coercive (or deterrence) diplomacy requires that the coercing (or deterring) power convince the adversary that it has both the will and the capacity "to inflict considerable damage upon something which [it] values more than the subject of the dispute."[28] Indeed, in order to effectively pursue a posture predicated upon the premises of deterrence and coercion, the initiator of these strategies must convince the antagonist of the high cost of persisting in its behavior.[29] To paraphrase Jervis, the success of the deterrence effort depends largely on the existence, in the mind of the target state, of an asymmetrical "balance of intrinsic interests" favoring the initiator of the strategy.[30] Such an asymmetry in the inherent value that each actor places on the issue at stake constitutes a major prerequisite for the establishment of a favorable "balance of resolve," which reflects the readiness of both sides to absorb costs and undergo hardship in defense of their interests. This, in turn, almost invariably guarantees that the deterring side will ultimately prevail in the encounter.[31]

In an attempt to shed light on the actual determinants of power within the American-Israeli framework, an auxiliary set of preconditions for the effective pursuit of coercive diplomacy should be incorporated into the analysis. Central among these is the need to establish a broad infrastructure of political support (both at home and in the "target state") for the coercive measures implemented. Thus, in the same way that the likelihood of successful coercion is greater "if one side is more strongly motivated by what is at stake than its opponent," so it is essential for the coercing side to be backed by sufficient domestic (as well as external) support that would provide the necessary legitimacy for the course adopted. In the absence of "sufficient enthusiasm" among significant sectors of the population in the initiating party, the initiator of coercion may feel constrained to actually pursue "only minimal objectives."[32]

In other words, coercive diplomacy is never implemented in a political and social vacuum and must be continuously preoccupied not only with the need for consolidating favorable balances of interest and resolve, but also—and perhaps even more importantly—with the task of creating a favorable "balance of legitimacy," namely, of a wide and pervasive complex of beliefs that envisages the use of coercive measures as justified and necessary.[33]

This divergent delineation of the intrinsic interests of both parties, which helps shape and determine the balance of resolve (and which affects the balance of legitimacy in less direct and tangible ways), becomes fully manifest once the initiator of deterrence or coercive diplomacy threatens to encroach upon the opponent's core values and interests. When such an acute threat is perceived by the social and political leadership of the "target state," one can expect defiant and recalcitrant behavior on the part of the victim to persist even in the face of strong and comprehensive pressures. For if the target of coercive diplomacy is convinced that it has everything to lose and that compliance may endanger certain basic principles of its foreign or defense policy, this party—whose actions precipitated the crisis—is likely to demonstrate a higher level of resolve than the deterring (or coercing) party: "Strongly motivated by what it has at stake," it will fiercely resist the pressures exerted and may ultimately prevail in the encounter despite its relative inferiority in terms of power capabilities.[34]

In such asymmetrical instances, coercive diplomacy will not induce the victim state to acquiesce. Instead, it will result in the creation or consolidation of a "sense of community and solidarity in the target state,"[35] thus providing its leadership with a broad domestic infrastructure of support for its defiant, intransigent posture. As a result, the costs of persisting in the coercive course may become so high that the initiator—and not the target—will ultimately be forced to acquiesce. Paradoxically, then, it is clear that considerable value deprivation may lead to social and political integration rather than to disintegration, with the national will becoming "a social amalgam of many components."[36] As the literature on such cases of economic sanctions as the American posture of economic coercion vis-à-vis Cuba (which was inaugurated in July 1960) clearly demonstrates, the relative balance of capabilities between the initiator and the victim of coercive diplomacy is unlikely in itself to determine the outcome of the encounter. In the words of Steven Rosen:

> Castro's victory in Cuba, the Communist victory in China, and perhaps even the revolutionists' victory in the American colonies were won by sheer persistence in the face of overwhelming odds. In each case, a highly committed party exhausted a materially stronger opponent by making the costs of victory exceed the privileged party's willingness to suffer.[37]

And as Klaus Knorr further elaborates:

> Many governments can appeal to the public need to stand together in solidarity, when foreign aggression is economic as when it is military. It is

even possible that some societies regard yielding to economic pressure as more ignominious than yielding to military pressure.[38]

In analyzing the components of crisis bargaining, George and Simons argue that "coercive diplomacy at any given situation may be facilitated by, if it does not require, genuine concessions to an opponent as part of a *quid pro quo* that secures one's essential demands."[39]

Although obfuscated or ignored by several proponents of rational deterrence theory (who are exclusively preoccupied with threats of punishments as a means of persuading an adversary not to challenge the status quo), the carrot of inducement, which is incorporated into coercive diplomacy for the purpose of eliciting a positive, cooperative response, may prove critical in encouraging a settlement by reducing the opponent's disinclination to comply with what is demanded from him and by increasing his willingness to live with the status quo. Thus, in addition to the status quo power's overriding need to influence its adversary's value structure by convincing it that its basic demands are not going to be granted, it may have to offer substantive concessions and compromises. These are designed to increase the opponent's estimate of the benefits associated with certain patterns of behavior, without attempting to affect its estimate of the costs associated with other forms of undesired behavior. In other words, the implementation of a successful coercive or deterrence strategy is contingent upon an optimal mixture or equilibrium between threats and conciliation, or between intimidation and accommodation.[40]

To illustrate, during the months that preceded the Japanese attack on Pearl Harbor, the posture pursued by the Roosevelt Administration toward Japan incorporated most premises of a "pure" coercive posture. It was assumed (particularly by Secretary of War Henry L. Stimson and Secretary of the Treasury Henry Morgenthau, Jr.) that the imposition of a series of increasingly severe economic sanctions would ultimately serve as the most effective deterrent against Japanese military aggression. The decision of July 26, 1940, to impose an embargo on shipments of scrap iron, aviation fuel, and petroleum products to Japan; the decision of July 25, 1941, to freeze Japan's assets in the United States; the imposition, on August 1, 1941, of a total embargo on Japanese trade, and the irreconcilable "Ten Point Plan" of November 26, 1941 (which included the demand that Japan evacuate its troops from China without delay), were the major manifestations of the uncompromising course of American diplomacy in the Pacific before the Japanese attack. However, since there was no simultaneous attempt to conciliate Japan on major issues, this posture of long-term deterrence was doomed to failure.[41] Indeed, the Stimson-Morgenthau formula for "firmness and boldness," when translated into a rigid, inflexible policy of severe economic sanctions, established an asymmetrical balance of motivation favoring Japan. Confronted with an irreconcilable coercive drive, "a desperate Japanese government chose the desperate, low-confidence strategy of war with the United States."[42] Devoid of any positive inducements, this pure coercive course ultimately provoked Japan into challenging the status quo by striking at Pearl Harbor despite the high risks inherent in this recalcitrant strategy.

In other words, although the risks of launching a military campaign against the United States were perceived by the Japanese as high (relative to the prospective benefits), this could not deter them from ultimately challenging the status quo in the Pacific. It is, therefore, clear in retrospect that American decisionmakers

> failed to formulate a carrot and stick that sufficed to overcome the strong unwillingness of the Japanese government to accept demands to curtail its aggressive activities in Asia. . . . Deterrence failed in the end because Roosevelt's effort at coercive diplomacy completely boomeranged. The ambitious objectives which he pursued by means of this strategy backed the Japanese government into a corner without leaving open an acceptable way out.[43]

Turning from the context of the 1941 Far Eastern Crisis to the less belligerent and combative, albeit emotion-laden and highly tense circumstances of American-Israeli relations as they unfolded during the period under consideration, it is clear that on those occasions where the carrot of inducement was at all incorporated into American strategy toward Israel during the years 1953–1956, it did not substantially mitigate the posture pursued, but comprised—at most—nothing more than a tactical gesture or a face-saving device. By comparison, during the period 1957–1962, a broader spectrum of accommodative components of American strategy came to increasingly dominate the landscape of American-Israeli relations at the expense of less benevolent facets and tenets. These coercive dimensions and elements progressively subsided into the background of the framework, having an ever diminishing impact upon the actual dynamics of American behavior in the American-Israeli sphere.

In other words, whereas, during the first term of the Eisenhower Presidency, the American approach toward Israel was closely patterned on the premises of the almost pure version of coercive strategy, with the cluster of accommodative elements and inducements constituting but a marginal component in American behavior, this propensity to rely upon the principles of deterrence and coercion as the administration's main bargaining tools vis-à-vis Israel gradually subsided during the years 1957–1962. Instead, both the Eisenhower Administration, during its second term in office, and the Kennedy Administration, became increasingly predisposed to employ two considerably more accommodative strategies toward Israel. The first strategy, which is termed by George "bargaining strategy" and which refers to an effort to achieve, through negotiations, an explicit, specific exchange that is usually carried out by the two parties simultaneously,[44] surfaced during Eisenhower's second term in the White House, and was later—during the Kennedy era—augmented and reinforced by an even more reassuring strategy which is called a "strategy of reciprocity," or "tit-for-tat."[45]

Although both strategies can be depicted as an exchange of "positive sanctions,"[46] they differ from each other in terms of the time factor and the extent to which their respective proponents are prepared to take risks for the sake of setting in motion a mutually beneficial process of confidence-building and tension-reduction within the American-Israeli dyad. Thus, while the more circumscribed and cautious bargaining strategy seeks to minimize risks by insisting on a concurrent tradeoff between the parties (namely, on a specific change in Israel's policy in the Arab-Israeli zone as a prerequisite for modifying the American posture on arms sales to the region), the more optimistic strategy of reciprocity is predicated upon the willingness of one side to take a unilateral cooperative initiative in the hope (but not the certainty) that "it will encourage the other side to take a conciliatory action in return."[47] According to this reassurance strategy—which was evident in President Kennedy's decision of August 1962 to sell to Israel Hawk anti-aircraft missiles in the hope of inducing the Ben-Gurion Government to soften its position on several controversial issues—the specific terms of the exchange are not negotiated between the parties "and are left somewhat *diffuse*, and the action that constitutes the reciprocation comes later, *not simultaneously*."[48] In other words, the initial conciliatory action (or promise of it) is not withdrawn in this strategy even if reciprocity does not follow.

Thus, whereas the bargaining strategy is based on a notion of an automatic, built-in linkage between two reciprocal and concurrent decisions, the strategy of reciprocity evolves around a considerably more amorphous form of linkage, one lacking concreteness and immediacy and confined strictly to the level of expectations or the "psychological environment."[49] While falling considerably short of a dramatic unilateral gesture (which is termed by Stein "suasive reverberation,"[50] and is designed to profoundly affect—with a single stroke—public opinion both at the regional and global levels), the strategy of reciprocity can be thought of as a reassuring measure, which is intended—through the initiation of a new policy line or action—to affect the risk calculation of the beneficiary. It is expected that the inauguration of a conciliatory posture through the offering of inducements will encourage him to reciprocate in kind and embark on a more accommodative posture, particularly when the reassuring act is broadly perceived as an inherently valid indication of the initiator's strategic intentions rather than as a signal that could easily and cheaply be manipulated.[51]

In the context of American-Israeli relations, the analysis will focus on instances of expected reciprocity, in which the Kennedy Administration initiated a major reassuring measure (namely, the sale to Israel of the Hawk missiles) in the hope (but without any guarantee) that Israel will reciprocate in the Arab-Israeli sphere by softening some of its traditional positions, particularly those pertaining to the question of the Arab refugees.[52] As Princen observes in his analysis of the interests and resources of the U.S. as a "principal mediator" in the Middle East:

> For the principal mediator, the target of intervention is *payoff structure* and the intervention objective is to *enhance incentives* for agreement. . . . It can rearrange payoffs to create an acceptable zone of agreement. . . .
>
> It can 'expand the pie;' it can arrange a credible deadline so a better outcome in the future is unlikely; or it can offer an insurance scheme or security guarantee to reduce risk.[53]

Thus, in assessing the effectiveness of the strategy of reciprocity as implemented in the specific global and regional circumstances and conditions of 1961 and 1962, an effort will be made to identify cross-issue, extended linkages between certain American reassuring moves, and the nature and magnitude of the Israeli response within the bounds and framework of the Arab-Israeli predicament. Did Israel even marginally modify either its Palestinian policy or its nuclear posture as a result of President Kennedy's decision to sell it sophisticated arms? Can one identify any form of "positive linkage" between this about-face of American traditional policy and any subsequent changes in the Israeli behavior or *modus operandi* in the Arab-Israeli sphere in general or in the Palestinian zone (or the nuclear zone) in particular? In other words, did the gradual shift of American diplomacy, during the Kennedy era, from an initial strategy of weak or vague commitment to Israel's security (which is termed by Snyder as an alliance strategy of defection [D]), to a strategy of strong commitment and support (which is defined by Snyder as an alliance strategy of cooperation [C]), result in an increase or decrease of Washington's bargaining leverage over Jerusalem?[54]

In seeking to explain the broad dynamics of American policy toward Israel as it was shaped and implemented during the decade 1953–1962, the cooperative premises of the strategy of reciprocity, and particularly the notion of positive, cross-issue linkage, will be juxtaposed with the earlier, less benevolent posture predicated on a different kind of linkage: on negative cross-issue linkage,[55] designed to induce Israel to avoid, or desist from, aggressive behavior in the Arab-Israeli sphere. In this context, the analysis will attempt to determine the relative effectiveness of the carrot and the stick, or of the reassuring strategy of reciprocity as contrasted with the punitive strategies of deterrence and coercive diplomacy in precipitating the desired change in Israel's mode of conduct. Was Israel more sensitive to the pain inflicted or threatened or to the reward offered, or was its behavior largely derived from a cluster of intrinsic factors and definitions as to what its core security interests entailed and required? In other words, to what extent did Israel modify certain basic tenets of its policy toward its neighbors as a direct or indirect result of either the exertion of American pressure or the offering, by the U.S., of tangible inducements?

Although the following analysis of American policy toward Israel, as it was shaped and delineated during the decade 1953–1962, will be largely premised on the notion of change as an incremental, phased, and unobtrusive process, in the course of which certain "background images"[56] or preliminary perceptions of the environment progressively recede into the background in the face of mounting discrepant information which indicate, in the aggregate, that they have become outdated or divorced from the forces comprising the "operational environment,"[57] an effort will be made to identify more specific turning points or "trigger events,"—those which precipitated immediate, and sometimes dramatic, frame-changes.[58] Among these are changes in the definition and assessment of the forces operating in the strategic environment of the Middle East. Specifically, it will be argued that by virtue of their magnitude and salience, such dramatic events as the Iraqi revolution of 1958 and its immediate regional ramifications profoundly affected the thinking and behavior of President Eisenhower and Secretary Dulles, and ultimately led them to reconsider some of their preconceived strategic perceptions, including their vision of Israel as a strategic liability. In other words, the following analysis will seek to establish that the shift from the sphere of certain abstract, general, and amorphous preexisting perceptions and expectations to the tangible and specific context within which a number of regional crises unfolded, constituted an impetus or a catalyst for modifying some of Washington's initial visions of the Middle East, which had evolved around the notion of a broadly-based defense organization as an effective multilateral bulwark against Soviet encroachment. Did the direct encounter with the revolutionary forces in the Middle East contribute directly to the administration's decision to abandon its initial desire to forge a multilateral regional alliance and instead to proceed incrementally, by consolidating agreements on bilateral rather than multilateral bases? And was Israel's emergence as a strategic asset to the U.S. inextricably linked to the lessons which the Eisenhower Administration drew from its 1958 engagement?

In an effort to answer these questions and shed light on the dynamics of American policy toward Israel during the period 1953–1962, the following analysis will focus, in chapter 2, on President Eisenhower's initial perceptions of, and policies toward Israel as they unfolded from 1953 to 1956. Then, in chapter 3, these initial visions of the region will be juxtaposed with the emerging cluster of "immediate images,"[59] which were progressively shaped and delineated between 1957 and 1960 as a result of the administration's inability to translate into regional reality its preconceived "background images."[60] The fourth chapter will seek to shed light on the process by which these tentative, recently established "immediate images" were transformed into a newly consolidated paradigm, which envisaged Israel as a strategic asset and a close regional ally of the U.S., and which became fully evident in August 1962, when President Kennedy decided to sell the Hawk missiles to Israel. In this context, the analysis will concentrate on two issues: the ill-fated American effort to engender a tradeoff between the Hawk sale to Israel and a reassessment of Prime Minister Ben-Gurion's attitude toward the Johnson Plan for comprehensively resolving the problem of the Palestinian refugees, and the President's determined effort to induce Israel to agree to a system of periodic inspection of its nuclear site in Dimona. The fifth chapter, the epilogue, will attempt to broaden the perspective by linking the developments and processes that had been instrumental in forging the American-Israeli alliance with certain developments that took place on the Israeli domestic scene more than three decades later, and that can potentially turn the clock back to the early 1950s in terms of the very essence of American-Israeli relations.[61]

II

THE UNITED STATES AND ISRAEL, 1953–1956
Divergence Dominates

We were in the present jam because the past Administration had always dealt with the area from a political standpoint and that had created a basic antagonism with the Arabs. That was what the Russians were now capitalizing on. . . . It is of the utmost importance for the welfare of the United States that we should get away from a political basis and try to develop a national non-partisan policy. Otherwise we would be apt to lose the whole area and possibly Africa, and this would be a major disaster for Western Europe as well as the United States.

—Vice President Richard M. Nixon, October 18, 1955
(Quoted from the memorandum of his conversation with several
Cabinet members)

An examination of President Eisenhower's first term in the White House indicates that in his approach toward Israel, he relied almost exclusively on the strategies of coercion and deterrence or, to use George's terminology, on negative cross-issue linkages, as the means by which to force Israel into abandoning certain core tenets of its security posture. Specifically, it was expected that the use of these strategies would result in unilateral Israeli territorial concessions in the Negev, in the cessation of retaliatory raids by Israel against Egypt and Jordan, and in its acceptance of an unspecified number of Palestinian refugees. In other words, Israel's compliance with the demands was not directly linked, during this period, to any promise of a major concurrent or future American reciprocal move such a the delivery of arms or the granting of *unilateral* American security guarantees.

Instead, these demands were exclusively embedded in a welter of threats of political, economic, and even military sanctions and punishments, unless Israel adopted "a conciliatory attitude" and an abiding desire "to reduce area tensions and thus minimize the danger of an outbreak of hostilities."[1]

However, for all its determination to "exert upon Israel strong pressures,"[2] the administration completely failed in its drive to implement a strategy of long-term, extended deterrence, as Israel remained defiant and recalcitrant throughout this period, unwilling to even marginally modify the basic premises of its security posture regardless of the costs threatened. And while this strategy fell short of a pure deterrence (or coercive) endeavor, the inducements offered or promised to Israel (such as the willingness to offer guarantees as a supplement to the settlement of the Arab-Israeli dispute) were so qualified, opaque, or marginal that their attractiveness was vastly reduced in the eyes of Israel's policymaking elite. On the other hand, on those rare occasions when the administration—faced with a perceived acute regional crisis—implemented a strategy of immediate deterrence toward Israel (as was the case in the course of the 1953 Water Crisis and the Suez Crisis of October 1956), it was largely successful in precipitating the desired Israeli behavior. Apparently, the level of American determination and resolve in seeking to accomplish its objectives was higher against the backdrop of the unfolding crisis episodes, which threatened to escalate into a broader confrontation engulfing the two superpowers, than it was in the absence of these emotion-laden, highly menacing circumstances, when the range and magnitude of the sanctions contemplated or implemented was far more limited. The success of the strategy of immediate deterrence did not spill over, however, beyond the specific and constrained parameters of such isolated events as the Water Crisis or the Suez Crisis and may have even weakened long-term, extended deterrence by increasing Israel's grievances and determination to fight in order to change a situation that is expected to deteriorate. As Jervis points out in exploring the linkages between these types of deterrence: "the success of immediate deterrence can weaken general deterrence in the future by increasing the loser's grievances—leading it to fight in order to change a situation which has become intolerable or is expected to deteriorate."[3]

Notwithstanding this difference, in neither the largely abortive attempt of the Eisenhower Administration to achieve long-term deterrence, nor the considerably more successful effort to pursue the strategy of immediate deterrence vis-à-vis Israel (in the context of such encounters as the Water Crisis of October 1953 and the Suez Crisis) did the forces affiliated with the special relationship paradigm play a significant role in seeking to constrain Washington's decisionmakers. And although the representatives of the paradigm did occasionally manage to marginally restrict the administration's ability to maneuver and its latitude to choose (as was the case during the final phase of the Suez Crisis), they could not modify the strategic outcome of the confrontation, nor could they change the premises and beliefs upon which American diplomacy was continuously shaped and delineated. Similarly, on a variety of secondary issues that became the focus of criticism and complaint by pro-Israeli forces (among which were the Saudi Arabian refusal to allow Jews to enter the country, the Arab boycott against American businesses dealing with Israel, and the Egyptian refusal to allow Israeli nonmilitary cargoes through the Suez Canal despite agreements to the contrary), proponents of the special relationship paradigm (particularly on Capitol Hill) were largely incapable of altering either the administration's indifferent approach or the uncompromising policies of individual Arab states.

As to the administration's continued failure to coerce Israel into abandoning some of the basic principles that guided its security policy it is clear that this inability to effectively pursue a long-term deterrence posture did not greatly reflect the efforts of any organizational representative of the special relationship paradigm to constrain or block the administration. Rather, it was the outcome of the asymmetrical perceptions held by the two leaderships about the nature of certain core interests. With the balance of the core intrinsic interests at stake favoring Israel, the Israeli leadership remained unwavering (unlike its American counterpart) in its determination to hold onto its basic initial positions, regardless of the costs involved.

The memorandum of the conversation that took place on April 8, 1953, between Israeli Foreign Minister Moshe Sharett and Assistant Secretary of State for Near-Eastern, South Asian and African Affairs, Henry A. Byroade, sheds light on these incompatible perceptions as well as on the asymmetry in the relative balance of interests and motivation:

> [Foreign Minister Sharett said that] to make territorial concessions to the Arabs would not bring about peace but would, on the contrary, whet the Arabs' appetite for more territory. Mr. Byroade pointed out that some of Israel's present territory was acquired by force of arms but the Foreign Minister explained that [this] territory . . . was obtained because the Arab states refused to accept the partition plan and invaded Palestine to attack the Jews. Territory can only be taken away from Israel by force of arms, the Foreign Minister added . . . Mr. Byroade asked whether his under-

standing of Israel's position as enunciated by the Foreign Minister means
Israel would make no territorial concessions and that the refugees must all
be settled elsewhere than in Israel. The Foreign Minister replied "definitely." . . . Mr. Byroade suggested that since neither Israel nor the Arab
states appeared willing to devise a plan for peace, the United States might
have to make its own plan—and it was probable that neither side would
like it. Foreign Minister Sharett said that he wished to warn anyone de-
vising a plan which included depriving Israel of territory that the plan
would have to include the sending of a military force to support it. The
Foreign Minister then added that considering territorial changes in the
concept being discussed would mean that Israel must immediately stake
out claims to land in the Arab states in order to be in a bargaining position if for no other reasons.[4]

As this heated exchange makes clear, the coercive American rhetoric,
which sought to establish an "intrinsic negative linkage"[5] between Israel's refusal to consider unilateral territorial concessions to its neighbors,[6] and a future American initiative to impose a settlement upon the
protagonists, did not precipitate any change in the basic Israeli approach, which continued to be closely patterned on the premises of a
classic bargaining strategy, and thus continuously insisted on specific, explicit and *simultaneous* tradeoffs and exchanges between Israel and the
Arab world. Thus, whereas Assistant Secretary Byroade repeatedly attempted—in the course of this meeting—to coerce the Israeli foreign
minister into adopting the premises of the strategy of reciprocity and
agree to unilateral concessions on a variety of core issues such as boundaries, Palestinian refugees, and the status of Jerusalem in the hope that
this would provide the impetus for a process of conflict reduction and
eventual accommodation in the Arab-Israeli sphere, Foreign Minister
Sharett remained fully and irrevocably committed to the principle of
concurrent symmetry in terms of scope and magnitude between any
such Israeli action and the Arab or American reaction:

> The Foreign Minister . . . said that if the [Arab] boycott [is] lifted it would
> enable Israel to earmark funds to pay compensation to the refugees, or,
> should a special loan be raised for this purpose, Israel would, with funds
> derived from the lifting of the boycott, repay the loan over a period of
> time. Mr. Byroade said he does not see how peace can be achieved unless
> Israel makes some gesture to Arab public opinion and that he hoped the
> Foreign Minister would be able to suggest something.[7]

Not only was the course of this conversation characteristic of the general, innate nature of American-Israeli relations during this period, which were permeated with tension and fraught with disagreement and misunderstanding, but its inconsequential outcome reflected the recurrent failure of a strategy that relied almost exclusively upon coercive tools and methods while avoiding any significant concrete and tangible reassuring accommodative measures vis-à-vis Israel. Indeed, a review of the conversation between Secretary of State Dulles and Foreign Minister Sharett, which took place on November 21, 1955, more than two and a half years after Secretary Assistant Byroade had unsuccessfully tried to set in motion a peacemaking process on the basis of certain Israeli unilateral territorial concessions, indicates that the respective expectations and negotiating strategies of the two parties remained essentially intact, although the American side had now a more concrete notion of the nature of the desired Israeli withdrawal (which reflected the Anglo-American "Alpha" plan) than was the case on April 21, 1953. Thus, whereas Secretary Dulles repeatedly insisted that "the Israeli Government must be prepared to make some concessions in the Negev which would make possible an area of contact between Egypt and the other Arab States," and that "we must know that there is flexibility if we are going to be in a position to push things along,"[8] Foreign Minister Sharett remained firm in insisting that the idea of "cutting a belt of land out of the Negev . . . [was] not fair and [that] the Israeli Government should not be asked to do so," and that any progress toward regional accommodation had to be based on the principle of a simultaneous tradeoff (namely, on the premises of the bargaining strategy) rather than on the notion of unilateralism (namely, on the premises of a strategy of reciprocity that expects—but can by no means guarantee—that the unilateral conciliatory move will be reciprocated): "If it was a question of give and take," the Foreign Minister further observed, "it could be discussed, but . . . Israel could not give up vital points . . . nor could it agree to something that would result in cutting Israel in two."[9]

Notwithstanding the differences in terms of the specific peace strategies advocated and the desired course and direction of Israel's defense and foreign policy, which continuously strained the relationship between Prime Minister Ben-Gurion and Foreign Minister Sharett (and which culminated in Sharett's forced resignation from the government in June 1956), they both shared an unwavering opposition to a strategy of unilateralism and supported instead (though with different levels of enthusiasm) the symmetrical and simultaneous bargaining strategy in the

Arab-Israeli sphere. Faced with this unwavering Israeli refusal to predicate its peace posture upon the belief that a unilateral concession on its part would ultimately trigger a mutually beneficial process of conflict reduction, the Secretary of State resorted to harsh coercive threats, which were not augmented by any explicit or implicit promise of compensation or inducement:

> . . . We must know whether Israel would be willing to make concessions or not. If "no" is the last word, then Israel is putting us all in great peril. If we have to make a choice of sticking with Israel in the face of all that the Middle East is to the safety and continued existence of the free world, Israel will be forcing us to make a very grave choice. . . . If Israel says no then the possibility of a settlement is off and we shall all have to face the consequences.[10]

For all these hardly veiled threats of political isolation and an imposed settlement, Foreign Minister Sharett remained irreconcilably committed to the principles of symmetry and mutuality as the cornerstones of any viable bargaining process between Israel and its neighbors. According to the memorandum of the conversation,

> Mr. Sharett said that Israel, by its geographic position, is the hub of the area and this imposes an obligation on it to be a good neighbor which it intends to be if the Arab States would only be good neighbors. Israel has offered to provide communication facilities for the Arabs across [its] territory, following a settlement, but giving up its sovereignty over present . . . territory, to meet a whim of [Egypt's President Gamal Abdel] Nasser, is another matter. Who can tell what Nasser would then go on to request? It would be the beginning of a slippery slope.[11]

As these statements make clear, during the period 1953–1956, the landscape of American-Israeli relations was clouded by incompatible negotiating strategies, which reflected in turn fundamentally different priorities, concerns, and objectives. However, despite the vast asymmetry in the political, military, and economic resources within the American-Israeli dyad, the pursuit, by the United States, of a harsh coercive posture (based on the premises of negative cross-issue linkage) was insufficient to bring about the desired outcome. Devoid of any meaningful inducement, this long-term policy ultimately faded into the background without having accomplished even a fraction of its original design while leaving the dovish Foreign Minister Sharett empty-handed in his effort to prevent or constrain some of the retaliatory measures adopted by Israel vis-à-vis Egypt and Jordan. And although the architects of American

Middle East policy clearly recognized that their posture toward Israel was unbalanced, they held onto their preliminary regional images and beliefs until a volatile and recalcitrant regional environment forced them, during President Eisenhower's second term, to reassess their strategic premises and policies. In the words of Assistant Secretary Byroade, which illustrate this continued refusal to integrate a significant accommodative component into the American coercive behavior within the bounds of the American-Israeli framework:

> Some time ago the Israelis approached me with a request that we allow them to make a commercial purchase of 24 F-86 jet fighters. The only act required by the United States would be to grant export licenses. I have been in fact searching some way to reassure the Israelis . . . [but] have come to the conclusion that I cannot conscientiously recommend such a course, as I believe it is clearly against United States' overall interests in the Middle East.[12]

It was only against the backdrop of a series of acutely menacing regional conflagrations and crises, which directly threatened global stability, as well as vital American strongholds and interests in the Middle East, that American diplomacy managed to overcome the strong Israeli disinclination to acquiesce in the pressures exerted. However, even on these occasions, while the administration demonstrated a high level of resolve and determination in its drive to defuse the situation and control the risks of escalation (as was the case in the course of the Suez Crisis of 1956), and in the process was prepared to impose drastic economic sanctions upon Israel, some reassurances to Israel—albeit of a partial or tactical nature—had ultimately to be integrated into the predominantly coercive bargaining structure in order to guarantee Israeli compliance.[13]

In seeking to elucidate the conceptual origins from which this reliance on the strategies of deterrence and coercion as the administration's major bargaining tools vis-à-vis Israel derived during the period 1953–1956, it is clear that this predilection for threatening and bellicose rhetoric (which was accompanied by such irreconcilable policies as the continued refusal to supply Israel with arms) did not reflect any idiosyncratic predispositions or proclivities. Rather, it was predicated upon a specific cluster of structural-realist premises and beliefs, which may be termed "pure bipolar-confrontational." These assumptions revolve around the notion that international crises are seldom local, isolated phenomena, but rather elements within a worldwide Communist effort to disrupt the global balance of power and thereby threaten the security of the United States.[14]

Convinced that events halfway around the globe automatically have a direct impact on America's core interests, "pure bipolar-confrontational" policymakers tend to view any adverse turn of events anywhere as an ironclad manifestation of a premeditated Communist conspiracy intended to directly endanger the United States.[15] Believing that the Cold War confrontation was inherent in the revolutionary and predatory character of the Soviet Union, the advocates of this orientation underscore the need to stand firm and resist any attempt at encroachment, whatever its location might be. Fully and irrevocably committed to the premises of deterrence and coercion, they perceive international politics as a bipolar, "zero-sum" game, in which the Soviet Union was invariably viewed as "the chief enemy of world order."[16] An indeed, in the thinking of President Eisenhower and Secretary Dulles, who exemplify this approach, "all international actors were divided into two camps—the free world and its Communist antagonists."[17]

In view of this world-wide dichotomy and the nature of Soviet intentions, any local event or crisis was invariably perceived by the Eisenhower Administration as but a facet of a larger and acutely threatening phenomenon, whose significance lay beyond the regional boundaries within which it unfolded.[18]

A memorandum of the conversation, which took place in Cairo on May 11, 1953, between Secretary Dulles and the Egyptian leadership, elucidates the essence of this "pure bipolar-confrontational" national security approach. According to the transcript of the meeting,

> The secretary [said] . . . that new administration's policies will be based on the Communist threat. The Communists already rule one-third of the world. [Dulles] referred to Communist activity in Indo-China as evidence that Communists seek further expansion. The death of Stalin did not change Communist philosophy which, like a religious creed, keeps on and on. . . . The U.S. considers the Middle East to be a danger area which heretofore has been somewhat neglected by the U.S. . . . In the Stalin-Hitler conversations of 1940, the U.S.S.R. placed as the center of Soviet aspirations the "general area of the Persian Gulf." The Germans objected to this Soviet claim and thus the U.S.S.R. risked a terrible war for this objective. This happened once; the U.S. believes that it could happen again and that the Middle East might be the next area of danger.[19]

And indeed, motivated by the vision of a worldwide Communist threat to the global balance of power, and alarmed by the rapid fall of all the East European states to Soviet domination, the Eisenhower Administration embarked on a policy that sought to encircle the Soviet Union with states allied to and supported by the West. In the Middle East, which was fully incorporated into this bipolar-confrontational vision, this strategic goal was to be accomplished by strengthening the defense of the Northern tier states as the first step toward forging a security alliance among such regional powers as Egypt, Turkey, Iraq, and Pakistan.[20]

Perceived as critical "because of its geopolitical importance and the value of its oil resources to Western Europe,"[21] the Middle East quickly emerged, in the thinking of President Eisenhower and Secretary Dulles, as a major front in the global effort to contain Soviet penetration and encroachment:

> The Near East possesses great strategic importance, as the bridge between Europe, Asia and Africa. The present masters of the Kremlin, following the lead of past military conquerors, covet this position. . . . It came as a surprising shock when the Chinese people, whom we had counted as friends, fell under Communist domination. There could be equally dangerous developments in the Near East. The situation calls for urgent concern.[22]

In addition, since 1948, the Abu Sueir air base in Egypt had been regarded by American strategists as vital for "the American strategic bomber offensive" against the Soviet Union at the outset of a general war, thus further reinforcing the perception of the region as critical to the defense of the West. Indeed, by virtue of its relative proximity to Soviet strategic targets, the Abu Sueir base was continuously looked upon by the American (and British) military leadership as the ideal site from which "an atomic air offensive could be launched before the Soviets overran the Middle East."[23]

The policy prescription derived from this perception of the Soviet threat to Western interests in the Middle East (and of the strategic importance of the region as the optimal springboard for the launching of military operations against the Soviet Union in the event of a general war between the two blocs), which was further reinforced by the growing American recognition that the British decision to gradually disengage from the region created new opportunities for Soviet diplomacy in its quest for new strongholds, was clear and unequivocal. In order to prevent these "dangerous developments" and disruptive processes, it was essential for Washington to try to induce such regional powers as Egypt and Iraq to align themselves with the United States in the all-encompassing confrontation with Soviet designs by providing them with generous military and economic support. The first step in this direction was taken on April 21, 1954, when the governments of the United States and Iraq exchanged letters inaugurating a program of direct American military aid. However, the administration refrained from formally joining such regional alliances as the pact between Turkey and Iraq, which were concluded under British auspices.[24]

This preoccupation with the role assigned to the Arab world in blocking, through a series of bilateral and multilateral defense alliances, a political or military Soviet thrust into the Middle East, led the Eisenhower Administration to adopt a highly reserved attitude toward Israel, the power which—by virtue of its continued conflict with the Arab world—distracted the region from the all-important mission of assisting American diplomacy in its drive to combat the highly threatening vision of Soviet penetration. As a Department of State Position Paper, composed on May 7, 1953, clearly asserted: "Arab-Israeli differences and the part played by the United States in the establishment and support of Israel contribute very substantially to . . . lack of progress in strengthening the defense of the Near East."[25] And indeed, in his meeting of May 15, 1953, with Syrian leader Adib al-Shishakli, Secretary Dulles quickly discovered that, in the thinking of his Syrian host, the resolution of "the overall problem of Israel" was a precondition for Arab participation "in any regional defense plan."[26]

This insistence on the need to rapidly and comprehensively resolve the Arab-Israeli predicament in a way that would reflect Arab preferences and positions as a prerequisite to the consolidation of a broadly based Arab security alliance against the Soviet Union was echoed in Cairo, Riyadh, and Beirut. Throughout the Middle East, the need to unify for the sake of effectively containing Soviet encroachment was downgraded by and subordinated to what was perceived as the more urgent need to solicit American support for terminating the Arab-Israeli dispute along traditional Arab lines. Clearly, concern for the global balance of power has played but a marginal role in the alliance choices of the regional actors in the Middle East. Preoccupied with, and acutely sensitive to threats from proximate power rather than from aggregate power, such states as Egypt and Syria remained largely oblivious to threats from the strongest powers in the international system while focusing instead on threats that originated in their geographic proximity, such as the perceived Israeli menace.

That the recognition of the Arab order of priorities fully permeated American thinking on the Middle East and was incorporated into the cluster of objectives the Eisenhower Presidency sought to promote is evident in the numerous statements and policy initiatives that followed Secretary Dulles's exploratory mission to the region of May 1953, and that reflected American determination to proceed toward containment via the route of regional accommodation. In the words of Assistant Secretary Byroade:

> Some of [the Arabs] are fearful. In certain areas the fear of one's neighbor exceeds that from any other direction. It is a surprise to many Americans that Soviet encroachment and imperialism is not recognized in parts of the Middle East as the primary danger. Some in the Middle East see an enemy much closer at hand. They turn their thoughts and actions not toward the security of the whole region but to [the] security of one against the other, and they thus present a picture of disunity of purpose which is being exploited by the agents of the Soviet Union.[27]

And as Secretary Dulles himself acknowledged in addressing, on June 1, 1953, the members of the National Security Council (NSC):

> The prestige of the Western powers in the Middle East was, in general, very low. . . . [Nevertheless] we could regain our lost influence if we make a real effort. *The great difficulty was the complete preoccupation of the Arab states with their own local problems and their lack of understanding and interest in the threat posed by the Soviet Union.*[28]

The political implications of this vision were clear and unequivocal. In order to incorporate the Arab world into Washington's strategic designs, it was essential to endorse at least some of the basic Arab positions concerning the appropriate means of resolving the Arab-Israeli conflict, and at the same time to refrain from any pro-Israeli move or gesture. The fear of Arab defection and alienation clearly overshadowed, in the thinking of Washington's policymakers, any considerations patterned on the special relationship paradigm. Perceived as directly contradicting the bipolar-confrontational premises of the American national interest, the notions incorporating the special relationship paradigm were outweighed by a cluster of national security convictions and beliefs.

This propensity to downgrade or obfuscate the premises comprising the special relationship paradigm was further reinforced by the pervasive vision of Israel as a socialist society dominated by a "leftward" orientation and continued ideological attachment to Marxist ideology.

The fact that, during the period immediately following the establishment of Israel, there was still "a lingering anti-American feeling" in Israel, and that such leaders as Golda Meir were reluctant—on ideological grounds—to commit themselves to a pro-American posture and believed that neutrality between East and West could ideally serve Israel's interests, added another layer to President Eisenhower's predisposition to approach Israel with utmost suspicion and unabated reservations.

And although the Israeli leadership opted, after the outbreak of the Korean War in June 1950, to formally abandon its "nonidentification" posture, and instead to adopt an explicit pro-American course (which became fully evident on July 2, 1950, when an extraordinary Israeli Cabinet meeting unanimously adopted a resolution that supported the American position), this reorientation of Israeli diplomacy could not in itself erode this deeply held and broadly based cluster of beliefs, which depicted the Israeli political system as largely committed "to Bolshevik ideology."[29] These beliefs remained intact in subsequent years despite the determined Israeli effort to side with the U.S. on a number of highly controversial international issues. In the case of the Korean War, for example, the Israeli Cabinet decided, in August 1953, to endorse the American position and thus to abstain when voting was taken in the United Nations on the issue of whether or not to include India in the Korean Peace Conference established to define the parameters of a Korean settlement. Despite the initial desire of Foreign Minister Sharett and several other members of the Cabinet to join the Asian bloc in supporting India's participation at the conference, they ultimately accepted the position of Prime Minister Ben-Gurion. The Prime Minister argued that unless the issue at stake involved vital Israeli security interests, not even a shadow of doubt regarding Israel's allegiance and foreign policy orientation should remain when the matter was defined as directly and inextricably linked to American interests, credibility, or prestige. (Ultimately, the motion to include India at the conference was defeated by the Political Committee of the U.N. During the voting, which took place on August 27, 1953, Israel was the only Asian power that did not support India).[30]

None of these demonstrations of Israel's unwavering commitment to American global objectives and policies in defiance of an entire cluster of regional considerations and priorities had any impact upon the thinking of Secretary Dulles. Nor could they even marginally erode his belief that there existed an irreconcilable gap between the national interest paradigm and the special relationship orientation. Repeatedly, the Secretary of State portrayed an apocalyptic, acutely menacing picture of the repercussions that were bound to result from a reliance, in the shaping of American regional strategy, upon the logic and very essence of the special relationship paradigm:

We do not think arms shipments to Israel [are] the answer to Israel's vulnerability in the face of Soviet shipments to the Arabs because it would alienate the Arabs and result in cutting off Arabian oil. This in turn would greatly weaken Europe economically and bring NATO to a standstill. All the gains of the Marshall Plan would be canceled and Europe would be faced to turn to the Soviet Union for economic survival and for its oil imports. *Thus we would save Israel but lose Europe.*[31]

Thus depicted as detrimental to the overriding goal of enticing such major regional powers as Egypt and Iraq to contribute to the defense of the West against Soviet encroachment, the special relationship paradigm quickly faded—during the first term of the Eisenhower Administration—into the background of American-Israeli relations, with little impact on the actual shaping and course of American diplomacy. Not only was Israel excluded from any discussion of the regional security system, which the administration began to forge as soon as it took office in 1953, but it was also denied military aid, security guarantees, and even some less tangible gestures of friendship and empathy.

Therefore, while in 1949 Israel had become a recipient of technical and economic aid from the U.S. (under the auspices of the Export-Import Bank, the Food-for-Peace Program, and the United States Technical Assistance Plan), it was continuously denied access to more comprehensive aid programs under the auspices of the Marshall Plan. Nor was the administration prepared to implement "Operation Stockpile," according to which vital strategic supplies were to be stockpiled in Israel, or to integrate Israel into the framework of the "Operation Gift" program, which appropriated direct grants in aid to states that publicly proclaimed their alignment with American global security efforts (as Israel did in July 1950).

Seeking to construct a broadly based, inter-Arab "structure of containment" in the Middle East, the administration regarded such initiatives as the idea of an American "security contract" with Israel, the plan to store American strategic supplies in Israel, and the proposal to include Israel in the United States Off-Shore Procurement Program (whose administrators were authorized to place massive orders for military and civilian supplies on behalf of American forces overseas) as incompatible with the American national interest, and thus as inherently detrimental to the overriding desire "to advance [the administration's] understanding with the Arab world, and with Egypt in particular." This desire was translated into specific action on November 6, 1954, when the administration concluded a $20 million economic aid agreement with Egypt. However, the administration's desire to extend military assistance to Egypt could not be implemented because the Egyptian president refused to comply with the standard Congressional requirement that an American military mission (the Military Assistance Advisory Group) administer the program in Cairo. Convinced that the establishment of a military alliance with a Western power would symbolize foreign occupation and thus abort his entire nationalist drive (as well as his posture of "positive neutralism"), President Nasser remained adamant in his refusal to accept any formal, direct, or explicit forms of strategic cooperation with the U.S., although he agreed to secretly receive logistical and organizational advice through the CIA between 1953 and 1954.

Against this backdrop of incompatible regional visions, Israel's security was a secondary concern for the American leadership and could therefore be fully addressed (in the form of formal security guarantees) "only as a supplement to the overall settlement of the Arab-Israeli dispute" and not (as Israel continuously demanded) as "a preliminary to that end."[32]

This vision of an unbridgeable gap between the two paradigms, which was predicated upon the pervasive perception of the very essence of the special relationship paradigm as incompatible with the promotion of American national security and core regional interests (which led Secretary Dulles, on numerous occasions, to question the legitimacy of the lobbying efforts of the organized representatives of the special relationship paradigm, and to state that the U.S. "would not become an Israeli prisoner"), was repeatedly and forcefully articulated by leading members of the Eisenhower Administration, and formed the conceptual infrastructure for a number of specific moves and policy initiatives. Thus a Department of State Position Paper from May 7, 1953, asserted that "the American partnership with Israel has been a lopsided arrangement, with the United States giving massive aid and support while receiving little or nothing in return." "One reason for this situation," the paper reasoned, "is the existence of heavy and effective Zionist pressure, which has been brought to bear on both the Executive and Legislative branches of the American Government. Courses of action designed to strengthen the overall position of the United States in the Near East have been sidetracked or so cluttered up with 'compensating favors' that they have not brought the desired improvement."[33]

Similarly, in the course of the meeting that took place on May 14, 1953, in Tel-Aviv, between Secretary Dulles and Israeli Prime Minister

David Ben-Gurion, the Secretary "expressed [his] conviction that without [the] goodwill and confidence of [the] Arabs, the United States would not be able to play [a] useful role in [the] area. Dulles explained "that [the] Arabs feel [that the] Roosevelt and Truman Administrations [were] so subject to Jewish influence that [the] Arab viewpoint [was] ignored. Decisions [were] often taken under pressure [from] United States Jewish groups, which felt they had [the] right [to] exercise influence because of [their] contribution to election victory." According to the memorandum, the Secretary further maintained that "the new administration . . . was elected by [an] overwhelming vote of the American people as a whole and [it] neither owes that type of political debt to any segment nor [does it] believe in building power by cultivating particular segments of [the] population."[34]

Less than a month later, on June 9, 1953, Assistant Secretary Byroade—in his meeting with Israeli Ambassador Abba Eban—went even farther in portraying a picture of inherent irreconcilability between the two paradigms, and in underscoring the regional and global repercussions of continued rivalry in the Arab-Israeli zone:

> If only Israel and Arab relations were concerned, the problem would be relatively easier. What is at stake, however, is the possible loss of all Western influence in the Middle East, including oil, airfields, etc. *The decline in influence has resulted . . . from Western support of Israel, and we are quite concerned about it.* . . . In Egypt it was apparent that the East-West conflict was happening on another planet as far as the Egyptians were concerned. . . . The American people and the American Congress should realize that the United States and the West are not in a position to exert much influence on the Arab world today. It is in Israel's interest . . . to have us retain a position of influence in the area.[35]

Two and a half years later, this innate propensity of the Eisenhower Administration "not to be influenced," in the formulation of the American posture toward Israel, "by internal considerations," and thus to "downplay the relationship [with Israel]" and instead to predicate American diplomacy exclusively upon the premise that a broad inter-Arab coalition against the Soviet effort "to restrict oil supplies" from the Middle East to Europe was still a viable option, remained intact. Although President Nasser profoundly resented the Baghdad Pact initiative from its inception, viewing it as a means to perpetuate Western domination in the Middle East and to hamper any sincere movement toward Arab unity, and concluded a major arms deal with Czechoslovakia in September

1955, members of Washington's foreign policy elite continued to believe that "President Nasser could still be steered toward the West."[36] Convinced that "Arab goodwill" could still be won, Secretary Dulles, in his press conference of October 4, 1955, could not bring himself to condemn the September 1955 arms deal. Unwilling to consider coercive, retaliatory measures vis-à-vis Egypt, he asserted: "It is difficult to be critical of countries which, feeling themselves endangered, seek the arms which they sincerely need for defense."[37] Indeed, the reliance on coercive measures and tools was strictly confined, during the administration's first term, to the American-Israeli dyad. As Secretary Dulles pointed out to Foreign Minister Sharett in the course of their October 30, 1955, meeting: "The United States . . . would make every effort to immunize the Arab states against the Soviet danger." Precisely because of this goal, "any unilateral action in Israel's favor would be liable to aid Soviet expansion among the Arab states."[38]

Despite the wealth of evidence indicating that Egypt would remain irrevocably opposed to the Baghdad Pact, and that the regional security visions of the administration could not be reconciled with Egypt's ambitions and inter-Arab policies, American diplomacy tenaciously held onto its preconceived belief that Egypt could still become a major component of its containment design. Committed to his belief that there was nothing irreversible in the September 1955 arms deal, Secretary Dulles would continued to pursue (until the summer of 1956) an accommodative course toward Cairo, in the hope that it would ultimately "woo Nasser away from the Russians."[39] As soon as the September 1955 arms deal was announced, he even offered Egypt a new deal with much lowered terms of payment—an offer Egypt rejected.

Similarly, a juxtaposition of the premises from which American policy toward Israel derived in late 1955, and the basic images from which the initial American posture within the American-Israeli framework was shaped and delineated during 1953, reveals a striking continuity in thinking and behavior. More specifically, in his conversation with the Egyptian Minister for Foreign Affairs, Mahmoud Fawzi, which took place on May 11, 1953, Secretary Dulles observed that "it was essential" to work out a Middle Eastern policy on the basis of [the] enlightened self-interest of the U.S. as a whole [rather than the] self-interest of particular groups of Americans."[40]

This determination to ignore the premises of the special relationship paradigm remained unchanged in October 1955. Thus in a meeting, which took place on October 21, 1955, between Secretary Dulles and

Senator Walter F. George (D., Georgia), the Secretary reiterated his long-standing vision of a dichotomy between the national interest paradigm and the special relationship paradigm, with the latter depicted as the main obstacle to the accomplishment of a broad cluster of vital security objectives. One month after the conclusion of an unprecedented arms deal between Egypt and the Eastern bloc, and almost three years after the administration had forcefully set out to disassociate itself completely from the premises of the special relationship paradigm by adopting "an attitude of reserve" toward Israel,[41] Secretary Dulles remained unabated in his conviction that the recent decline in American influence in the area and the failure to induce Egypt to adopt a pro-Western posture resulted from pervasive Arab beliefs that the premises of the special relationship paradigm had played a formative role in the shaping of the original American approach to the region. According to the Secretary's own account of the meeting:

> We discussed the situation in the Near East. [Senator George] felt that it was very serious. I agreed that it had come about largely because we had in the past dealt with these matters on a domestic political basis [in defiance of] the interests of the United States. I said that President Eisenhower and I had tried to carry out a policy in the interests of the United States and I felt that it would be necessary to adhere to that, although circumstances might arise which would make it costly from a political standpoint.[42]

On the very same day, in his conversation with Attorney General Herbert Brownell Jr. and Treasury Secretary George M. Humphrey, Vice-President Richard M. Nixon expressed identical views, asserting that any gesture in support of Israel was detrimental to basic geostrategic American interests in the region. According to his memorandum of the meeting:

> I said I wished to discuss certain aspects of the Near East situation which had political implications. We were in the present jam because the past administration had always dealt with the area from a political standpoint and had tried to meet the wishes of the Zionists in this country and that had created a basic antagonism with the Arabs. That was what the Russians were now capitalizing on. I said I thought it of the utmost importance for the welfare of the United States that we should get away from a political base and try to develop a national non-partisan policy. Otherwise we would be apt to lose the whole area and possibly Africa, and this would be a major disaster for Western Europe as well as the United States.[43]

Oblivious to the wave of Arab nationalism and anti-Western senti-ments, which swept the Middle East and effectively sealed the fate of the effort to solicit the support of such powers as Egypt for Washington's containment endeavor, and convinced that Egypt could still be induced to adopt an accommodative posture toward Washington, the adminis-tration was predisposed to interpret the September 1955 arms deal be-tween Egypt and Czechoslovakia as an undisputed proof that it had failed to sufficiently distance and disassociate itself from Israel rather than as an indication that the effort to integrate Egypt into the frame-work of the Baghdad Pact was doomed to failure. Notwithstanding the persistent American effort to accommodate Egypt (that had been amply demonstrated in Washington's willingness, in 1954, to provide econom-ic and military assistance to Nasser, and to help mediate the Anglo-Egyptian base settlement), the American leadership remained convinced that the September 1955 arms deal reflected its failure to avoid the ap-pearance of favoring Israel over the Arab states and did not originate, therefore, in the dynamics of Egyptian nationalism and neutralism. As Secretary Dulles pointed out to a group of Congressional leaders, whom he met on April 10, 1956:

> We believe that we could prevent a war in the Near East by the Arabs. The Arabs have felt that they could not depend on the U.S. in view of Zionist pressures, which can be brought to bear in this country. If we can demon-strate that we can pursue an independent policy, we can prevent the out-break of war in the Middle East. We should try to save Israel in these ways rather than by taking steps whereby the U.S. and the U.S.S.R. would be facing each other in a deteriorating situation in the Middle East.[44]

Not until the summer of 1956 was this continued propensity "to tempo-rize regarding Egypt" in the wake of President Nasser's tilt to the East-ern bloc, partially abandoned.[45] Infuriated over the Egyptian decision, of May 16, 1956, to recognize the People's Republic of China, the ad-ministration decided, on July 19, 1956, to withdraw its offer to help fi-nance the construction of the Aswan Dam. In response, President Nass-er nationalized the Franco-British owned Suez Canal Company, thus transforming a bilateral dispute into a severe multilateral crisis.

For all this growing American disenchantment with the course of Egyptian diplomacy (which was manifested in the Anglo-American Omega initiative), no change in the basic parameters of the American strategy toward Israel was forthcoming, as Washington remained adamant in its refusal to either provide Israel with military assistance or to offer Jerusalem unilateral security commitments as part of an intricate bargaining strategy. The recognition, which increasingly permeated American thinking during the months that preceded the Sinai Campaign of October 1956, that "Nasser [was] no longer entitled to the preferential treatment he has been getting [from the U.S.],"[46] did not lead to a reexamination of the basic premises from which the basic posture toward Israel was delineated and shaped. Instead, continuously and vehemently opposed to the very essence of the special relationship paradigm, the architects of American Middle East diplomacy remained—throughout President Eisenhower's first term—committed to their initial coercive posture of negative linkage, unwilling to incorporate any significant reassuring inducement into their irreconcilable course.

Indeed, not only did the administration remain, during the period 1953–1956, adamantly opposed, in theory and rhetoric, to the very logic and core of the special relationship paradigm, but also many of its concrete and tangible moves and policies within the American–Israeli dyad reflected this unabated conviction that "backing Israel might be very costly to vital United States national interests."[47] As Secretary Dulles advised the American Ambassadors in the region, the effort "to bring about a transition from the present armistice regime governing relations between the Arab states and Israel to formal peace" should be pursued by American diplomacy "in a manner not unduly jeopardizing other U.S. area objectives, notably area defense arrangements." What was essential, therefore, was to avoid any discrepancy or inconsistency between the goals of seeking "agreements on settlements of issues [stemming] from the Arab-Israeli conflict," and of soliciting Arab support and participation in the all-encompassing mission of containing Soviet penetration and encroachment.[48]

In attempting to resolve—or at least mitigate—the Arab-Israeli predicament as a springboard toward accomplishing its major objective of forging a broad Middle Eastern security alliance, the Eisenhower Presidency consistently predicated its posture toward Israel upon the assumption that a series of unilateral Israeli concessions on core issues constituted the only feasible way to achieve an Arab-Israeli accord. Such an accord, in turn, was perceived as necessary for preventing further Soviet penetration of the region. Focusing on such emotion-laden, highly charged questions as Israeli's immigration policy, permanent boundaries, the Palestinian problem, and Israel's strategy of retaliatory raids into Arab territory, it sought to coerce Israel into acquiescing in the American demands by threatening to decrease or suspend economic aid (including loans from the Export-Import Bank), by continuously refusing to supply Israel with arms, and by collaborating with the British in an effort to jointly define the territorial parameters of a settlement.

On several occasions, in the course of highly threatening regional crises, and in an effort to disassociate itself completely from Israel, the administration opted to carry out the threat of economic sanctions. For example, in October 1953, at the peak of the Water Crisis between Israel and Syria, the President suspended the $26 million that had been earmarked as a grant of economic aid under the Mutual Security Act of 1953 (a sum designed to cover the first six months of the fiscal year 1953–1954).[49] Concurrently, the administration prohibited the use of U.S. grant-in-aid funds for the payment of the debt.

Three years later, in the wake of the Israeli onslaught on Egyptian forces in the Sinai Peninsula, the administration decided to suspend the ongoing negotiations between the Export-Import Bank and the Israeli Government on a $75 million loan, to suspend its Food Surplus Agreement with Israel, and to hold in abeyance an economic and technical assistance program (these sanctions were lifted in March 1957, after Israel had completed its withdrawal from the Gaza Strip and Sharm-el-Sheikh). It also contemplated—but ultimately ruled out—such sanctions as the imposition of a maritime blockade against Israel and the freezing of all private aid.

Despite these instances, for the most part the administration relied on deterrence and coercive threats—explicit or veiled—as its major tactical tools in seeking to influence Israel's actions and policies toward its neighbors without attempting to change the bargain from distributive to integrative and thus without seeking "to find creative ways to benefit both sides."[50]

In their advocacy of an asymmetrical posture in the Arab-Israeli sphere, U.S. policymakers, irrevocably committed to their belief that the special relationship paradigm was incompatible with the American regional and global national interest, assumed that Israeli policy was designed—according to a typical position paper, which was drafted in the Bureau of Near Eastern, South Asian, and African Affairs on November 23, 1953—"to coerce the Arabs into 'peace' on Israeli terms, or to prevent the restoration of stability in the belief that the present unsettled situation in the Near East is in Israel's best interests." "Unable to show the realism required for a successful adjustment into the Near Eastern environment," the assessment continued, Israel resorted to "heedless and provocative acts."[51] Believing that Israel might be "deliberately trying to break the armistice open on the theory that that was the only way to get a better arrangement,"[52] the administration remained oblivious to the scope and magnitude of the *fedayeen* raids on Israeli villages and settlements (on both the Egyptian and Jordanian fronts), which precipitated a series of massive and horrendous retaliatory raids on Jordanian villages (and later on Egyptian command posts in the Gaza Strip).

Viewing Israel's strategy of retaliatory raids (which, in 1953, culminated on October 15 in the devastating raid on the Jordanian village of Qibya) as "deliberately provocative to the Arabs" and as premeditated actions, which were carried out against a backdrop of "a relatively quiet period [along the Israeli-Jordanian border],"[53] the administration failed to consider both the underlying and immediate causes of this Israeli posture. Thus, although the Qibya raid resulted in more than sixty civilian casualties and the destruction of some forty-five houses, it had been preceded by a *fedayeen* attack on the village of Yahud near Petah-Tikva, in which a mother and her two children were killed.

Invariably committed to the belief that "Israel has been over-aggressive, over-insistent on what it wants and too eager to achieve immediate goals,"[54] Secretary Dulles and Assistant Secretary Byroade asserted on numerous occasions "that Israel has embarked on a deliberate policy of fomenting border disturbances" in an effort "to bring about, through the use of force, a revision of the armistice machinery" and thus to impose upon the Arab states "permanent arrangements" from a position of strength.[55] Maintaining, in a memorandum drafted by Assistant Secretary Byroade on June 3, 1954, "that the real danger today lies in some foolish move on the part of Israel," the Assistant Secretary further elaborated: "The Israeli military authorities have maintained and to some extent increased a deliberate policy of retaliation which is not overruled by the civil government."[56] Although the Israeli strategy of retaliatory raids on both the Jordanian and Egyptian fronts was formulated, at least in 1953 and 1954, as a strictly defensive posture intended to deter the Jordanian and Egyptian authorities from supporting or acquiescing in the *fedayeen* infiltration into Israel, the administration remained wedded to its preconception, according to which "the Israelis have embarked on a deliberate policy of making things worse in the hope that by doing so they may . . . force peace on the Arabs."[57]

It was only in the aftermath of the September 1955 arms deal between Egypt and Czechoslovakia that Israel—in defiance of the continued American threats and pressures—abandoned its posture of intermittent, sporadic retaliatory raids and adopted instead the more ambitious and offensive concept of preventive war against Egypt as the core of its new strategy. In the thinking of Israeli Prime Minister Ben-Gurion, concern over the ever-escalating *fedayeen* raids merged with, and was further reinforced by security considerations related to the future military balance of power between Israel and Egypt. As a result, far from becoming resigned to an unpleasant reality, the Israeli leadership—faced with an American refusal to supply arms to Israel even in the wake of the September 1955 Egyptian-Czechoslovak arms deal (and with the failure of its deterrence vis-à-vis Egypt and Syria)—became increasingly predisposed to challenge the status-quo before the full impact of the arms deal between Egypt and Czechoslovakia drastically altered the very essence of the regional strategic environment. Believing that such a challenge would buy Israel a much-needed respite, during which the impact of the expected victory in the Sinai Peninsula would suffice as a deterrent against both small- and large-scale forms of harassment and encroachment, the Israeli Prime Minister predicated his confrontational posture (particularly after the resignation of Foreign Minister Sharett) upon the conviction that Israel's strategy of retaliatory raids had outlived its usefulness in view of the growing problem of *fedayeen* infiltration and the expected disruption of the military balance of power between Egypt and Israel. (During the period immediately following this arms deal, it similarly became evident that Army Chief of Staff Moshe Dayan's preferred strategy of trying to provoke the Egyptians into launching the first strike through a series of ever-escalating retaliatory raids had failed to accomplish its objective).

Against the backdrop of this acutely threatening regional landscape, Ben-Gurion ultimately adopted the view that only a large operation coming close to the scale of an all-out war could resolve—at least temporarily—Israel's security predicament: "After the arms deal . . . the Egyptian threat [to Israel] began to loom strategic. . . . In October [1955], the Egyptian announcement of the Czech deal was followed by Israeli failure to secure American . . . arms." As a result, Ben-Gurion ordered Dayan to make plans and prepare the IDF (Israel Defense Forces) to capture the Straits of Tiran and possibly the Gaza Strip and Northern Sinai as well. This was a major conceptual leap from the earlier plan to capture part or all of the Gaza Strip. It envisaged a large military operation, designed to drastically modify Israel's strategic environment rather than to end infiltration.[58] Perceived as directly threatening Israel's vital security interests, the arms deal between Czechoslovakia and Egypt, therefore, proved to be the major precipitant in Ben-Gurion's decision to strike Egypt in the Sinai Peninsula. As Troen elaborates:

There is considerable evidence that it was the arms deal between Czecho-slovakia and Egypt . . . that caused a fundamental change in his thinking about the dangers from Egypt and convinced Ben-Gurion to go to war. He concluded that this agreement would directly threaten vital Israeli security interests through the introduction of large quantities of modern weapons and the projection into the region of Soviet power, a force he deemed dangerous and hostile to Israel. It was especially these new circumstances that would require taking the field against the Egyptians. Ben-Gurion defined his task as ensuring that the coming conflict would be conducted under conditions that would be most favorable to Israel.[59]

Indeed, the Israeli nightmare was that once the sophisticated weapons Egypt had started to receive from the Eastern bloc in 1955 were fully absorbed into the Egyptian army, Israel would face a formidable enemy possessing—according to Dayan—"both the capacity and will to launch a devastating blow [which] could potentially put an end to the Israeli dream of a national homeland." As Dayan further observed:

It was clear to us in Israel that the primary purpose of this massive Egyptian rearmament was to prepare Egypt for a decisive confrontation with Israel in the near future. The Egyptian blockade, her planning and direction of mounting [*fedayeen*] activity against Israel, Nasser's own declarations, and now the Czech arms deal left no doubt in our minds that Egypt's purpose was to wipe us out, or at least win a decisive military victory which would leave us in helpless subjugation.[60]

The Sinai Campaign was intended to eliminate this perceived threat to the very existence of Israel by destroying the Arab world's potentially strongest army, and by seriously weakening the Nasser regime. Highly motivated to combat this frightening vision of Arab military superiority, which entailed the searing prospects of "the liquidation of Israel," and increasingly exasperated with the failure of the strategy of limited retaliatory raids as a means for curbing armed military infiltration into Israel, Ben-Gurion and Dayan remained undeterred by continued American warnings and threats, including the threat to militarily intervene in case Israel disrupted the territorial status quo. That Israel had been denied any American arms during the period preceding the Sinai Campaign served to broaden its perceived freedom of action. As Prime Minister Ben-Gurion fully recognized, any American-Israeli arms deal would have required ironclad Israeli commitments not to use American weapons for offensive purposes.

Israel's lack of even a small margin of strategic depth, along with its geographic attributes and vulnerabilities that could have made the task of protecting its major population centers against a full-scale Arab military offensive an insurmountable one, was a major factor in the Israeli decision to take the initiative and thus start the war on Egyptian territory. Indeed, in the minds of the Israeli leadership, the fear that the strategic balance of power between Israel and Egypt was bound to change in the aftermath of the September 1955 arms deal was further compounded by a cluster of geostrategic concerns and beliefs that revolved around the conviction that—by virtue of the proximity of Israel's population centers to its borders—it could ill-afford to absorb the first Arab strike and had therefore to adopt an offensive military strategy.

In the same way that, on the regional level, the Sinai Campaign can be viewed as "a declaration of the failure of [Israeli] deterrence" and as a recognition that the threat of continued Israeli reprisal was not deterring, so did the Israeli onslaught of October 29, 1956, expose—within the American-Israeli framework—the futility of the long-term, extended deterrence posture the administration had pursued toward the Ben-Gurion Government from its very inception.[61]

The fate of the administration's posture of long-term extended deterrence was therefore now sealed. With the balance of intrinsic interests and motivation favoring Israel, the exclusive American reliance upon threats and other forms of denial and coercion could not induce the Israeli Government to acquiesce. Not only did this posture of deterrence and coercion ultimately provoke, rather than restrain, Israel but also, in the process, it deprived the moderate faction within the Israeli leadership (led by Foreign Minister Sharett) of any leverage or bargaining power in its quest to prevent escalation and war. Denied any American "carrot," this group remained empty-handed in its effort to pursue the diplomatic option within the Egyptian-Israeli framework and had ultimately to watch from the sidelines (after Sharett's forced resignation from the government in June 1956) as the region drifted into the 1956 conflagration.

The fact that, during the period preceding the October 1956 onslaught, about 55 percent of capital imported to Israel originated in the United States, "made her extremely dependent on the decisions [of the Eisenhower Administration]." Furthermore, Israel's enormous trade deficit made the country acutely dependent on external sources of finance.[62] Nonetheless, in the absence of any American incentive or inducement (and against the backdrop of the momentary coalescence of Israeli, French, and British antagonism toward Egypt during the summer and autumn of 1956, which enabled Ben-Gurion to launch his war with Anglo-French political protection and French aerial cover), Israel perceived the costs of compliance as unacceptable, with the expected benefits of noncompliance outweighing the advantages of compliance, and with the bargaining range becoming increasingly constrained by the less menacing no-agreement alternative.

Indeed, it was this strategic convergence between Israel and President Nasser's European opponents (with France becoming, in 1956, a close strategic ally, providing Israel with arms and political support) that provided Israel with the necessary compensation for American support, thus reducing for Israel the costs of defiance and recalcitrance.

In adopting this recalcitrant course, the Israeli leadership was capable of projecting a credible image of unity and resolve. Indeed, the government enjoyed a broad margin of legitimacy and public support on security matters: the activist approach of the dominant Labor camp on the eve of war was backed by 62 percent of the Jewish vote. Therefore, Prime Minister Ben-Gurion was able to implement his preventive strategy with the conviction that this confrontational posture would be opposed only on the periphery of the Israeli political system.[63]

Still, the growing recognition, which became apparent as early as on October 21, 1955, "that there was a great danger that the Israelis might precipitate a war with Egypt while they felt they were still stronger and without awaiting a time when Soviet arms might make the Arabs the stronger,"[64] that "the Israelis despaired of continuing their existence within their present boundaries and would even risk World War III to improve their general situation,"[65] and that "the imminent shift in Israel's security policy, which will greatly increase the possibilities of general hostilities in the area, could still be avoided by the supply of a minimal number of modern jet fighters,"[66] did not precipitate any reorientation of the American arms sale policy toward Israel. Indeed, despite its recognition of the expected long-term ramifications of the September 1955 arms deal, and despite Ben-Gurion's and Sharett's strong pleas that the U.S. guarantee that the balance of military power within the Egyptian-Israeli dyad not be disrupted, the administration remained fully committed to its initial irreconcilable posture of refusing to supply arms to Israel. As Secretary Dulles elaborated on October 20, 1955, in a meeting of the NSC:

> For the United States to sponsor an arms race between Israel and the Arab states would be a very futile action. For one thing, Israel, with its small territory and population could not absorb more than a certain

amount of armaments, much less than the Arab States with their large territories and populations. . . . Accordingly, our best course of action is to assume that the arms deal between the Soviet Bloc and Egypt was a 'one-shot affair' and [respond] in the negative to all of Israel's [arms] requests. . . . In any event, we would probably lose out in backing Israel because in the long run the Arab States can absorb much more armament.[67]

As these words amply demonstrate, none of Ben-Gurion's warnings that unless provided with a "security treaty" as well as "jet planes comparable to MiGs, tanks and naval aircraft," Israel could resort to a preventive war against Egypt out of "disillusionment" and desperation,[68] led Secretary Dulles to reconsider the premises on which his strategy toward Israel had been shaped and delineated. Thus in his October 26, 1955, meeting with the Israeli Prime Minister after turning down Israel's requests for arms and security guarantees, the Secretary of State reiterated his belief that "Israel ought [to] seriously consider the extent of sacrifice it [was] willing to make to obtain a settlement."[69] This advice was repeatedly augmented by a spate of deterrence threats which asserted that a deliberate strategy of escalation by Israel along the Arab-Israeli borders in an effort "to coerce the Arabs into acquiescence" and ultimately impose a settlement from a position of relative strength, "would not be tolerated by the Western powers."[70]

The Israeli invasion, on October 29, 1956, of the Sinai Peninsula unequivocally exposed the fallacies inherent in this irreconcilable posture and made it abundantly evident that the pursuit of a long-term strategy of extended deterrence, devoid of any tangible inducements, rewards, and reassurances, could not overcome Israel's strong disinclination to compromise on vital security issues. Indeed, when the issues at stake were perceived by the Israeli leadership as inextricably linked to its very survival and well-being, Secretary Dulles's demands that "the security of Israel [should] better be assured by means other than an arms race," and that it should therefore predicate its quest for security "upon the international rule of law,"[71] quickly faded into the background of the American-Israeli dyad without significantly influencing Israel's strategic behavior in the Arab-Israeli zone (and without providing any ammunition to such moderate leaders as Foreign Minister Sharett, who were opposed to some of the comprehensive and drastic retaliatory raids Ben-Gurion and Dayan were continuously advocating). The fact that France provided Israel with an umbrella of military and political support on the eve of the Israeli attack reduced the risks inherent in the Israeli posture of defiance.

The American opposition to the Israeli strategy of retaliatory raids (which, in October 1956, merged with the considerably more comprehensive strategy of preventive war), which precipitated—in the wake of the Israeli onslaught of October 29, 1956, against Egypt—a series of punitive measures against Israel, was only one facet, fully integrated into a broad complex of attitudes, predilections and policies which, in the aggregate, formed a coherent American posture toward Israel between 1953 and 1956. One of the main tenets of this posture, which was closely patterned on the logic of Washington's approach to the issue of retaliatory raids, was the question of Israel's permanent boundaries with its neighbors. The continued American preoccupation with this core issue (which, in 1955, culminated in a joint American-British territorial plan) reflected the belief that by coercing Israel into unilateral territorial concessions, a window of opportunity would be opened, not only for defusing the Arab-Israel dispute but also for winning Arab support and cooperation in the all-important drive to contain Soviet penetration and encroachment. Indeed, from the moment of its inception, the administration looked upon a unilateral Israeli territorial concession (or a decision to restrict Jewish immigration and reduce the size of the Israeli army) as a confidence-building measure destined, by virtue of alleviating the persistent Arab fear of Israel's expansionist designs, to encourage the Arab world to enter into a negotiating process with Israel and thus to reduce conflict. Maintaining that "in the present situation the Israeli Government should not allow the contribution, which it can make to a settlement, to stand in the way of a settlement," the administration was uninhibited in addressing the adverse consequences that were bound to result from continued Israeli intransigence.[72] In the words of Assistant Secretary Byroade, in the absence of "a gesture on the part of Israel . . . it may be necessary for the United States to formulate a [peace] plan because it is in our interest that peaceful conditions return to the Near East and with us that is a primary objective."[73]

It is against the backdrop of this continued threat of imposing upon Israel the terms of peace that the American long-term posture of extended deterrence and coercion concerning the territorial components of a settlement unfolded during the period 1953–1956. Initially, the specific territorial parameters and demarcation lines of the envisaged settlement remained largely amorphous. Instead, American diplomacy focused on the need to extract from Israel either a commitment to the principle of territorial concessions or a pledge to limit the flow of Jewish immigration as measures expected to lay to rest Arab concerns that Israel harbored expansionist plans. (On occasion the administration added to these confidence-building measures a third component: the demand that Israel reduce the size of its army). The administration perceived these two issues—Israel's permanent boundaries, and the scope of immigration into Israel— as interchangeable by virtue of its belief that an unlimited flow of Jewish immigrants would ultimately result in an expansionist drive by Israel, designed to occupy the necessary space for accommodating its rapidly growing population. Fully committed to the Arab view that "there was a real and dangerous fear of Israeli expansion" throughout the Arab world,[74] leading members of the administration called upon Israel "to remedy [this] fear" by reexamining its "policy of encouraging large-scale immigration, taking into consideration [its] economic absorption capacity, [the] political effect on neighbors (i.e., Arab fears of expansion) and the inconsistency of this policy with [its] present attitude toward Arab refugees."[75] As a Department of State Position Paper, which was drafted on May 7, 1953, stated: "The Arab states continue to believe . . . that Israel harbors additional territorial ambitions and they fear that continued immigration into Israel will stimulate the desire for more territory. . . . It will undoubtedly be necessary for the United Sates to exert considerable influence on Israel to secure a modification in certain of its policies."[76]

One month later, in his June 9 conversation with Israeli Ambassador Eban, Assistant Secretary Byroade reiterated this basic argument although, on this occasion, he explained the prospects of Israeli expansion in terms of Israeli needs rather than opportunities. According to the memorandum of his conversation with Ambassador Eban, the Assistant Secretary said "that in his opinion . . . the Arabs do believe . . . that one day Israel will be forced to expand. There is the feeling in the Arab world that if, for example, the Soviet Union should permit the departure of Jews from Communist countries and if they should find their way to Israel, Israel would be forced to expand its frontiers to make room for them."[77]

Almost a year later, in his policy address of May 1, 1954, Assistant Secretary Byroade expressed identical thoughts and concerns:

A constant [Arab] fear is . . . of a greatly expanded immigration. These fears are enhanced by the knowledge that the only limitation imposed by the state on immigration into Israel is, in fact, the total number of those of the Jewish faith in the entire world. The Arabs know the capacity of the territory of Israel is limited. They see only one result—a future attempt at territorial expansion—and hence warfare of serious proportions.[78]

Oblivious to the fact that, in view of the British White Paper of 1939, which severely restricted Jewish immigration to Palestine from Europe on the very eve of the Holocaust, the entire issue of immigration into Israel had become an acutely sensitive and central question for Israeli leaders, comprising the *raison d'être* for the establishment of the state, Assistant Secretary Byroade remained relentless in his continued challenge of one of the basic tenets of Zionism. He similarly continued to urge American Jews to reduce their support of Israel, thus forcing it to become fully integrated in the region. "When we ask the Arab states to accept the existence of the State of Israel," Assistant Secretary Byroade argued in his May 1, 1954, address,

> it seems only fair to me that they should have the right to know . . . the magnitude of this new state. They look upon it as a product of expansionist Zionism which—regardless of any promise or paper treaty—will ultimately commit aggression to expand to suit its future needs. . . . Israel should see her own future in the context of a Middle Eastern state—and not as a headquarters of world-wide groupings of peoples of a particular religious faith, who must have special rights within and obligations to the Israeli state.[79]

One week later, in a speech in Chicago on May 7, 1954, Byroade was even more explicit in demanding that the Law of Return be modified in order to prevent unlimited Jewish immigration into Israel, and that Israel assure the Arabs that it was not planning military operations to expand its borders.[80]

Despite the recalcitrant and defiant Israeli reaction in the face of these demands (which was clearly manifested in Sharett's parliamentary address of May 10, 1954, in which he stated that "there is no way that anybody can force us to accept an agreement contradicting either our existence or our historical mission to serve as a safe haven to all Jews in distress"), and notwithstanding its vehement refusal to either reassess its immigration policy or accept the principle of a unilateral territorial concession, this welter of American demands and coercive threats did not subside, but was in fact transformed in subsequent months into a concrete and detailed American territorial posture predicated upon the principle of Israeli territorial concessions as the panacea for an overall settlement.

Believing that "peace could come only if the Israelis took the initiative," and that continued tension along the Arab-Israeli front was bound to result in the "loss of all Western influence in the Middle East, including oil, airfields, etc.,"[81] the administration, in early 1955, decided to collaborate with Britain for the sake of jointly defining the parameters of a Middle East settlement. Motivated by a realization that an Arab-Israeli accommodation was essential for safeguarding Jordan's territorial integrity, for consolidating the position of the West in the region, and ultimately for establishing a Middle East defense organization, the British Foreign Office fully shared the American vision of peace as necessitating significant Israeli territorial concessions. Convinced that a settlement failing to satisfy Arab demands was bound to result in the growing isolation of Baghdad and Amman in the Arab world and will thus generate additional resentment toward Britain throughout the region, the British Undersecretary for Middle Eastern Affairs, Evelyn Shuckburgh, who initiated the joint venture, was even prepared initially to proceed beyond the parameters of the American position in advocating that Israel concede the entire Negev area in return for retaining Western Galilee. Ultimately, however, he acquiesced in the less extreme concept of the "kissing triangles." Culminating in a plan which was code-named "Alpha," this concept envisioned the establishment, in the Israeli Negev, of two triangular sections that would link Egypt to Jordan. The apices of these triangles would touch the Arava Road several miles north of Eilat, thus linking the two halves of the Arab world, the African and Asian.

According to the draft of the plan, completed on July 14, 1955 (and incorporated into Secretary Dulles's address of August 26, 1955, to the Council on Foreign Relations, in which the Alpha Plan was inaugurated), "the idea . . . is that Israel should cede to Egypt a triangle of territory with its base on the Egyptian frontier and another triangle with the base on the Jordanian frontier. . . . We can see no way of reconciling the vital interests of both parties in the Negev except by this principle."[82]

And as Secretary Dulles explained to Israeli Foreign Minister Sharett on November 21, 1955:

> The Israeli Government must be prepared to make some concessions in the Negev, which would make possible an area of contact between Egypt and the other Arab states. . . . And the compensation to Israel from affecting a settlement would outweigh any loss of territory. . . . The Israeli Government should not take the position of saying that it will not consider a solution that might be worked out. . . . If Israel says no then the possibility of a settlement is off and we shall all have to face the consequences.[83]

Two and a half weeks later, in a second meeting between Secretary Dulles and Foreign Minister Sharett, the Secretary of State was equally explicit and unequivocal in alluding to the envisaged Israeli territorial contribution to a settlement. According to the memorandum of the December 6, 1955, conversation, "the secretary said that the Israeli-Egyptian Armistice Agreement provides that the armistice lines were to be without prejudice to the question of ultimate boundary decisions. The secretary said that he believes there are ways of avoiding this chamber of horrors and still provide land communication between Egypt and the rest of the Arab world."[84]

Notwithstanding the belief that "the U.S. was now in a position to put pressure on Israel," and that the Israeli Government "would not jeopardize public and private aid to Israel from the United States,"[85] the American and British expectations that the Alpha Plan would provide the impetus for an accelerated process of regional accommodation failed to materialize. In the absence of any concurrent reassuring measures or inducements, the administration's pursuit of a posture of extended coercion proved abortive. Viewing the territorial issue as a core security question, Prime Minister Ben-Gurion and Foreign Minister Sharett remained vehemently and irreconcilably opposed to the territorial components of the Alpha Plan regardless of the costs involved. As was the case during the April 8, 1953, encounter between Assistant Secretary Byroade and Foreign Minister Sharett, the Israeli leadership predicated its reaction to the plan upon the principle of simultaneous and symmetrical exchanges between Israel and its neighbors. Fully committed to its initial bargaining strategy, it was therefore unequivocal in rejecting demands based on the premise of unilateral Israeli concessions despite the "severe complications" in Israel's relations with the Western powers, which the Israeli leadership expected to result from its defiance and irreconcilability. In the words of Prime Minister Ben-Gurion: "Israel will not consider a peace offer involving any territorial concessions whatsoever. The neighboring countries have no right to one inch of Israel's land. In peace negotiations we will consider mutually-agreed border adjustments to the benefits of both sides. We are willing to meet Nasser in any way, but not on a basis of a plan calling for any part of Israeli territory to be torn away for the benefit of her neighbors." In view of the proximity of Israel's centers of population to its borders, Ben-Gurion further asserted that any settlement that involved a unilateral Israeli concession "would be suicidal."[86]

Indeed, against the backdrop of the persistent American refusal to provide any short-term assurances or compensations to Israel (in the form of bilateral security arrangements or the sale of arms), Jerusalem remained unwavering in its opposition to the Alpha Plan, referring to it as a prescription for "a built-in deadlock."[87] Insisting on specific American measures that would reduce the dangers to Israel inherent in any unilateral concessions as well as in the Egyptian-British agreement of October 19, 1954 (according to which Britain agreed to terminate its presence in the Suez Canal region, and thus remove a crucial buffer between Egyptian and Israeli forces), Israel remained irrevocably determined "to reject [the Alpha Plan's territorial components] even if we are told that there is no other way to reach a settlement." As Prime Minister Ben-Gurion further observed on May 14, 1955, in referring to the architects of Alpha: "if you want to take the Negev—you will have to fight. Our army will confront yours. . . . Any attempt on the part of Britain to force Israel to withdraw from territories it now possesses will require the deployment of troops to accomplish this objective. Under such circumstances, Israel would fight." [88]

None of these arguments and threats precipitated change in the American approach. And while the administration was prepared to consider multilateral guarantees to Israel after "a general settlement" had been reached on the basis of unilateral Israel concessions, it looked upon such a commitment as "the biggest American carrot," which should not, therefore, "be given away" prematurely, namely, before "a general agreement [on such issues] as water, Arab refugees, territorial adjustments, and [the] status of Jerusalem" had emerged.[89] As for the unilateral guarantees or a defense treaty, Secretary Dulles—who wished to avoid a confrontation with Egypt over the issue—reiterated his conviction that the administration would not be able to obtain Senate ratification for the idea "in the current state of tension which prevailed between Israel and its neighbors."[90]

Ultimately, with the balance of intrinsic interests at stake favoring Israel, and with Egypt remaining highly critical of the Alpha Plan (Egypt maintained that the proposed Israeli concessions were too minimal), the architects of Alpha were forced to suspend their entire initiative.

It was not that the planners of Alpha were unaware of Israel's position with regard to the Negev, but they "definitely failed to sense the intensity of its attachment to that part of the country. For the founding fathers of the Zionist state . . . the Negev was not merely . . . a barren territory . . . but an embodiment of the whole difference between Israel as a normal state with a future and Israel as an unviable enclave." Instead of providing the Israelis with a sense of security that would allow them greater flexibility, Alpha confronted them "with alarming international pressures which only consolidated their determination never to exchange their strategic self-reliance for outside guarantees of any kind.

The fact that the plan refrained from even mentioning the conclusion of full peace with the Arabs certainly did not facilitate Israel's readiness for territorial concessions."[91]

Unable to coerce Israel into acquiescence (and to induce Nasser to publicly endorse Alpha), the administration ultimately abandoned its efforts to comprehensively resolve the Arab-Israeli conflict. Instead, it adopted an incremental peacemaking strategy, which was most clearly manifested in the futile attempt of former Deputy Defense Secretary Robert Anderson to set in motion a process of conflict-reduction in the Egyptian-Israeli sphere. Code-named the Gamma Plan, Anderson's mission of late 1955 and early 1956 (which originated in earlier CIA efforts to arrange a meeting between President Nasser and a high-ranking Israeli official) consisted of a series of shuttles between Cairo and Jerusalem, designed to clarify positions, narrow differences between Israel and Egypt, and pave the way for a summit meeting between President Nasser and Prime Minister Ben-Gurion.

However, it quickly became evident that despite the repeated American warnings of the "severe repercussions," which would follow from its continued refusal "to show flexibility" on the territorial issue, Israel remained strongly opposed to any a priori unilateral concessions. Thus it repeatedly insisted that peace could be established only on the basis of the political and territorial status quo. Whereas Egypt's position was "that the boundaries would have to be revised in Arab favor, and that Israel would have to accept in principle the return of the Arab refugees," Israel remained committed to the view that the boundaries established by the 1949 armistice should not be altered, although it was prepared to consider "*mutual* minor border adjustments that would help resolve local problems such as villagers' access to land or water." Repeatedly, Prime Minister Ben-Gurion warned that Israel would resist militarily any attempt to coerce it into relinquishing territory.[92]

Furthermore, maintaining that no intermediary could explain Israel's positions on substantive issues as convincingly as Israel's representatives themselves, the Israeli Prime Minister looked upon direct Egyptian-Israeli talks (preferably at the highest level) as an essential prerequisite for success, which would also help reduce the tension between Cairo and Jerusalem.

For all of Anderson's initial optimism, the American emissary soon realized that these Israeli predilections and positions could not be reconciled with the Egyptian posture, as President Nasser remained unwavering in his refusal to either directly negotiate with Israel, stabilize the perilous situation along the Egyptian-Israeli border, or reconsider the "triangles" concept. Maintaining that opposition to peace with Israel in the Arab world was pervasive and violent, the Egyptian President reiterated that he risked being assassinated, as King Abdullah of Jordan had been, if direct contacts with Israel were initiated. On the other hand, Israel remained irreconcilably committed to its view that direct contacts with Egypt were necessary in order "to dispel the distrust presently prevailing between the parties . . . and to stabilize the cease-fire."[93]

Ultimately, deprived of any margin of maneuverability, Anderson decided—in late March 1956—to terminate his mission. As was the case with the Alpha Plan, the Gamma initiative could not provide the impetus for progress toward conflict resolution or even crisis management within the highly tense Egyptian-Israeli framework. In Touval's words:

> As it became clear that the [Anderson] mediation could not serve the goal of containing or limiting Soviet penetration, the American willingness to exert itself in the search for peace faded away. In other words, in this case the mediation attempting to reach an Egyptian-Israeli agreement was in part an instrument used in the pursuit of another and more important goal. Once the U.S. concluded that the positive incentives offered to Egypt—the aid for constructing the Aswan Dam and qualified American support for Egypt in the negotiations with Israel—failed to produce the results hoped for, both incentives were withdrawn.[94]

Notwithstanding its salience and centrality for Prime Minister Ben-Gurion and Foreign Minister Sharett, the territorial issue was only one facet within the broad complex of positions and policy lines initiated and supported by the Eisenhower Administration during its first term in office in an effort to allay Arab lingering suspicions that American policy had been invariably determined "by efforts made on the American domestic political scene."[95] Thus, in addition to its continued preoccupation with the territorial components of a settlement, the administration devoted considerable attention to other core issues, including the highly charged predicament of the Palestinian refugees. Concerning the emotion-laden refugee question, the persistent American demand that Israel accept the principle of repatriation and thus agree to settle, in the Negev and the Western Galilee, an unspecified number of Palestinian refugees, was met with a staunch Israeli opposition. Thus although Assistant Secretary Byroade, in his conversation of June 9, 1953, with Israeli Ambassador Eban, addressed the problem "in general terms only,"[96] Israel remained unmoved, insisting—in the words of Foreign Minister Sharett—that "to do so would only open up the whole refugee question and would encourage in the refugees a hope which could not be materialized."[97]

Two years later, when the issue was raised once again as an integral part of the Alpha Plan, the balance of interests and resolve remained in Israel's favor. Convinced that its acceptance of the principle of repatriation would result in a massive flow of Palestinian refugees which, in turn, would ultimately threaten its very existence as a Jewish state, Prime Minister Ben-Gurion was irreconcilable in rejecting the proposal that Israel absorb 75,000 refugees at a rate of 15,000 a year. Instead, he reiterated Israel's readiness to compensate the refugees for the property they had left behind as part of a broad multilateral assistance program.

Ultimately, notwithstanding the residual American hope that in view of the "Soviet entry into the picture," Israel "would . . . play, from now on, the part of a good neighbor of the Arabs and not seek to maintain itself by its own force," and would therefore seek "a negotiated settlement" while it "still had a military equality,"[98] it became clear in subsequent months that in the absence of any significant inducement or a symmetrical negotiating framework, the persistent pursuit of a coercive posture that threatened core Israeli values and interests was doomed to failure. Thus contrary to Secretary Dulles's belief that "the full significance of the changed situation [in the wake of the Czech-Egyptian arms deal] would be reflected in [more accommodative] Israeli attitudes,"[99] the September 1955 arms deal had a diametrically opposite impact upon Israel's *modus operandi*. By virtue of further reinforcing and solidifying a pervasive Israeli vision of growing isolation and potential vulnerability, it provided a major trigger or impetus which—together with such American initiatives as the Alpha Plan—precipitated a defiant Israeli strategy, which culminated in the October 29, 1956, preventive onslaught against Egypt.

Thus, with the political option subsiding into the background of the Arab-Israeli framework in the aftermath of the failure of both the Alpha and Gamma Plans, what was left for American planners was to prepare a broad repertoire of comprehensive economic and military sanctions, to be imposed upon Israel in case it initiated war.

Finally, even on such issues as the right of transit in the Gulf of Eilat (Aqaba), where the Israeli position was perceived by the administration as valid and legitimate, President Eisenhower and Secretary Dulles refused to take action after Egypt disrupted, in 1954, Israeli commercial traffic in the Gulf. When Israel tried to force the issue by sending a ship (the *Bat Galim*) through the Suez Canal in September of 1954, the administration expressed anger at the Israeli action and acquiesced in Egypt's impounding of the ship. It further warned Israel "not to seek . . . the settlement of specific issues by force, such as the right of transit in the Gulf of Aqaba."[100]

As the preceding analysis sought to demonstrate, the American posture toward Israel from 1953 to 1956 was patterned on a broad cluster of strategic premises and beliefs, which evolved around the need to consolidate a multilateral regional security alliance in order to effectively contain Soviet encroachment. In view of unabated "Arab-Israeli tensions," these strategic imperatives were viewed as incompatible with the idea of the "inclusion of Israel into any regional grouping."[101] Indeed, in its desire to win the support and goodwill of the Arab world, the administration was careful not to incorporate any of the premises of the special relationship paradigm into its policy toward Israel. In the process, not only did it scrupulously avoid "the preferential treatment [of Israel],"[102] but it also remained irrevocably committed to a posture of long-term deterrence and coercion toward Israel, which included a continued effort "to use U.S. influence to secure . . . some concessions by Israel [as a means of] securing Arab-Israeli boundary settlements," "to urge Israel to accept a limited number of Arab refugees," "to progressively reduce the amount of economic aid furnished to Israel," and "to deter Israel from embarking upon aggression as a preventive measure while she has military superiority."[103]

For all this American desire to implement a policy of long-term extended deterrence and coercion toward Israel and thus to decouple its regional behavior from any linkage with the special relationship paradigm, it ultimately became evident that the balance of the intrinsic interests at stake favored Israel. As a result, highly motivated and determined to defy American pressure, it managed to prevail in most of the encounters with the administration. Israel's alliance with France on the eve of the 1956 conflagration, under the terms of which Israel received the weapons systems the Eisenhower Administration had continuously refused to supply, provided the Ben-Gurion Government with an adequate compensation and an added inducement to maintain its defiant course.

In this context of constant confrontations between Washington and Jerusalem, the role of the representatives of the special relationship paradigm was at best marginal. Not only did the President and his entourage repeatedly express their unwavering determination to ignore the premises of the special relationship in the shaping of American policy toward Israel, but they tended to view the efforts of the representatives of the special relationship paradigm to exert pressure upon the administration as illegitimate activities which, according to Secretary Dulles, "would be counter-productive" if they were not stopped.[104] As the Secretary of State further elaborated in his March 2, 1956, conversation with Ambassador Eban: "The more the friends of Israel try to exert pressures against the administration, the more difficult it is to convince the Arabs that they do not need to turn to the Soviets. All the activities that friends of Israel customarily resort to in whipping up pressure . . . do not help to create a basis for understanding and cooperation between our two Governments."[105]

In view of this initial dichotomy between the American national interest and the special relationship paradigms, it is clear not only why the forces affiliated with the latter largely failed in their attempts to either constrain or redirect American policy toward Israel, but also why leading administration officials resorted to harsh and irreconcilable rhetoric in alluding to the organizational representatives of the special relationship paradigm. In the words of former Assistant Secretary Byroade (who in May 1955 was appointed American Ambassador to Egypt), which illustrate the unbridgeable gap separating the two paradigms from one another:

America never has been able to understand the Arab-Israeli issue . . . and there has been nothing in America to match the distortion of the Zionists. We now have a situation, however, that the American people can understand—and that is the threat from the Soviet Union in this part of the world. The problem of Israel and of Zionism at home can be put in the proper context for the first time . . . in such a way as to practically break the back of Zionism as a political force.[106]

And indeed, not only did such prominent representatives of the special relationship paradigm as Rabbi Abba Hillel Silver, Chairman of the American Zionist Council, remain empty-handed in their continued efforts to modify the American posture on such issues as the sale of arms to Israel (as the outcome of his April 26, 1956, meeting with President Eisenhower indicates), but they were also occasionally maneuvered by the administration into performing the role of a liaison with the Israeli Government, thus becoming the unofficial representatives of the Eisenhower Presidency rather than the independent advocates of the special relationship.[107] Deprived of continuous access to the top levels of the administration, and torn by incessant rivalries and friction, the leadership of the American Jewish community was hardly in a position to effectively constrain the administration during the entire Eisenhower era. As Alteras points out, "although Jewish leaders would make the rounds of the State Department and at times would be received by the President, they were listened to politely but failed to influence the decision makers in moving away from 'impartiality.' "[108] Indeed, despite Rabbi Silver's "very strong plea,"[109] of April 26, 1956, that the administration agree to sell arms to Israel, no change in the traditional posture of the Eisenhower Presidency was forthcoming. According to Secretary Dulles's account of the conversation, "I said that we did not want our policy to seem to be made by the Zionists. . . . The president said that he was not going to be influenced at all by political considerations and if doing what he thought right resulted in not being elected, that would be quite agreeable to him."[110] And while several Jewish leaders echoed Rabbi Silver's concern over the American position, this activity did not amount, during the entire Eisenhower era, to a serious legitimacy crisis for the Administration.

Thus, notwithstanding the lobbying efforts of several Jewish leaders and organizations in support of Israel during the Suez Crisis, the administration remained relentless in its drive to coerce Israel into completing its withdrawal from the Sinai Peninsula. Motivated by a desire to quickly defuse the acutely menacing regional situation precipitated by the Israeli onslaught of October 29, 1956, President Eisenhower remained fully and irrevocably wedded to his view that the only way to prevent Moscow from escalating the crisis was to compel Israel to acquiesce by progressively raising the costs of noncompliance and procrastination. And while a number of prominent Jewish representatives of the special relationship paradigm strongly defended the Israeli position, several other leaders became increasingly critical of Israeli policy as the crisis in American-Israeli relations approached its confrontational phase.[111] The remarks of Nahum Goldmann, President of the World Jewish Congress, in a letter to Prime Minister Ben-Gurion of November 7, 1956, shed light on the inability of the backbone of the special relationship paradigm to unanimously confront the administration in an effort to constrain its margin of maneuverability and range of coercive measures contemplated vis-à-vis the Israeli Government:

> With regard to Israel's refusal to move from Sinai or even to transfer its positions to an international force. . . . I must tell you that it is impossible to mobilize an American-Jewish front to support this posture. If there will be an open dispute between Israel and the US Government on this point

[and] if this should lead to cessation of the [United Jewish Appeal] and Bonds, I foresee great difficulties in renewing these enterprises. . . . What is needed is a step that will prevent an open split with Eisenhower.[112]

At that time, the U.S. Jewish community was not yet a viable, cohesive, and well-organized political force. This fragmentation contributed to the failure of its sporadic efforts to reorient the course of American diplomacy toward Israel.

It is true that another traditional representative of the special relationship paradigm, the U.S. Congress, was occasionally successful in limiting the scope of the coercive measures contemplated or implemented vis-à-vis Israel.[113] Nonetheless, Congress completely failed in its quest to change the basic direction and course of the administration's policy toward Israel. Thus on February 6, 1956, in response to a joint letter from several members of the House of Representatives (which was sent on February 3, 1956), calling upon the administration to supply arms to Israel, Secretary Dulles expressed his belief that "the security of Israel [could] . . . better be assured by means other than an arms race," and that it should therefore predicate its quest for security "upon the international rule of law."[114]

The activities of the AFL-CIO which—during the Suez Crisis—called for the continued Israeli civilian presence in the Gaza strip, similarly failed to induce change in the administration's strategy.[115] This strategy continued to be predicated upon the notions of extended deterrence and coercion as the administration consistently refused to integrate into its policy toward Israel any of the basic premises of the special relationship paradigm.

That this long-term strategy of extended deterrence and coercion ultimately failed to accomplish its objectives is, of course, quite a different matter and cannot be attributed to the efforts of the forces affiliated with the special relationship paradigm to modify Washington's Middle East policy.[116]

III

The Emergence of Strategic Convergence

The heart of the matter . . . is the urgent necessity to strengthen the bulwarks of international order and justice against the forces of lawlessness and destruction which currently are at work in the Middle East. We have been glad that Israel shares this purpose, as illustrated by your deeply appreciated acquiescence in the use of Israel's airspace by United States and UK aircraft in their mission in support of Jordan. . . . We believe that Israel should be in a position to deter an attempt at aggression by indigenous forces, and are prepared to examine the military implications of this problem with an open mind. . . . The critical situation in the Middle East today gives Israel manifold opportunities to contribute, from its resources of spiritual strength and determination of purpose, to a stable international order.

—SECRETARY OF STATE JOHN FOSTER DULLES, AUGUST 1, 1958
(Quoted from his letter to Israeli Prime Minister David Ben-Gurion)

A first glance at American-Israeli relations as they were delineated during President Eisenhower's second term suggests that the administration remained committed, during the period 1957–1960, to most of the background images and derivative policy lines that had previously characterized its thinking and behavior on both the global and regional levels. Thus, in the same way that its initial strategy and approach to the Middle East had been predicated upon an acutely threatening vision of the Soviet Union as an expansionist and aggressive power whose forays into the region endangered a broad complex of vital American interests, so did the administration remain invariably committed to the belief that "the security interests of the United States would be critically endangered if the Near East should fall under Soviet influence or control."[1] Similarly, the administration was still motivated, in its attitudes and policies toward Israel, by a desire to allay the unabated, lingering Arab suspicions that the forces affiliated with the special relationship paradigm continuously played a major role in the shaping of the American posture toward Israel, as they had since its inception. As Secretary Dulles pointed out in his conversation with Ambassador Eban on October 31, 1957:

> Our great problem . . . was that we were tagged as supporters of Israel and Zionism, while the Soviet Union claimed to be against them. This was a liability for us to carry in the Arab world. The way to escape it was to make the Arabs see that the Soviet Union was a greater danger than Israel.[2]

As the most appropriate means of accomplishing this goal, the Secretary again called upon Israel, as he had on numerous other occasions in previous years, "to try hard . . . to avoid any actions tending to revive Arab fears of Israel . . . and drive home to the Arabs the realization that the real danger comes from the Soviet Union."[3] The specific policy lines that derived from this overriding need were closely patterned on earlier American ideas and plans. Thus in his June 24, 1957, meeting with Levi Eshkol, the Israeli Finance Minister, Secretary Dulles sought to establish a negative linkage between Israel's continued "open-door policy toward immigration," and the level of economic aid:

> Whether Israel should have an immigration policy which could recreate economic problems might be a matter for Israel to decide but this question had international repercussions. There was the apparently genuine concern of the Arabs at increased immigration into Israel and its implications with regard to possible territorial expansion. This concern would be heightened if the United States provided financial support for such immigration.[4]

In addition to this long-standing, unabated opposition to the Israeli "policy of accepting all the Jews who wished to come to Israel," which distracted "the Arabs from the Soviet Union, the real danger to the area,"[5] the administration remained committed—albeit with an ever-diminishing enthusiasm and conviction—to its initial policy of refusing to sell arms to Israel, thus avoiding, during its entire tenure, the offering of a major reassuring inducement to Israel (and a potential powerful leverage on Jerusalem's behavior).

These elements of continuity notwithstanding, a careful review of the period 1957–1960 suggests that beneath the facade of consistency, the American posture toward the region in general, and toward Israel in particular, gradually changed. This transformation reflected the premises of the January 5, 1957, Eisenhower Doctrine (which underscored the need to establish a regional network of *bilateral* security arrangements between

the U.S. and individual Middle-Eastern parties) and was specifically precipitated by the cumulative impact of a sequence of regional developments and crises (which unfolded in 1957 and 1958) upon the thinking
and behavior of the American leadership.

As a result of these developments, the perception of Israel as a potential strategic asset to the United States came to increasingly permeate
the cognitive map of Washington's policymakers. And although this perceptual shift was never transformed into concrete, compatible action on
most core issues, it did establish the conceptual infrastructure that later
enabled President Kennedy to complete the swing of the pendulum and
thus to convert the latent and unobtrusive into an explicit and manifest
American posture.[6] In other words, while the administration continued
to adhere to several tenets of its preliminary policy within the American-
Israeli dyad, it became increasingly predisposed to abandon most of its
coercive tactics.

Nor were these tenets any longer integrated into a coherent, multifaceted plan. Confined largely to the level of the symbolic and ritualistic, the
administration's posture in the Arab-Israeli zone was ultimately that of
abandoning any hope that a settlement—partial or comprehensive—of
the Arab-Israeli conflict was feasible during its tenure. Confronted with a
turbulent and volatile regional environment, in which the Arab-Israeli
conflict comprised but one among many cleavages and disputes, the
Eisenhower Presidency was forced to abandon its preexisting vision of an
Arab-Israeli peace as a prerequisite for ensuring Arab unity and support
in the encounter with Soviet expansionism. Indeed, faced with a plethora of regional factors and crises, among which were the issues of Arab nationalism, neutralism, anticolonialism, and incessant inter-Arab rivalries
(which included an intensive and enduring Egyptian-Iraqi rivalry, and an
equally deep feud between Saudi Arabia and Iraq), the administration
gradually came to realize that its initial propensity to approach regional
instabilities exclusively through the lens of the Soviet threat to Western interests was divorced from a highly dynamic regional context. It was thus
the administration's learning experience and inability to superimpose its
global perspective and broad East-West considerations upon the Middle
East that precipitated a major reassessment of Washington's regional approach during President Eisenhower's second term.[7]

Contrary to the very detailed Alpha Plan, the result of a prolonged
and intensive search for a comprehensive settlement, Secretary Dulles realized—two years after the plan had been inaugurated—that "the problems of the area . . . were difficult of solution even without the Russians."

As the memorandum of his August 6, 1957, meeting with Ambassador Eban further stated, the Secretary "did not feel hopeful as to the prospects of an overall early settlement, since there was too much evil loose in the area. Therefore, we must live with the problems on a crisis-to-crisis basis, perhaps until there was a basic change in Soviet thinking."[8]

This shift in American regional predilections, priorities, and perceptions inevitably affected Washington's vision of Israel, although not its policies toward it. Thus, while some of the earlier tenets of the administration's policy (such as the demand that Israel restrict Jewish immigration) remained intact, they were for the most part addressed intermittently and in isolation, without being integrated into any coherent and coercive design, and without the sense of urgency that had precipitated their original delineation. With the hope of achieving Arab unity and of consolidating a broadly based regional coalition against the Soviet threat receding into the background against the regional backdrop of incessant inter-Arab cleavages and pervasive hostility toward the West and the colonialist legacy, there was no need to persist in the effort to secure Arab goodwill by coercing Israel into territorial concessions. Confronted with a regional setting that remained defiant (or indifferent) to American objectives, American diplomacy was ultimately forced to shift gears and thus to set aside its initial multilateral approach in favor of a less ambitious bilateral approach that laid the groundwork for cooperating with *any* regional power predisposed to oppose Soviet penetration.

In other words, with the acutely menacing vision of Arab defection to the Soviet orbit becoming partially realized despite the early American effort to ignore, or set aside, the basic premises of the special relationship paradigm, the President and his entourage became increasingly prepared to reassess their preexisting premises, including the view of Israel as a strategic liability and as an impediment to Washington's regional plans. While the goal of defending the remaining pro-Western strongholds against Soviet encroachment continued to preoccupy the American leadership during the years which followed the Suez Crisis, the fact that it adopted an *ad hoc* and particularistic approach to concrete issues and crises as they unfolded (no longer seeking to integrate them into a broader security alliance) implied that the perception of Israel could be decoupled now from the cluster of regional considerations and concerns in which it had been inextricably embedded. Thus was the regional and multilateral downgraded and set aside in favor of the local and the bilateral.

A clear illustration of this growing propensity to deviate—at least on the conceptual level—from the initial American approach toward Israel is provided by a juxtaposition of three messages which involved the Reverend Edward L. R. Elson of the National Presbyterian Church in Washington, who was a close friend of both the President and Secretary Dulles. According to Reverend Elson's recollections, President Eisenhower informed him that in March 1953, "some Zionist officials called at the White House, and in their visit attempted to enlist the new president's interest in Israel." As he further disclosed on September 22, 1968:

> The president turned to them and inquired whether they were visiting him as representatives of Americans or representatives of some other foreign interest. Then he turned to them and pointed to a map of the world and indicated to them the great Arab land bridge between the continents of Asia, Europe and Africa. He told them in no uncertain terms that whoever had the friendship of the people of this land bridge astride these three continents would in any worldwide conflict have the advantage, and that . . . friendship in this area was essential to the maintenance of stability and world order.[9]

Four years later, as the American-Israeli crisis over Israel's withdrawal from the entire Sinai Peninsula reached its climax, this perspective remained unchanged. Thus, in an effort to mobilize Christian support for the administration's coercive course vis-à-vis Israel, Secretary Dulles, in his telephone conversation of February 22, 1957, with Reverend Elson, observed that "it would help if something could be said in the pulpit [in support of the administration's position]." The Secretary further said "that if the Jews have the veto on US foreign policy, the consequences will be disastrous. The future of the UN was at stake. . . . A country could not seize what did not belong to it and then hold out for assurances."[10] Seeking to counterbalance the forces associated with the special relationship paradigm, the Secretary reiterated his conviction that these forces and organizations were pursuing policies that were incompatible with the American national interest.[11]

However, less than a year and a half after portraying this picture of an unbridgeable gap between the American national interest paradigm and the special relationship paradigm, in a letter to Reverend Elson on July 31, 1958, Secretary Dulles's words were suddenly permeated with empathy and sympathy toward Israel. Drafted in the course of the Lebanese and Jordanian crises, the letter reflected the total American disillusionment with the course of Egypt's policy, as well as the growing realization that, since Arab hostility toward Israel was profound and broadly-based, any expectation that the Arab-Israeli predicament would

wither away and sink into oblivion as a result of a determined American
peacemaking effort, was unrealistic:

> In any conversation with an Arab, *he* is the one that brings up the subject
> of Israel. Underlying all Arab thought is resentment toward the existence
> of Israel and an underlying determination, some day, to get rid of it. . . .
> It is necessary to remember that it is antipathy against that state, practi-
> cally universal among all Arabs, that provides fertile ground for Nasser's
> hate propaganda.[12]

The corollary of this modified perception was clear. While American
diplomacy still hoped to defuse or resolve aspects of the Arab-Israeli
conflict, it became increasingly prepared to reassess its preconceived
view that comprehensive peace between Israel and its neighbors was feasible, and could provide the needed impetus for achieving Arab unity
and support in the all-important encounter with Soviet designs. With the
perception of comprehensive peace as a viable policy goal fading into
the background, the rationale for coercing Israel into acquiescence became equally questionable. Not only did the posture of extended deterrence and coercion that had been pursued from 1953 to 1956 fail to influence Israel's basic strategy in the Arab-Israeli sphere, but in view of
the unabated Arab hostility toward Israel, the administration become
convinced that the prospects of mitigating the dispute or of effectively
side-stepping it for the sake of promoting its containment agenda in the
region were dim. As Secretary Dulles acknowledged in his July 31, 1958,
letter to Reverend Elson:

> I never fail, in any communication with Arab leaders, oral or written, to
> stress . . . that belief in God should create between them and us the com-
> mon purpose of opposing atheistic Communism. However, in a conver-
> sation of this kind with King [Ibn] Saud [of Saudi Arabia], he remarked
> that while it was well to remember that the communists are no friends of
> ours, yet Arabs are forced to realize that Communism is a long way off, Is-
> rael is a bitter enemy in our own backyard.[13]

As was the case during the early years of the Eisenhower Presidency,
the perception of Israel held by leading administration officials during
the President's second term was closely patterned on a broad complex of
global and regional beliefs and expectations. However, while previously
the vision of Israel as a strategic liability to the U.S. had been a byproduct of the overriding American desire to solicit the support of all *major*
Arab powers in a joint defense posture against Soviet encroachment,

now, during a time when it was becoming increasingly evident that the broad multilateral approach could not provide the impetus for progress, the very essence of the bilateral approach—which progressively came to dominate the administration's thinking—reflected a desire to cooperate individually and separately with any regional power that was aware of or threatened by the Soviet expansionist drive. And while this growing recognition of the need to rescue and assist the remaining islands of pro-Western orientation did not trigger an immediate and dramatic change in the specific American posture, it nevertheless created a new lens through which Israel's regional role could now be assessed.

Further reinforced by the growing willingness of the Eisenhower Presidency to decouple its activities in the Middle East from the strains and anxieties of the Arab-Israeli predicament and thus to avoid a direct and simultaneous entanglement with the complex of highly controversial, emotion-laden issues comprising the core of the dispute, this new bilateral orientation was based on a differentiated view of the specific circumstances existing in each zone rather than on a monolithic and homogenous vision of the region as a whole. As the President observed as early as on November 23, 1956: "We are in a period in which we can strengthen our bilateral arrangements with the various Arab countries, not being so bound as in the past by the Arab-Israeli dispute."[14]

Although confined initially to Arab parties, it was this premise of bilateralism that laid the groundwork for the eventual development of security ties between Washington and Jerusalem. Indeed, with the perception of an inextricable linkage between the individual and the collective, or between the particular and the general, subsiding into the background, the American leadership became increasingly predisposed—in the aftermath of the Suez Crisis—to abandon its original perception of Israel "as an obstacle to the attainment of American objectives."[15] As Spiegel further asserts:

> In the crisis atmosphere of the post-Suez era, Eisenhower and Dulles were no longer wooing the whole Arab world to gain allies in the conflict with the Soviet Union. Now they were intervening in intra-Arab affairs to assure that those individuals and forces inclined to reject Soviet influence either rose to power or remained in authority.[16]

It was in this revised context that Israel—which had demonstrated impressive military capabilities during the Sinai Campaign—came to be gradually viewed as a power that could contribute, albeit unobtrusively and indirectly, toward the accomplishment of those objectives. Against the backdrop of the growing perceived threat to the very existence of such pro-Western regimes as Jordan and Lebanon, the administration could not remain oblivious to the potential value of Israel as a counterbalance to the forces of radical Arab nationalism. In terms of pure balance of power considerations, any regional actor with an abiding interest in preventing the collapse of the remaining pro-Western strongholds had now to be at least quietly encouraged and supported by the U.S. Not only was Israel, by virtue of its strategic interests, geographical proximity, and proven military capabilities increasingly depicted—in the aftermath of the Suez Crisis—as a power that could provide invaluable assistance to the U.S. and Britain in their efforts to protect such besieged entities as the Hashemite dynasty of Jordan, but it came to be looked upon in Washington as having a significant deterring potential vis-à-vis Egypt and Syria. During the President's first term, Israel had been the target of his posture of long-term extended deterrence and coercion;now it became one of the regional vehicles for reinforcing American deterrence strategy vis-à-vis such powers as Egypt and Syria, which were looked upon in Washington as Soviet proxies. And although no formal, bilateral security ties between Washington and Jerusalem were established, a tacit understanding regarding the nature and magnitude of the threat to regional stability did emerge between President Eisenhower and Prime Minister Ben-Gurion, transforming a highly conflictual, emotion-laden structure into a more benign framework.

As we shall soon witness, the severe regional crisis of July 1958, which was precipitated by the Iraqi revolution, provided the impetus for converting this subdued, implicit and tacit understanding into an explicit—albeit narrowly defined—collaborative strategic course, designed to rescue the besieged Hashemite Kingdom of Jordan. And while this modified perception of Israel as a potential strategic asset to the U.S., capable of deterring the regional proxies of "International Communism" from disrupting the balance of power, did not yet result—during the Eisenhower era—in a revised American policy on such issues as the sale of arms to Israel, it helped eliminate much of the strain that had characterized the first Eisenhower term, and thus laid the groundwork for the future reorientation of American strategy toward Israel. As Ambassador Eban observes, in the aftermath of the July 1958 crisis, "the United States developed a sharper sensitivity than before toward the problems of Israel's defense." "The road was open," he concludes, "for a more dignified and prosperous period in American-Israeli relations."[17]

It would, however, be left to President Kennedy to close the gap that still separated the operational from the perceptual, and thus to predicate the specific American posture within the American-Israeli framework upon the vision of Israel as an ally in the struggle "to contain Soviet-backed revolutionary Arab nationalism."[18]

Two months after the Suez Crisis had waned with the completion of Israel's withdrawal from the Sinai Peninsula and the Gaza strip, a sequence of inter-Arab crises began to disrupt the region, which would culminate in July 1958. These crises repeatedly demonstrated to the architects of American Middle East diplomacy that their initial hope of forging a broad multilateral security organization incorporating all major Arab parties was completely divorced from the actual dynamics of the region.[19] On April 10, 1957, King Hussein of Jordan, reacting to pro-Nasserist threats to his throne, dismissed Prime Minister Sulayman al-Nabulsi, and declared that Jordan was threatened by "International Communism." Alarmed by the increasingly radical policies of the al-Nabulsi Cabinet, which established diplomatic relations with the Soviet Union, recognized Communist China, and expressed willingness to accept Soviet military and economic aid, King Hussein moved forcefully to confront his domestic opposition. In addition to Prime Minister al-Nabulsi, he ousted several high-ranking military officers, including Chief of Staff Ali Abu Nuwar, and placed Jordan under martial law.[20] Furthermore, viewing the independence and territorial integrity of Jordan as vital, the President, on April 26, dispatched the Sixth Fleet to the eastern Mediterranean as a display of American support for the Hashemite Kingdom. Three days later, the administration granted Jordan $10 million in emergency aid, which included a variety of military equipment. Two months later, Jordan received an additional $20 million.[21]

Ultimately, the U.S. posture of strong deterrence proved effective, as the King quickly suppressed domestic opposition while Egypt and Syria—the King's chief adversaries—refrained from any direct intervention on the side of the anti-royalists. Although Israel remained on the sidelines throughout the crisis, it reiterated its intention to seize the West Bank of the Jordan should King Hussein be toppled or lose control over events. Fearing that an Israeli intervention in the crisis would exacerbate an already tense situation by injecting the strains of the Arab-Israeli predicament into a fundamentally different regional context, the President adopted an unusually conciliatory rhetoric toward Prime Minister Ben-Gurion, assuring him that American policy "embraced the preservation of Israel."[22] And while this pledge fell considerably short of the formal security guarantees Israel had been seeking in vain, Eisenhower's words clearly underscored his awareness that Israel had the potential of aborting, or vastly complicating, American plans and designs.

In the administration's thinking, Israel had, therefore, to be at least marginally reassured as a means of safeguarding its continued restraint in the face of domestic divisiveness and turmoil across its eastern border. The administration, which had relied upon the strategy of long-term extended deterrence as its preferred approach for influencing Israel, was now prepared—in view of the imminent danger to the very existence of the pro-Western Hashemite Kingdom—to set aside its accommodative posture toward Egypt and Syria for the sake of implementing immediate deterrence in a quintessential inter-Arab context. Against this altered regional backdrop, Secretary Dulles's tone and negotiating style vis-à-vis Israel were markedly different from his earlier uncompromising and irreconcilable rhetoric. According to the memorandum of his April 24, 1957, conversation with Ambassador Eban,

> The secretary . . . wanted to tell the Israelis our thoughts with respect to his efforts. . . . There might be a deliberate provocation of Israel by anti-Hussein forces. . . . The secretary . . . welcomed Israel's council. . . . We were not warning Israel. . . . If the US decided to act . . . it would be useful if Israel were prepared.[23]

One week later, in his meeting with the Israeli Ambassador, Acting Secretary of State Christian A. Herter was even more explicit and uninhibited in referring to the emerging strategic convergence between Washington and Jerusalem, which called for continued consultations. According to the memorandum of the conversation,

> Mr. Herter noted that . . . we had made abundantly clear to the states of the Near East the fact that United States foreign policy embraced the preservation of the state of Israel. We were prepared to reaffirm this to those states should we feel that the situation required it. We hoped to continue our consultations with Israel on problems affecting the Near East. . . . We appreciated Israel's deep concern over developments of such importance to her and we hoped that we could work together toward solutions of the many problems of the Near East.[24]

Clearly, in view of the highly menacing possibility that the remaining pro-Western strongholds in the Middle East would soon succumb to the pressures of Arab nationalism, the preliminary vision of Israel as a strategic liability gave way, in the immediate aftermath of the Suez Crisis, to a new image of Israel as a power that was now capable of providing assistance—by deed or by inaction—to the administration in its revised and redirected deterrence posture.

Four months after the Jordanian Crisis had subsided, administration officials were forced to focus their attention on an increasingly disturbing situation in Syria, where the government moved to intensify its military and economic ties with Moscow. (By 1957, Syria was receiving from the Soviet Union an estimated $60 million in tanks and other military hardware). Fearing that the Damascus government might "fall under the control of International Communism and become a Soviet satellite,"[25] the administration dispatched Deputy Undersecretary of State Loy Henderson to confer with the leaders of Lebanon, Jordan, Turkey, and Iraq. Concurrently, it expedited arms shipments to Turkey and Iraq and committed itself to protecting their rear flank against any potential Soviet threat.[26] Determined to prevent Syria from committing "any acts of aggression against her neighbors,"[27] the President decided, late in September 1957, to intensify the pressure on Damascus by sending, as he had in the course of the Jordanian Crisis, the Sixth Fleet into the eastern Mediterranean. He also ordered the redeployment of American aircraft from Western Europe to the U.S. base at Adana.

Combined with the concurrent concentration of about 50,000 Turkish troops along the Syrian border as well as the mobilization of the Iraqi and Jordanian armed forces, these deterrence measures ultimately helped to defuse the crisis, although the more ambitious American objective of toppling the Syrian regime (by encouraging "Syria's neighbors to participate in an attack against her in order to react to anticipated [Syrian] aggression"[28]) failed to materialize in subsequent months.

Although the Syrian Crisis did not precipitate a dramatic and immediate reorientation of the specific American posture toward Israel, it further reinforced the lessons drawn in the wake of the Jordanian Crisis of April 1957. Specifically, faced with the pressing need to provide support to Syria's neighbors as a means of guarding the entire region against engulfment by the forces of radicalism and Arab nationalism, the administration could no longer ignore the potential strategic value of Israel as a viable bulwark against continued Communist aggression. Nor could it ignore the threat to Israel's security, which was inherent in the growing military ties between Syria and Egypt. Indeed, against the backdrop of the Syrian defection to the Soviet orbit and the possibility—which was viewed in Washington as imminent and real—that Damascus would engage in provocative acts against its neighbors, including Israel, American decisionmakers became increasingly predisposed to view Israel as both a potential victim and a potential strategic asset to the U.S. As had been the case in the course of the Jordanian Crisis, Secretary Dulles's references to Israel during, and in the aftermath of the Syrian Crisis, were permeated with empathy and sensitivity to Israel's security predicament. As the Secretary of State told Senator William F. Knowland (R., California) on August 30, 1957: "They [the Israelis] might not be indefinitely acquiescent if they thought that the Soviet orbit would be extended to Syria and then to Jordan, thus with Egypt virtually surrounding Israel by land."[29]

Similarly, whereas—during the first term of the Eisenhower Presidency—Israel had been continuously portrayed as an inherently aggressive entity whose actions were designed to provoke its neighbors into another round of hostilities, it was now depicted as the likely target of Syrian (and Egyptian) provocation. As Secretary Dulles observed in his September 11, 1957, meeting with Senator Mike Mansfield (D., Montana):

> It was likely that the Syrians would engage in extreme provocation against Israel in an effort to precipitate Israeli retaliation. . . . If [the Syrians] precipitate an Israeli attack against themselves they would be able to bring the whole Arab world on their side and the question of communist penetration in the area would be forgotten.[30]

Indeed, contrary to the Secretary's initial conviction that the Arab fear of Israeli expansion was real, he was now motivated by the belief—which surfaced for the first time in the course of the Jordanian Crisis—that such Arab parties as Egypt and Syria were cynically manipulating and exacerbating the Arab-Israeli dispute as a convenient means of obfuscating and disguising their own aggressive designs. As was the case during the Jordanian Crisis, the unfolding Syrian Crisis and the prospects of the establishment of a staunchly pro-Soviet regime in Damascus prompted Israel to seriously consider the option of military intervention. However, in view of the fact that the administration employed a broad spectrum of deterrence and coercive tactics vis-à-vis Syria, and in the process even encouraged Syria's Muslim neighbors to mobilize against the Syrian regime, the Ben-Gurion Government ultimately decided to accept the American view and avoid any overt involvement in the crisis. (It was feared in Washington that such an involvement could result in the undermining of the pro-Western governments in Iraq, Jordan, and Lebanon[31]). And while the American compensation for Israel's restraint fell considerably short of a formal security commitment, it did surpass—in terms of the rhetoric used—the highly delimited bounds of the first four years of the Eisenhower Administration. As Secretary Dulles remarked, on September 12, 1957, to Ambassador Eban, while the American commitment to Israel "might not have the same weight as a formal expression, we thought that Israel . . . need not believe that the United States would be indifferent to an armed attack from any quarter."[32]

These words were echoed on the following day by President Eisenhower, who noted that Prime Minister Ben-Gurion "should have no doubt of the deep US interest in the preservation of the integrity and independence of Israel."[33] Convinced that President Nasser "was an aider and abettor of [recent developments in Syria]," and "that there was no hope for Nasser as a means of retrieving the situation in Syria,"[34] the administration repeatedly indicated—in the course of the crisis—that it had abandoned all remaining, residual hope that Egypt could still be induced to reconsider its foreign policy orientation.[35]

From the onset of the crisis, President Nasser had expressed solidarity with Syria and continued to support the regime in Damascus unconditionally "against any external threat," while asserting that any attack on Syria "would be considered an attack on Egypt." Washington viewed this policy as conclusive evidence that Egypt had become an integral part of the Communist conspiracy to spread anti-Western and revolutionary sentiments throughout the Arab world.

This image became even more pervasive and menacing in October 1957, when President Nasser sent a small contingent of Egyptian troops to Damascus, thus signaling his unwavering commitment to his nationalist allies in Syria. As Secretary Dulles remarked on October 29, 1957, in his conversation with the President of the International Bank for Reconstruction and Development, Eugene Black:

> Nasser seemed to think that he could deal with impunity with the Soviets and did not appear alarmed as to where his policies might take him. . . . Egyptian blindness toward the danger of the Soviet Union had presented a barrier between Egypt and the United States. . . . Nasser's actions in recognizing Red China, in concluding the large arms deal with the Soviet Union, etc. had completely changed the situation with regard to our attitude toward him as an Arab leader.[36]

It is against this background of incessant cleavages and chronic instability in the Arab world, combined with the defection of such regional actors as Egypt and Syria into the Eastern orbit, that Israel came to be increasingly depicted as a viable island of stability in a turbulent and volatile environment and thus as a power that could potentially be incorporated—albeit unobtrusively and informally—into the administration's regional strategic plans.[37]

A clear illustration of this perceptual change in policy is provided by the account of the December 5, 1957, meeting between Secretary Dulles and Iraqi Prime Minister Nuri al-Said. When the Iraqi Prime Minister reiterated a theme that had been articulated by Secretary Dulles on numerous occasions in previous years, according to which most Arab states continued to view Israel as a major regional menace, Dulles sharply rebuked him, stating that "he felt [Prime Minister] Nuri al-Said was oversimplifying the question."[38] Similarly, when Prime Minister al-Said argued—as had Secretary Dulles during the first term of the Eisenhower Administration—that the necessary impetus for an Arab-Israeli peace was "an Israeli territorial gesture," combined with an Israeli willingness to absorb most Palestinian refugees, he was once again criticized by the Secretary of State, who forcefully asserted: "It does not solve problems to create new ones. 500,000 Jewish people could not be driven into the sea. . . . The clock could not be turned back. . . . People who were now in territory originally allotted to the Arabs could not be thrown out."[39]

The fact that, in the immediate aftermath of the crisis, such pro-Western Arab powers as Saudi Arabia, Jordan and Iraq, claimed to see "no clear threat to any other Arab state from Syria" and "began to speak reassuringly of the priority they gave to the concept of solidarity among the Arab states," provided yet another impetus for the administration to accelerate the search for reliable allies in its continued drive to contain those regional powers believed to be dominated by International Communism.[40]

And although the administration continued to refuse, during the months that followed the crisis, to cross the Rubicon and agree to sell arms to Israel, it repeatedly sought—as Secretary Dulles's November 12, 1957 message to Prime Minister Ben-Gurion demonstrates—to reassure Israel that it would resist any effort to infringe upon its territorial integrity.[41] Clearly, the growing compatibility between Washington and Jerusalem in terms of the perceived regional concerns and threats helped eliminate much of the strain and tension that had permeated the American-Israeli framework during President Eisenhower's first term in office. But while most coercive dimensions of American behavior vis-à-vis Israel receded progressively into the background of the relationship, this emerging strategic compatibility and convergence did not instantly precipitate congruent derivative policies, as the American-Israeli alliance remained, during the period preceding the July 1958 Jordanian Crisis, at an embryonic phase. Still, by the end of 1957, it had become clear that the initial American belief that "the effective defense of the region depended upon collective measures," and that "such measures . . . needed to be a natural drawing together of those who felt a sense of common destiny in the face of what could be a common danger,"[42] could not be translated into reality and had to be replaced by the much less ambitious bilateral defense strategy. This change opened a conceptual window of opportunity for Israel to become eventually integrated into the administration's revised and reformulated regional containment designs.

Against this changing backdrop, the dramatic events of July 1958 provided a major impetus for transforming the notion of U.S.-Israeli collaboration from the potential into the actual, albeit confined specifically to the Jordanian Crisis. Coming in the wake of the 1957 crises in Jordan and Syria and the American intervention in Lebanon, the crisis demonstrated that, despite the costs and risks in terms of Israel's relations with the Soviet Union, Prime Minister Ben-Gurion—unlike such traditional allies of the West as King Saud of Saudi Arabia—was prepared to contribute to the Anglo-American operation designed to rescue King Hussein from the surrounding forces of radical Arab nationalism.

Ironically, the crises of July 1958 in Iraq, Lebanon, and Jordan unfolded against the backdrop of a complete reversal of one of the major tenets of President Eisenhower's original regional strategy. Whereas the administration initially sought to promote a posture closely patterned on the desire to cement a broad inter-Arab coalition that would constitute an effective bulwark against Soviet encroachment, the formation, in February 1958, of the United Arab Republic between Egypt and Syria (the UAR) was perceived in Washington as an acutely threatening challenge to American interests and objectives.[43] Depicted as a means of mobilizing the entire Arab world against Western influence and as ironclad proof that Syria had fallen "under the control of International Communism," the February 1958 merger helped consolidate, in the minds of President Eisenhower and Secretary Dulles, the image of President Nasser as "a demagogue," whose tactics and notions of pan-Arabism were similar "to Hitler's Pan Germanism."[44] As Secretary Dulles further elaborated in his statement of June 25, 1958:

> It was incredible to me that the US should be accused of 'imperialism' in the Middle East. Such charges were now coming from President Nasser, who has a highly volatile personality. At times he seemed calm and reasonable; at other times he was highly emotional, and whipped up Pan-

Arabism much as Hitler whipped up Pan-Germanism as a means of promoting an extension of his power. In the case of Lebanon, there was no
doubt [whatsoever] as to the activities of the United Arab Republic.[45]

Fully committed to the Munich analogy and to the belief that the intensifying internal crisis in Lebanon was not an isolated and local episode
but rather a manifestation of the world-wide drive of International
Communism to systematically undermine Western strongholds, Secretary Dulles once again predicated American policy upon the premises of
deterrence and coercion, albeit not in the direction initially envisaged by
American diplomacy. As the Secretary of State remarked to the United
Nations Secretary General, Dag Hammarskjöld, on July 7, 1958, "If
Nasser and his Soviet backers were to gain a victory in Lebanon while
we stood aside and looked in the other direction, the countries neighboring on the Soviet Union and on Egypt would be so shaken that the
effect could be very bad."[46]

The immediate crisis, which culminated in the American military intervention in Lebanon on July 15, 1958, was precipitated by a growing
friction between the American-backed Maronite President Camille
Shamoun, and the commander-in-chief of the Lebanese army, General Fouad Chehab. Convinced that President Shamoun intended to
amend the Lebanese constitution so that he could be reelected as president, General Chehab became an outspoken critic of the government,
and repeatedly expressed support for the ideas of Arab nationalism and
neutralism.[47] This political and constitutional crisis was further exacerbated in the wake of the assassination, on May 8, 1958, of a Lebanese
newspaper publisher who had been a severe critic of the Shamoun
regime. As the fighting in and around Beirut became more intense, reports that Syrian infiltrators were entering Lebanon and aiding the
rebel cause began to be circulated. Meanwhile, Syrian and Egyptian
radio broadcasts stepped up their attacks on President Shamoun and
called for his overthrow.[48]

Against the background of growing turmoil and escalating cleavage
between opposing factions and armed groups in Lebanon, the Iraqi revolution of July 14, 1958, can be thought of as the direct precipitant of
the American intervention. Perceived in Washington as an integral part
of the drive, launched by the forces and proxies of International Communism, to disrupt pro-Western governments throughout the Middle
East, the overthrow of the Iraqi monarchy and the assassination of the
Iraqi Prime Minister Nuri al-Said prompted the administration to inter-

vene militarily in the Lebanese civil war in a last-ditch effort to prevent President Nasser "from taking over the whole area."[49]

Believing that the Iraqi revolution could have a profound effect on the ongoing crisis in Lebanon by altering the balance of power in favor of the rebels, the administration was determined to act forcefully in order to prevent "the complete elimination of Western influence in the Middle East" and the regional chain reaction that could endanger the survival of conservative Arab regimes in Lebanon, Jordan, and Saudi Arabia.[50] Viewing the Lebanese scene as the stage on which the administration had to perform a leading role in the struggle against the forces of Arab nationalism, President Eisenhower, on July 15, 1958, dispatched 14,000 marines into Beirut.[51] In the President's words:

> It was better if we took a strong position rather than a Munich-type position if we are to avoid the crumbling of our whole security structure. . . . Our action [in Lebanon] would be a symbol of American fortitude and readiness to take risks to defend the values of the free world.[52]

Notwithstanding the risks involved, the intervention bore fruit. The landing of the marines in Lebanon, and the concurrent mediating mission of Deputy Undersecretary of State Robert Murphy, paved the way toward an early resolution of the internal Lebanese Crisis, which—in turn—precipitated the smooth withdrawal, in October 1958, of American troops without any Iraqi or Egyptian interference. Before the Lebanese Crisis had been defused, however, and against the backdrop of a highly charged, emotion-laden regional landscape, Israel's role in the British operation in Jordan started to unfold in mid-July. Since the American intervention in Lebanon was not conceived as an end in itself, but rather as the means of inspiring "the non-Nasser governments in the Middle East and adjoining areas,"[53] it had to be augmented by a series of tangible and concrete actions, designed to "reassure many small nations that they could call on us in times of crisis."[54]

One of these small powers, which had much to fear from the extension of Egyptian influence in the region, was the Hashemite Kingdom of Jordan. Confronted by an internal coalition of Jordanian and Palestinian nationalists, who were more receptive to President Nasser's revolutionary ideas than to any conservative, pro-Western views, the embattled King Hussein—who was profoundly alarmed by the Iraqi revolution—called upon both Britain and the United States to militarily intervene on his behalf.[55] The fact that Iraq had cut off its oil supplies to Jordan in the immediate aftermath of the revolution while Syria closed its border with the

Hashemite Kingdom further exacerbated King Hussein's predicament and convinced Secretary Dulles that "the Jordanian situation [was] rapidly becoming extremely dangerous."[56]

Notwithstanding the growing recognition that the very survival of the Hashemite Kingdom was at stake, and that an American refusal to proceed beyond the constrained parameters of the Lebanese scene was bound to adversely affect "not only the neighboring Arab area but also . . . peripheral states such as Libya, Sudan and Iran,"[57] the administration remained firmly opposed to the very idea of a direct military intervention in Jordan. Believing that such a move "would undoubtedly give rise to an intensified wave of anti-Western feelings on which Nasser could capitalize,"[58] the President refused "to give the British a blank check" and thus to commit himself "to act with them in Jordan and possibly Iraq."[59]

As President Eisenhower further elaborated in his July 14, 1958, telephone conversation with British Prime Minister Harold Macmillan, in which Macmillan urged him "to do a lot of things together": " . . . I would not want to go further [than Lebanon]. . . . If we are now planning the initiation of a big operation that could run all the way through Syria and Iraq, we are far beyond anything I have the power to do constitutionally."[60]

This reluctance to expand American military involvement, which was primarily predicated upon the fear of becoming alienated throughout the region, was expressed once again on the very same day. In his July 14, 1958, meeting with the British Chargé d'Affaires in Washington, Lord Samuel Hood, Secretary Dulles remained unimpressed with the Ambassador's plea that the U.S. join Britain in a military operation designed to rescue the besieged King Hussein. According to his account of the conversation:

> I told Lord Hood that this was a totally new question, not covered by our present military planning, and that I did not therefore feel that at the moment we could either give King Hussein the assurance he sought or accept the British suggestion that we urge him to request the assurance at once. . . . I said that I could not give any considered view of what to do about Jordan without consulting our military and political advisers but that my off-hand thought was that Hussein has a better chance of putting through without Western military assistance than with it.[61]

Ultimately, despite President Eisenhower's conviction that "to lose would be far worse than the loss of China, because of the strategic position and resources of the Middle East,"[62] and despite the pressures exerted by Britain and Saudi Arabia, the administration remained firm in its decision to confine its military activity to Lebanon. It did support, however, the British decision to dispatch from Cyprus to Amman 2,200 paratroopers to protect the capital city, King Hussein, and Western interests in Jordan in the face of the Nasser-fomented domestic insurgency.[63] It also agreed to ship to Jordan vital strategic materials.

It was precisely at this crucial strategic juncture, on the very eve of the deployment to Jordan of the British Sixteenth Parachute Brigade, that Israel was called upon to play a supportive role in the operation.

At first glance, the role assigned to Israel—of permitting the British and American airlift into Jordan through Israeli airspace—may appear marginal and relatively insignificant, as it did not commit any Israeli troops to the defense of the Hashemite Kingdom. Nonetheless, the decision to grant overflight rights to British and American aircraft en route to Amman precipitated an acute crisis in Israeli-Soviet relations, with the Soviet Union resorting to harsh and threatening rhetoric in an effort to coerce Prime Minister Ben-Gurion into reassessing his position.[64] Furthermore, the Israeli decision to permit the overflights despite the risks involved diametrically contradicted the attitude of Saudi Arabia, which was perceived in Washington as a major regional bulwark in the confrontation with radical Arab nationalism. In the aftermath of the Iraqi revolution, King Saud contacted the Eisenhower Administration and asked for Western intervention in Jordan, Lebanon and Iraq. As Secretary Dulles reported to President Eisenhower on July 14, 1958: "Two messages have come from Saudi Arabia. King Saud demands action at once, stating that if the United States and the United Kingdom do not act now, they are finished as powers in the Middle East."[65]

Notwithstanding this Saudi insistence that the administration act forcefully to contain the revolutionary tide sweeping the region (which was also manifested by King Saud's threat that unless the West intervened, Saudi Arabia would be forced to acquiesce in President Nasser's ambitions), King Saud refused to allow Britain the use of the American airfield in Dhahran for resupply,[66] nor did he agree to grant Britain and the U.S. overflight rights.[67]

Faced with the unwavering Saudi determination that the Western powers pull the chestnuts out of the Middle Eastern fire without involving them directly in any strategic move against Iraq, Egypt, or Syria, and deprived of any other viable option, the administration—which feared the imminent collapse of the Hashemite Kingdom—increasingly looked upon the Israeli overflight clearance as a major strategic contribution to its effort to prevent a drastic disruption of the regional balance of power in the wake of the Iraqi revolution. As Secretary Dulles acknowledged in his July 21, 1958, meeting with Ambassador Eban: "We appreciate Israel's acquiescence in the airlift to Jordan. We were trying to find alternatives but the matter was very difficult." Impressed with Israel's willingness to defy the Soviet Union and contribute to the Jordanian operation, the Secretary was uninhibited in alluding—in the same meeting—to the American commitment to the survival of Israel:

> Our action with respect to Lebanon should give Israel confidence that we would respond in similar circumstances to an Israeli appeal. . . . If there should be a meeting at which there would be a definition of vital interests, we would not agree to the exclusion of Israel. This would be unthinkable.[68]

Thus, although excluded from the initial American vision of a broad regional security alliance, Israel became, in July 1958, a *de facto* partner of the Western powers in their drive to prevent the collapse of the fragile and embattled Jordanian regime. With Saudi Arabia unwilling to cooperate with the operation it wholeheartedly supported, and with the continued erosion of British power and prestige, Israel emerged as the only regional power prepared to take risks for the sake of "relieving the situation in the area."[69]

Further reinforcing the lessons derived from the regional crises of 1957, the Jordanian Crisis of July 1958—which was indeed defused shortly after the British intervention—provided a major impetus for modifying American perceptions of the role assigned to Israel in the effort to implement an effective deterrence posture against the forces of radicalism and pan-Arabism. Specifically, contrary to the preliminary vision of Israel as a strategic liability to the U.S.—which was premised on the basic dichotomy between Israel and the Arab world—the administration came to fully recognize, in July 1958, that the Arab-Israeli predicament comprised but one facet within (and occasionally downgraded by) an entire cluster of ideological, political, social, and nationalistic inter-Arab divisions and rivalries. In this respect, the 1958 Jordanian Crisis can be thought of as the "trigger event,"[70] which provided the impetus for completing the swing of the perceptual pendulum from Israel as a strategic liability and an impediment to American regional designs, to Israel as an indispensable asset to American and British strategic plans and objectives. In Jervis's terminology, Israel's behavior in the course of the crisis was perceived by the administration as an index, namely, as an inherently credible indication of behavior, which was inextricably related to certain basic dimensions and characteristics of the

Israeli operational code which—as such—could not be manipulated or misused for the purpose of projecting a misleading image.[71]

Thus, rather than an isolated episode of limited significance, the Jordanian Crisis came to be viewed as the focal point from which an entire cluster of core Israeli values, attitudes, and preferences could reliably be elucidated. Indeed, by dramatically exposing the discrepancy between the preliminary, and quite abstract, strategic premises adhered to by the administration during its first term in office, and the concrete, tangible and operational regional circumstances that became fully evident to President Eisenhower and Secretary Dulles in July 1958, the Jordanian Crisis led Washington's policymakers to reframe the entire regional situation and thus to give priority to the actual and observable over the potential and hypothetical.[72] Seeking to minimize the losses to the West from the sequence of regional crises that culminated in the July 1958 Jordanian Crisis, American policymakers opted to set aside their initial hopes that a broadly based regional alliance could effectively deter Soviet encroachment for the sake of adopting a less ambitious posture which replaced the optimal with the feasible. With any residual expectations that a broad regional alliance could still be consolidated fading rapidly into the background, the administration therefore became increasingly predisposed to pursue a bilateral rather than a multilateral strategy and thus to collaborate individually and separately with any regional power—including Israel—that was willing and able to contribute to the accomplishment of the highly desired goal of containment, albeit unobtrusively and indirectly. Indeed, in view of the limits of American willingness and ability to mobilize public and Congressional support for militarily intervening in such locations as Iraq and Jordan, the need to rely on regional allies became a major imperative for American strategy. With most pro-Western powers unwilling or incapable of even marginally contributing to this mission, it is hardly surprising that the Israeli role in the Jordanian Crisis was viewed by American decisionmakers and strategic planners as a useful precedent, which would pave the way toward the formulation of a new, and more realistic, regional strategic doctrine.

This revised vision of Israel's role in the aftermath of the crisis was most clearly articulated in a memorandum entitled: "Factors Affecting U.S. Policy Toward the Near East," which was submitted, on August 19, 1958, to the NSC by the NSC Planning Board. In a section entitled: "Should the United States Reconsider its Policy Toward Israel?" the paper stated:

It is doubtful whether any likely US pressures on Israel would cause Israel to make concessions which would do much to satisfy Arab demands, which—in the final analysis—may not be satisfied by anything short of the destruction of Israel. *Moreover, if we choose to combat radical Arab nationalism and to hold Persian Gulf oil by force if necessary, a logical corollary would be to support Israel as the only strong pro-West power left in the Near East.*[73]

Whereas, during the first term of the Eisenhower Administration, American diplomacy predicated its coercive posture toward Israel upon the belief that territorial concessions on its part would be the panacea and the key to an early resolution of the Arab-Israeli conundrum, it was now predisposed to question the very feasibility of such a settlement regardless of the territorial costs to Israel: "We must reckon with the possibility that if Nasser were deprived of anti-Western foci for his policy, he might turn to the revival of Arab-Israeli tensions as a lever for whipping up nationalist fervor in order to achieve his ends."[74]

Indeed, whereas, during the first half of the decade, Israel had been continuously viewed as the main obstacle to the formation of a broad inter-Arab security alliance linked to the West, the sequence of crises that erupted in Syria, Jordan, and Lebanon in 1957 and 1958 convinced the administration that it was "Arab nationalism in the radical form represented by President Nasser's movement" that posed the most serious and immediate threat to Western interests and designs. The corollary of this newly established perception of President Nasser as a leader who was committed "to policies of assassination and murder, and to the destruction of the integrity of sovereign states through indirect aggression abetted from outside" was the urgent need to deter Egypt's aggressive designs by encouraging Israel "to contribute, from its resources of spiritual strength and determination, to a stable international order."[75]

The recognition that, in addition to its valuable role of permitting the U.S. and Britain the use of its airspace, Israel could play a balancing role vis-à-vis Egypt and thus help deter President Nasser from any direct effort to topple the Jordanian regime, surfaced on several occasions in the course and aftermath of the Jordanian Crisis, and reflected a dramatic change in the American perception of the entire regional landscape. Whereas Eisenhower and Dulles had in the past vehemently opposed Israel's pursuit of a deterrence posture toward Egypt, fearing that it could set in motion a highly dangerous escalatory process, they came around in July and August 1958 to support precisely this strategy, both in the context of the Jordanian Crisis and in the broader context of the continued Egyptian threat to the regional balance of power. In view of the imminent menace to the very existence of both the Lebanese and Jordanian regimes (and of Saudi Arabia's refusal to directly or even indirectly challenge Egypt or Syria), the administration—which repeatedly expressed concern over "this general weakness of pro-Western [Arab] governments"[76] in the area—became increasingly prepared to look upon Israel as the only regional power capable of deterring and restraining Cairo's ambitions. On occasion, the President even toyed with the idea of enticing Israel to launch a military strike against Egypt. Thus on July 16, 1958, at the height of the Jordanian Crisis, and provided with evidence which indicated that President Nasser had instructed his agents in Jordan to assassinate King Hussein and overthrow the Jordanian Government, President Eisenhower noted to Secretary Dulles "that the strategic action in the circumstances would be to turn Israel loose on Egypt, thus going for the head of the snake."[77] Similarly, at the National Security Council meeting of August 7, 1958, the President remarked that it was ironic that until recently "we were concerned with the possibility of an Israeli aggression against the Arab states" rather than with the opposite contingency. He added that "if we choose to combat radical Arab nationalism and to hold Persian Gulf oil by force if necessary, a logical corollary would be to support Israel as the only strong pro-West power left in the Near East."[78]

In most instances, however, the architects of American diplomacy recommended a less ambitious stratagem, namely, the use by Israel of the very same strategy of deterrence that for four years had been Washington's main means of trying to influence Israel's behavior in the Arab-Israeli sphere. Thus on August 8, 1958, in his meeting with British Chargé d'Affaires Lord Hood, Secretary Dulles remarked "that he saw some advantages in the existence of an Israeli threat [to militarily intervene in Jordan]."[79]

Similarly, in his meeting of August 12, 1958, with Foreign Minister Lloyd, Secretary Dulles underscored the value inherent in the pursuit by Israel of a deterrence posture vis-à-vis Egypt as a means of preventing President Nasser from exploiting a protracted state of turmoil and instability in Jordan:

> The secretary said that the question was that if Jordan collapsed, would the Israelis move in? *What was important was what the UAR [United Arab Republic] thought the Israelis would do. If the UAR thought the Israelis would touch off a big war, it was doubtful if the UAR would want Jordan.*[80]

Furthermore, on a number of occasions in the immediate aftermath of the crisis, the threat of an Israeli military intervention in Jordan was conveyed directly to Egypt in an effort to deter President Nasser from disrupting the Hashemite Kingdom. Contrary to the plethora of messages to the Egyptian leadership, which depicted Israel—throughout the period 1953–1956—as a potentially expansionist entity whose intransigent and irreconcilable behavior along the Arab-Israeli front constituted the main obstacle to peace, American diplomacy was now fully prepared to at least implicitly endorse and repeatedly use the "West Bank Scenario" (according to which Israel would occupy the West Bank of Jordan if the Hashemite Kingdom were on the verge of disintegration) as a potential deterrence weapon vis-à-vis Egypt. Thus on August 6, 1958, in the course of the meeting which took place in Cairo between Deputy Undersecretary for State and Political Affairs Robert D. Murphy and President Nasser, the American emissary was unequivocal in warning that an Egyptian intervention in Jordan would inevitably precipitate an Israeli drive to capture the West Bank. According to the memorandum of the conversation:

> I expressed [the] opinion [that] if UAR intervention should occur, Israel would attack and that would be [a] situation the US could not control. . . . Nasser became grave and reverted to the subject several times thereafter. He declared that we could be assured UAR and he especially were not promoting an uprising or disturbance in Jordan and did not intend to do so.[81]

Two weeks later, in his meeting of August 21, 1958, with Egyptian Foreign Minister Mahmoud Fawzi, Secretary Dulles was equally uninhibited in portraying a highly menacing picture of the regional repercussions that would be bound to result from the collapse of the Jordanian Monarchy. As the Secretary pointed out:

> If the situation in Jordan should be permitted to disintegrate, that would almost certainly bring about internal chaos giving rise to a real danger of renewed Arab/Israeli hostilities. . . . If the UAR really wanted to take over Jordan [it should take into account] the question of the likely Israeli reaction to the various contingencies.[82]

Two months later, in the wake of the evacuation of the British paratroopers from Lebanon and against the backdrop of the growing concern that Egypt would seek to exploit the power vacuum in order to overthrow King Hussein and install a pro-Nasserite regime in Amman, this hope that Israel could effectively deter President Nasser continued to dominate the thinking of Secretary Dulles, who was left now without any viable military option for coping with the crisis. As he remarked on October 31, 1958, to British Ambassador Caccia:

> Apparently, the UAR really believes that something will happen in the area of the Middle East and possibly that Israel will take over the West Bank of the Jordan now that British troops have departed. . . . [Since] the Israelis could mobilize very quickly . . . and take over the West Bank should they so desire . . . the UAR was particularly sensitive in this respect.[83]

Notwithstanding this growing perception of Israel as an important outpost of the Western bloc and as a power capable of deterring and restraining Egypt, and notwithstanding the impact which the Israeli decision to permit the British and American overflights en route to Jordan had upon the thinking of the President and his Secretary of State, it became clear in subsequent months that a gap continued to exist between perceptions and actual behavior. At least during the remaining two and a half years of the Eisenhower era, this growing convergence in terms of the strategic visions of the area between Washington and Jerusalem did not exceed—by and large—the level of the amorphous, uninstitutionalized, and discombobulated. While the seeds of comprehensive regional collaboration had been clearly planted during the turbulent days of July 1958, the American-Israeli alliance remained embryonic, lacking any explicit or formal definition of the converging interests and the derivative policies designed to promote them within the American-Israeli framework. Nor did this revised vision precipitate—during the Eisenhower Presidency— major and durable forms of strategic cooperation between the U.S. and Israel. More specifically, the recognition that "the situation in the Middle East has been substantially altered since our last consideration of an Israeli arms request," and that "the Israeli government has been helpful to us in such matters as the recent overflights to Jordan"[84] did not lead the administration to significantly modify such tenets of its regional policy as its long-standing refusal to supply advanced weapons systems to Israel. Thus, although it did agree, on August 26, 1958, to sell to Israel 100 anti-tank recoilless rifles "plus reasonable quantities of ammunition and spare parts," the administration remained committed to its basic policy "of not being a major supplier of arms to Israel."[85]

The fact that the Israeli Mossad provided the CIA—during the second half of the decade—with invaluable military, political and economic data about the Arab world, the Soviet Union, and the Eastern bloc, could not tip the scale in Israel's favor. While this uninterrupted flow of information concerning such developments as the beginning of the de-Stalinization process in the Soviet Union was perceived as yet another in-dication that Israel was capable of providing useful strategic services for the United States, it did not erode Washington's long-standing refusal to sell Israel sophisticated weapons systems.[86]

Insisting that large Israeli arms purchases "might adversely affect [the administration's] relations with the rest of the area," Secretary Dulles, in his meeting of October 2, 1958, with Israeli Foreign Minister Golda Meir, informed her of the administration's decision to turn down the Israeli request to purchase from the U.S. tanks, small submarines, electronic equipment, and anti-aircraft missiles.[87] Indeed, the American recognition that "recent events have brought the United States and Is-rael closer together"[88] did not result in any reorientation of American arms sale policy. Unwilling to become engaged in a regional arms race, and anxious to maintain a margin of maneuverability that would en-able the U.S. "to act as a mediator in any disputes that arise,"[89] the ad-ministration remained "reluctant to become a principal source of sup-ply for the area."[90] Thus, while American policymakers discreetly began, in the aftermath of the Jordanian Crisis, to encourage Iran, Turkey, and Ethiopia to join Israel in a "Little Entente" composed of the non-Arab states in the Middle East,[91] they refused to heed Israel's arms requests, maintaining that Israel already had "an overall quanti-tative superiority over the combined armed forces of the UAR, Iraq, Jordan, and Saudi Arabia."[92] And although Washington did agree, in the summer of 1959, to allocate to Israel $100 million in technical and financial assistance over the next two years, it still refused to conclude a major arms deal with the Ben-Gurion Government. Clearly, while most coercive elements and methods receded into the background of the American-Israeli dyad in the aftermath of the Jordanian Crisis, Presi-dent Eisenhower remained reluctant to cross the Rubicon and revise American "traditional [arms] policy."[93]

It was only in the wake of Prime Minister Ben-Gurion's meeting of March 10, 1960, with President Eisenhower that a window of opportu-nity was opened for Israel to purchase from the U.S. six batteries of Hawk anti-aircraft missiles. In the course of the meeting, the Prime Min-ister underscored Israel's vulnerability to an Egyptian air attack, main-taining that "at the present time Egyptian bombers can carry three tons of bombs, but that the new bombers they were getting from the Soviet bloc will be able to carry ten tons of bombs . . . and to destroy Tel-Aviv without too much trouble."[94]

In his March 13, 1960, meeting with Christian A. Herter, who had replaced the ailing Dulles as Secretary of State a year earlier, the Prime Minister repeated his request for the Hawk missiles, and emphasized their defensive nature as well as Israel's grave concern over the possibility of "a surprise air raid attack by the United Arab Republic," which "could destroy Tel-Aviv by two or three successive days of bombing," while making it "impossible for Israel to mobilize her ground forces for defense."[95] Contrary to numerous earlier instances in which Israeli statesmen and diplomats who sought military assistance from the U.S. were instantly turned down, Ben-Gurion's emotional plea for meeting Israel's urgent defensive needs impressed Secretary Herter. Believing that the prospects of promoting ambitious and comprehensive regional objectives which necessitated the collaboration of several Arab parties "were not encouraging,"[96] and faced with the collapse of his predecessor's dream of forging a broadly based inter-Arab security organization for the purpose of containing Soviet penetration into the region, Herter, unlike Dulles, was now prepared to decouple the American security posture toward Israel from the overall dynamics of American behavior, expectations, and objectives in the Arab world.

This willingness to review the Israeli request on its intrinsic merits and within the parameters of the American-Israeli-Egyptian triad clearly surfaced in the course of the March 13, 1960, meeting when Secretary Herter promised Ben-Gurion that the U.S. would consider the Israeli request "sympathetically and urgently."[97] When asked by the Prime Minister whether this reply "could be considered a positive one," Secretary Herter confirmed that "that [was] a fair assumption." Immediately afterward, however, he qualified this statement "to the extent of saying that this was a fair assumption unless factors which he did not now know about were brought to his attention."[98]

Despite Secretary Herter's conviction that "we should do something promptly in connection with Israel's needs for air defense equipment for use in the event of an attack by the UAR," and that "this means the supply of ground-to-air missiles,"[99] no change in the American position on the sale of arms to Israel was forthcoming. And although Secretary Herter most forcefully supported the sale to Israel of the Hawk missiles in the course of his meeting of July 27, 1960, with several of the Department's Middle East experts (including Acting Assistant Secretary of State for Near Eastern and South Asian Affairs, Parker T. Hart, Director of the Office of Near Eastern Affairs, H. Armin Meyer, and Undersecretary of State for Political Affairs, T. Livingston Merchant), he was ultimately persuaded by his subordinates to avoid any deviations from the traditional parameters of American arms sale policy. Indeed, the Secretary's assertions that "he found it difficult to understand why we are refusing to allow the Israelis to buy . . . the purely defensive Hawk missiles," and that "unless better arguments could be presented . . . he felt the Israelis should have the missiles"[100] were not translated into action at the end of the day.

While Secretary Herter's initial view was fully shared by Vice President Richard Nixon and by the Department of Defense, which warned—in a memorandum of June 14, 1960—that "if the recent rate of Arab arms acquisition continues, and unless the Israeli forces receive military assistance from some source, the Israeli military position vis-à-vis the neighboring Arab states will be jeopardized eventually,"[101] he did not insist that his advocated policy be implemented. Confronted with a united front of Department of State officials, who argued "that the Israelis were well ahead of the UAR in supersonic aircraft," that "introducing such spectacular weaponry in the area would have serious consequences in the form of an increased arms race, with the Russians backing Nasser," and that the Hawks' sale "would link us closely to Israel's security at the expense of our relations with the rest of the Arab world and to the benefit of the Soviets,"[102] Secretary Herter decided to acquiesce and thus to lend his support to the unanimous view of Undersecretary Merchant, Acting Assistant Secretary Hart, and Director of the Office of Near Eastern Affairs Meyer. According to the memorandum of the meeting, "after a general discussion of the question, the conclusion emerged that we would not provide the missiles to the Israelis."[103]

Despite this strategic victory by the Department of State bureaucracy, the Secretary apparently did manage to secure a tactical, face-saving achievement for himself in the encounter. Contrary to the recommendation of his advisers who "did not believe our answer to the Israelis should leave the door open," Secretary Herter "felt other considerations might suggest a delay of several months before closing the door completely."[104]

Even this victory, however, proved short-lived. Faced with continuous and relentless pressure, which was exerted by such Middle Eastern experts as Assistant Secretary of State for Near Eastern and South Asian Affairs, G. Lewis Jones, Director of the Office of Near Eastern Affairs Meyer, and Undersecretary of State Merchant, Secretary Herter was induced to seal the fate of the Israeli request only one week after his supportive view had been articulated.

On August 4, 1960, in a letter from the Secretary of State to Prime Minister Ben-Gurion, Israel's request was formally turned down.[105] Closely patterned on the arguments that had surfaced on July 27, 1960, in the respective presentations of Hart, Merchant, and Meyer, the letter incorporated their rhetoric and terminology. Maintaining that "the introduction of such spectacular weaponry into the Near East area [was bound] to contribute to an intensification of an arms race to the detriment of the states concerned,"[106] the message effectively brought to an end a long and intricate process of intergovernmental as well as intragovernmental bargaining. Despite the growing strategic convergence between Washington and Jerusalem, the administration was still unprepared to abandon certain basic premises of its traditional Middle Eastern policy. Nor was it willing to forgo its deeply held belief that a policy of even-handedness in the Arab-Israeli zone could prevent "the Arab countries" from further drifting into the Soviet bloc.[107]

Thus, in the same way that Assistant Secretary Byroade and the Office of Near Eastern Affairs managed—on several occasions in 1953 and 1954—to convince the reluctant Secretary Dulles to adopt strong and far-reaching coercive measures against Israel,[108] so did Secretary Herter ultimately acquiesce in the concerted pressures exerted upon him to prevent the sale to Israel of the Hawk missiles.[109] It would be left to President Kennedy to close the gap between perceptions and reality, and thus to translate into concrete and tangible policy measures what remained, to the very end of the Eisenhower era, an essentially undefined, unstructured, and embryonic partnership.

Although the Israeli expectations that the administration would approve the sale of the Hawk missiles failed to materialize, it is clear that, as the decade approached its end, the American-Israeli framework had become increasingly consensual. The recognition that the initial American objective of uniting the Arab world against the Soviet menace—which had dictated a reserved and detached posture toward Israel—could not be accomplished because of deep inter-Arab ideological and political rivalries and divisions had by then eliminated the perceived necessity to choose between the pursuit of a collaborative policy toward Israel and the promotion of the overriding goal of containing Soviet regional encroachment. Indeed, with Egypt, Syria and Iraq committed now to an irreconcilable anti-American course, there was no need any longer for American diplomacy to prove its lack of any pro-Israeli bias by retaining its coercive policy toward the Ben-Gurion Government. As Telhami notes,

while Israeli objectives were not achieved in the short term, events unfolding . . . after the Suez War seemed to turn the tide in Israel's favor. The
sudden upheavals in the Arab world against the West and the dramatic
rise in Nasser's popularity forced the United States into a role it did not
wish to play. Egyptian-American relations worsened, and Egypt became
preoccupied not with Israel but with what came to be known as the "Arab
Cold War."[110]

This transformation of American policy from its preliminary comprehensive regional approach to the considerably less ambitious coun-
try-by-country *modus operandi*[111] therefore enabled the administration to
increasingly decouple its relations with Israel from an entire cluster of
broad regional constraints and considerations. And while he remained
sensitive to the ramifications of some of his actions within the American-
Israeli dyad (as the August 1960 decision to turn down the Israeli request
to purchase from the U.S. Hawk missiles demonstrates), the President's
diminishing preoccupation with the broad regional context increased his
margin of maneuverability and latitude of choice in approaching Israel
and in assessing its contribution to the preservation and promotion of
Western strategic interests. In other words, the recommendation—incorporated into the statement of policy drafted by the NSC Planning
Board on June 17, 1960—that the U.S. "avoid for the present any active
efforts to enlist Arab nations in regional collective security arrangements,"[112] presented Israel with the chance to eventually become integrated into American designs as a recognized strategic asset.

Thus, whereas the administration remained staunchly opposed, during the period preceding the Suez Crisis, to the pursuit by Israel of a coercive course vis-à-vis Egypt, Syria, and Jordan, and was uninhibited in
its criticism of the Israeli strategy of retaliatory raids against its neighbors, it came to realize, in the aftermath of July 1958, the advantages for
the West inherent in an effective Israeli deterrence policy toward the
UAR. Hence, it reacted with relative equanimity and restraint in the face
of such massive Israeli raids as the infantry attack of January 1960 on
the Syrian positions in and around the village of Lower Tawfiq. Unlike
the administration's angry reaction in the face of earlier Israeli operations such as the Qibya raid of October 1953, it now adopted a low-key
approach toward Israeli border violations as well as its vigorous endeav-
or to complete the National (water) Carrier project in defiance of vehement Syrian opposition. In the case of the water dispute with Syria, the
administration—believing that the Israeli decision to move the site

where the water would be pumped from the Jordan to the northwestern corner of the Sea of Galilee was fully compatible with the framework of the Johnson Plan—quietly supported the Israeli position during its last two years in office.[113]

In addition to their growing sense of disillusionment with the diverse and dynamic political landscape of the Middle East, which demonstrated to the architects of American diplomacy that their preconceived hopes of quickly inducing the Arab world to fully cooperate with the West in the confrontation against the Communist menace were completely decoupled from a recalcitrant and turbulent regional setting, American policymakers came to reassess, during President Eisenhower's last year in office, their initial belief that the uninterrupted flow of Middle Eastern oil to Western Europe was crucial to the economic survival of the West.

Clearly, by 1960 it had become evident to the administration that not only was its preliminary goal of winning the goodwill and support of the Arab world an elusive vision, but that, in view of the recognition that "Near East oil (excluding Iranian oil) is no longer of quite as great importance to Western Europe as in 1958,"[114] its long-held premise that Middle Eastern oil was vital "not only to NATO but to the Western world"[115] was a somewhat outdated and obsolete assumption. Whereas, in previous years, Washington's policymakers had been convinced that the threat of "a cessation of oil [from the Middle East to Western Europe] would be just about as effective as [a Soviet threat] of atomic destruction,"[116] in 1960—against the backdrop of the initial success of the intensive interdepartmental effort "to retard Western Europe's dependence on Middle East oil and to reduce the effects on Western Europe of an emergency created by any complete or partial denial of Middle East oil resources"[117]—it could adopt a relatively relaxed and equananimous attitude toward Middle Eastern issues and parties.

Thus, by the end of the Eisenhower Presidency, most of the controversial issues that—during the first term of the administration—had continuously strained American-Israeli relations—subsided into the background. And while the two governments continued to disagree on such issues as the appropriate way for resolving the refugee problem, these disagreements did not lead administration officials to openly attack Israel's policy, nor did they result in a coercive course of the sort that had characterized the first term of the Eisenhower Administration. Convinced that the Middle East of the late 1950s was not ripe for an overall Arab-Israeli accommodation, and faced with a regional environment that remained largely oblivious to Washington's order of priorities, the administration was forced, in 1957 and even more so in 1958, to reconsider its overall strategy in the region, and thus to set aside its broad multilateral approach for the sake of adopting a minimalist bilateral strategy, which was most clearly embedded in the Eisenhower Doctrine.

In the process, while remaining fully committed to its bipolar-confrontational perspective, it came to realize that no single panacea could transform overnight a region, which was chronically permeated with friction and cleavage, into a cohesive front, united in purpose and determined to assist the U.S. in its drive to stem the tide of Soviet expansionism. And although this recognition did not entail the immediate formalization of the ties with all the regional powers that, like Israel, were prepared to collaborate with the American containment designs, it did provide the conceptual infrastructure for the future intensification and institutionalization of the American-Israeli security relationship. In other words, the fact that during the period 1957–1960 the administration had to considerably scale down its conflict resolution efforts, and instead was forced to devote most of its energy and attention to the management of a series of regional crises, inevitably reduced the potential for an open American-Israeli confrontation of the sort that repeatedly had clouded the relationship in previous years.

Whereas its continued effort, during Eisenhower's first term as president, to resolve the Arab-Israel dispute, led the administration to tackle head-on all the emotion-laden, highly charged questions that comprised the core of the predicament, and in the process precipitated a protracted and heated encounter with Israel over the terms of the settlement, the President's post-Suez decision to shift gears and focus on the need to manage and defuse the crises which, in 1957 and 1958, had erupted in Syria, Jordan and Lebanon, helped obscure the basic differences between Washington and Jerusalem regarding the parameters of the desired peace, and thus underscored the compatibility in terms of the perceived strategic interests and objectives between the U.S. and Israel. And while it was still reluctant to predicate its entire behavior in the Arab-Israeli zone on the logic and premises of this emerging strategic convergence, the Eisenhower Presidency paved the way for President Kennedy to complete and institutionalize the process.

Indeed, the shift—which became fully apparent in July 1958—from a strategy that had been closely patterned on the notion of a tight linkage between the American mode of conduct in the Arab-Israeli sphere and the prospects of accomplishing a broad complex of highly desired regional objectives, to an approach that sought to deal separately and sequentially with issues and crises as they arose without seeking to integrate them into one coherent and multifaceted design, implied that the U.S. and Israel could now cooperate within broadened security parameters.

Paradoxically, then, the diminution of the overall American vision and perspective, and the gradual move of American diplomacy to a decoupling or non-linkage strategy, entailed the prospects of a dramatic increase in the level of strategic collaboration within the bounds of the American-Israeli dyad. It also eliminated from the scene the pervasive and constant sense of urgency that had characterized the attitude of the administration in approaching the Arab-Israeli conflict during Eisenhower's first term (and particularly first year) in the White House.

Thus, although several of its activities during the late 1950s, such as its intervention of July 1958 in Lebanon, resulted from a perception of an acute and immediate threat to the regional balance of power, which necessitated an urgent American response, this perception remained confined to a sequence of sporadic and intermittent crisis episodes and did not spill over—as was the case during the period 1953–1956—to the broad complex of issues that comprised the very core of the Arab-Israeli conundrum. And while American diplomacy still hoped, during the second half of the decade, to promote an Arab-Israeli settlement, its actions were primarily designed to either stabilize a highly charged situation on the Arab-Israeli front, or to defuse certain isolated facets of the dispute (such as the American regional water plan) without seeking to comprehensively and forcefully confront all the root causes of the conflict, and without resorting to coercive measures vis-à-vis Israel in an effort to eliminate, with one stroke, all the stumbling blocks along the road to peace. "By early 1957," writes Schoenbaum, "official Washington took it for given that hopes for a comprehensive peace had died between Rhodes and Lausanne years earlier in the aftermath of the first Arab-Israeli war. Instead of peace, what Americans offered was the piecemeal pragmatics of crisis management. . . . With the American profile itself kept low to the ground."[118]

As a result, although the specific positions the administration supported remained essentially unchanged during the period 1957–1960, the perception of the appropriate mechanism by which these policies should be translated into reality, underwent a profound transition. Thus, contrary to Secretary Dulles's initial propensity to predicate his peacemaking posture in the American-Israeli sphere upon the premises of long-term deterrence and coercion, the behavior of both Dulles and his successor Christian Herter was patterned on the more benign premise of persuasion.[119] American diplomacy therefore became increasingly predisposed to downgrade the entire notion of comprehensive peace as a feasible, short-term contingency. Unlike the plethora of American statements and references to such aspects of the Arab-Israeli dispute as permanent boundaries, Palestinian refugees, and the division of water which, during the first Eisenhower term, reflected an unbounded determination to vigorously and forcefully promote an overall Arab-Israeli settlement, in later years the administration adopted an attitude of "benign neglect" toward the conflict.[120] It no longer attempted to integrate its positions on the various dimensions and ingredients of peace into a multifaceted and operational peace plan. And indeed, as the "Statement of U.S. Policy Toward the Near East," which was submitted on June 17, 1960, by the NSC Planning Board to the NSC clearly indicates, Eisenhower's official references to the Arab-Israeli dispute and its resolution did not proceed beyond the level of the general exposition of certain basic principles:

> Elements of the [Arab-Israeli dispute] which would have to be settled include: Establishment of the boundaries of Israel, settlement of the refugee problem, a UN review of the Jerusalem problem, equitable division of the waters of the Jordan River system, relaxation of trade and transit restrictions.[121]

Distracted by a welter of regional crises unrelated to the Arab-Israeli conflict, American decisionmakers ultimately abandoned their determined and assertive peace posture, and instead adopted an incremental and unobtrusive approach, while avoiding a direct and concurrent entanglement with all the political, territorial, ideological and social layers and tenets of the conundrum. As the June 17, 1960, memorandum of the NSC Planning Board recommended to the architects of American Middle East diplomacy: "Be prepared to accept a constructive settlement short of a formal peace treaty and addressed to only some rather than all the outstanding issues, and with some rather than all of the Arab states."[122]

Thus, while such emotion-laden, highly charged issues as the refugee question were addressed from time to time by administration officials, during the second term of the Eisenhower Presidency these references were no longer accompanied by any detailed or concrete plans for resolving the dispute of the sort that the American peace plan of August 1955 had sought to accomplish. On occasion, as was the case during

Vice President Nixon's meeting of March 13, 1960, with Prime Minister Ben-Gurion, the discussion revolved around the dangers to Israel inherent in any decision "to accept refugees prior to a peace settlement" without reviewing any other contingencies or options. Under such circumstances, observed the Vice President, Palestinian refugees would seek "to enter Israel for the purpose of stirring up more trouble there."[123] Similarly, in his reference of September 21, 1959, to the refugee problem, President Eisenhower confined himself to an expression of concern with "the situation of the Arab refugees," which he characterized as "an international disgrace," which ought to be tackled "more effectively."[124] The President did not elaborate, however, on how best to resolve this problem.

A final manifestation of this overall propensity of the Eisenhower Administration to avoid, during its second term in office, a direct and open confrontation with Israel can be found in the way in which Washington approached, in December 1960, the recently discovered fact that Israel was constructing a nuclear complex in Dimona with French assistance. Despite the administration's concern that Israel's nuclear activity might trigger a highly dangerous nuclear arms race in the Middle East, and despite the President's conviction—expressed in his meeting of December 19, 1960, with several cabinet members and representatives of the intelligence community—that "Israel should forthwith open the [Dimona] plant in order to assure that [it] conforms to peaceful purposes,"[125] no forceful and determined action was taken in order to guarantee that "qualified scientists from the International Atomic Energy Agency [IAEA]" are permitted "to visit the new reactor"[126] and that Israel's atomic energy program is indeed "devoted exclusively to peaceful purposes."[127]

Indeed, notwithstanding the "unequivocal" American opposition "to proliferation of nuclear weapons capabilities,"[128] and notwithstanding "the suspicions that Israel has aroused in many quarters"[129] and the conviction of CIA Director Allen Dulles, expressed on December 19, 1960, that "the Israelis seem to be trying to confuse this plant, which is a large production installation, with the very small research reactor [in Nahal Soreq] on which we are helping them,"[130] the administration, during its last month in office, adopted "a low-key approach"[131] toward Israel on the matter. Seeking to avoid a direct confrontation with Prime Minister Ben-Gurion in its last days in office, the lame duck administration in fact acquiesced in this development, preferring "to look the other way with regard to the Israeli case."[132] Lacking the time needed for setting in motion and orchestrating a coherent coercive strategy, and deprived of some of its power and leverages, the President decided to refrain from any public recrimination of Israel and instead advocated the use of quiet and conciliatory diplomatic tools as the most appropriate means of defusing the issue and obtaining satisfactory clarifications from Israel. As President Eisenhower pointed out on December 19, 1960: "Our message to Israel should be that we are confident, in view of . . . their statement that this is for peaceful uses, that they will permit . . . inspection."[133] And indeed, in its press announcement of December 21, 1960, the Department of State criticized "the American and world press" for "creating more excitement than facts as revealed by the Israelis warrant," and expressed its belief that "the Israeli atomic energy program as made public does not represent cause for special concern."[134]

While seeking to define the situation in a way that would limit Israel's margin of maneuverability and reduce any residue of ambiguity and doubt regarding the parameters of permissible and forbidden behavior, this "coupling strategy"[135] was pursued in a strictly nonconfrontational and nonthreatening fashion and was not incorporated into any deterrence or coercive design. Thus, in his meeting of December 24, 1960, with Prime Minister Ben-Gurion, American Ambassador Ogden R. Reid "noted that [the administration] did not wish to prolong or exaggerate [the nuclear] issue" and expressed satisfaction with the public and private assurances Israel provided concerning the "peaceful purposes of this reactor and Israel's atomic energy program."[136] Although the assurances the Prime Minister gave in his parliamentary address of December 21, 1960 (and in his meetings with Ambassador Reid), were partial at best, and did not include a formal commitment to make the reactor accessible to the safeguards system of the IAEA, American officials—in their eagerness to mitigate the crisis—interpreted Ben-Gurion's general and amorphous statements as sweeping and binding assurances that the new reactor "will be dedicated entirely to peaceful purposes."[137] Anxious to leave office with a clean slate, the President transformed the desirable into the real and tangible.

That by doing so he planted the seeds of misperception and misunderstanding that would haunt his successors in the White House in approaching the nuclear issue is, of course, quite a different matter. In any event, shortly after surfacing as a highly salient and potential source of strain and friction between Washington and Jerusalem, the nuclear issue subsided into the background without escalating into an open confrontation, but without effectively guaranteeing that the Dimona nuclear reactor was indeed constructed and designed in a way that fully and quintessentially reflected Prime Minister Ben-Gurion's visionary, if not utopian, message of December 21, 1960.

In conclusion, it is clear that the second half of the 1950s witnessed a progressive change in the American perception of Israel. With the initial vision of Israel as a strategic liability to American strategic designs receding into the background in the aftermath of the Jordanian Crisis of 1958, a new view had emerged, one that increasingly envisaged Israel as a potential asset of the U.S. by virtue of its ability to effectively deter the UAR from completely disrupting the Middle Eastern balance of power. Reflecting the recent changes in the regional strategic environment, and particularly the emergence of the UAR as a power closely linked to the Soviet Union in an effort to undermine American influence in such states as Saudi Arabia,[138] this gradual change was closely patterned on the national interest paradigm and cannot be even marginally attributed to the efforts of representatives of the special relationship paradigm to redirect the course of American diplomacy. Indeed, toward the end of the Eisenhower era, the initial gap that had separated the two paradigms from each other had largely disappeared, although this should by no means be interpreted as an indication that the forces associated with the special relationship paradigm had been successful in their persistent efforts to incorporate their preferences and recommended policies in the Arab-Israeli sphere into the official American course. In fact, Israel's Congressional allies, as well as the American-Israel Public Affairs Committee (AIPAC), which was established in February 1959, failed to accomplish their long-standing central objective, namely, the reversal of the administration's arms sale policy toward Israel. On occasion, as was the case in April 1959, they were even engaged in heated and stormy debates with administration officials, who remained unresponsive to Israel's demands that the U.S. agree to sell it the Hawk anti-aircraft missiles and to make Israel eligible for a multi-million-dollar military assistance credit under the Mutual Security Program.[139]

Thus, while the basic attitude of the Eisenhower Administration toward Israel did change gradually in the course of the period 1957–1960, this conceptual transition was not converted into those tangible and concrete measures that were continuously advocated by the organizations whose actions were predicated upon the premises of the special relationship paradigm. Incapable of softening the long-standing American opposition to "becoming a major supplier of arms to the area,"[140] or of inducing the administration to reassess such decisions and courses of action as the April 1959 decision (which was based purely on economic considerations) to eliminate from the Mutual Security Program $7.5 million of grant aid for Israel,[141] the organizational representatives of the special relationship paradigm remained largely in the background of the American-Israeli framework during the second term of the Eisenhower Presidency. Denied informal access to top administration officials and deprived of any significant influence on core and cardinal issues, the individuals and groups affiliated with this paradigm were confined to the sidelines without directly contributing to the formation of American policy toward Israel.[142]

As Burns observes, although Maxwell Rabb, Secretary to Eisenhower's Cabinet (who was the highest ranking Jew in the administration), did "maintain links to the American-Jewish community during the 1950s, the Israeli lobby had much less influence in the White House in the Eisenhower era than it had enjoyed during the Truman years."[143] And indeed, not only did AIPAC completely fail in its effort to revise American arms sale policy, but it also remained empty-handed in its attempt to prevent—in 1959 and 1960—the resumption of American food supplies to Egypt.[144]

Notwithstanding their overall inability to precipitate change in the basic American posture toward Israel, representatives of the special relationship paradigm did manage to win a few tactical victories in the Senate. For example, after Senator Ralph Flanders (R., Vermont) delivered a series of speeches in July and August 1958 calling for a reduction in the level of economic aid to Israel, he was confronted by a bipartisan group of Congressional leaders which was headed by Senators Lyndon Johnson (D., Texas) and William Knowland (R., California). The activities of this ad-hoc group, which were dramatically manifested in an emotional statement, which was made by Senator Hubert H. Humphrey (D., Minnesota) in support of Israel and of the activities of the United Jewish Appeal (which was attacked by Senator Flanders), were fully coordinated with the American Zionist Committee for Public Affairs (AZCPA).[145] Isaiah Kenen, Executive Director of AZCPA (and the founder of AIPAC), even drafted Senator Humphrey's message, which sealed the fate of Senator Flanders's initiative.[146]

Effective as these tactical moves, actions and stratagems were, these victories on Capitol Hill could not obscure the fact that on the strategic level, which pertains to the delineation of the basic tenets of American diplomacy, the proponents of the special relationship paradigm remained unsuccessful, during the entire Eisenhower era, in their efforts to channel American behavior into a course that would accommodate at least some of their premises and preferences.

IV

Convergence Dominates

The United States has a special relationship with Israel in the Middle East really comparable only to that which it has with Britain over a wide range of world affairs. But for us to play properly the role we are called upon to play, we cannot afford the luxury of identifying Israel . . . as our exclusive friend, hewing to the line of close and intimate allies (for we feel that about Israel though it is not a formal ally) and letting other countries go. If we pulled out of the Middle East and maintained our ties only with Israel, this would not be in Israel's interests.

—PRESIDENT JOHN F. KENNEDY, DECEMBER 27, 1962
(Quoted from the memorandum of his conversation with
Israeli Foreign Minister Golda Meir)

Contrary to the widespread belief that the Kennedy Administration drastically changed American policy toward Israel,[1] a careful review of Kennedy's first two years in the White House reveals a considerably more complex picture. While the new administration did augment the perceptual change that had taken place during Eisenhower's second term with concrete action, it also tried to accomplish certain objectives that the second Eisenhower Administration had downgraded or abandoned. The Kennedy Administration demonstrated a readiness to close the gap that still existed between image and reality, or between the growing perception of Israel as a strategic asset of the U.S., and the actual policy that the Eisenhower Administration continuously pursued on such issues as the sale of arms. However, from its very inception, the new administration demonstrated an abiding interest in the promotion of several policy goals (such as the comprehensive settlement of the Palestinian refugees), that the first Eisenhower Administration had vigorously promoted, albeit without relying—as Eisenhower had—on the tactics of deterrence and coercion. Not only did President Kennedy inject new life into policies and plans that had long been in abeyance, but also, at least some of his concerns in approaching Israel quintessentially reflected the sensitivities and preoccupations of his predecessor.

Deeply suspicious about the lobbying activities of the organizational representatives of the special relationship paradigm, the Eisenhower Administration did not hesitate—in its first years in office—to harass such Jewish organizations as the American Zionist Council (AZC) by demanding that their leaders register as "agents of a foreign government" and by threatening to abolish their status as tax-exempt organizations with the argument that the Jewish organizations were engaged in lobbying rather than charity activity.[2] Similarly, in numerous meetings with Israeli Ambassador Eban, Secretary Dulles warned that the exertion of "political pressures" by pro-Israeli groups upon the administration "would be counterproductive."[3] Repeatedly, he warned that "all the activities that friends of Israel customarily resort to in whipping up pressure—the paid advertisements, the mass meetings . . . the demands of Zionist organizations, the veiled threats of domestic political reprisals— do not help to create a basis for understanding and cooperation between our two Governments."[4] Viewing these activities as illegitimate and as inherently incompatible with the American national interest, the Secretary repeatedly expressed concern "over the fact that the Jewish influence here is completely dominating the scene." This influence, he argued, made it exceedingly difficult for the administration to demonstrate to the Arab world that it has "a foreign policy the Jews don't approve of."[5]

More than five years later, despite the vastly altered regional landscape, this desire to constrain, monitor, and occasionally intimidate the organizations associated with the special relationship paradigm remained intact. Thus, in 1962, acting in close cooperation with the Kennedy Administration, Senator J. William Fulbright (D., Arkansas), Chairman of the Senate Foreign Relations Committee, renewed the demand that the leaders of AIPAC should be forced to "register as foreign agents," and launched a comprehensive investigation into its activities and funding.[6] Concurrently, incensed by the publication of an article in *The Washington Post*[7] suggesting that American economic assistance to the UAR enabled it "to divert its own resources to purchase arms from the Soviet bloc," the Department of State involved the FBI in an investigation designed to identify "the source of information of [the] article."[8] Fearing that the article (and similar ones) could provide ammunition to the Congressional opponents of the administration's policy of continued economic assistance to the UAR under the auspices of the Foreign Assistance Act, the Department of State had no reservations in initiating a political inquiry, which established that the Israeli Embassy was the source of the information, and that it "has been in contact with members of the Congress on the subject."[9]

Yet another illustration of the basic congruity between the policies of the Eisenhower and Kennedy Administrations concerns their pattern of reaction in the face of repeated Israeli retaliatory raids against Egyptian, Syrian, and Jordanian targets. From its inauguration, the Eisenhower Administration was uninhibited in its condemnation of "border incidents perpetrated by Israel." Perceived as "a deliberate effort to provoke an engagement" with its neighbors, Israel's strategy of retaliatory raids in the face of repeated *fedayeen* infiltration had become, in the course of the period 1953–1956, a constant source of strain and friction between Washington and Jerusalem.[10] Repeatedly maintaining that there was a vast asymmetry between certain "small scale . . . acts of individuals and small [Arab] groups acting on their own responsibility and, on the part of the Israeli Government, a deliberate policy of reprisals," which was intended to trigger a major confrontation "while it still had military superiority," the administration resorted to harsh, irreconcilable rhetoric (occasionally accompanied, as was the case in October 1953, by coercive action) in an effort "to deter Israel from embarking upon aggression."[11]

Almost a decade later, although the strategy of retaliatory raids had been largely abandoned by Israel in the aftermath of the 1956 Sinai Campaign, the Kennedy Administration remained irrevocably committed to the posture pursued so vigorously during the first term of the Eisenhower Presidency and was therefore predisposed to strongly condemn Israel on those occasions in which it operated across its border against Syria and Jordan. Fearing, like his predecessor in the White House, that the adoption of "any posture other than strong opposition . . . to [the] Israeli tactics of retaliatory raids . . . would create strong feelings in the Arab world against the US for its abandonment of a well-established principle, important to maintenance of order in the area,"[12] President Kennedy was determined to disassociate himself from Israel's retaliatory strategy. "Were we to avoid a condemnation of Israel's retaliatory raid of March 16, 1962, across its border with Syria," observed James M. Ludlow, the United Nations Adviser to the Assistant Secretary of State for Near Eastern and South Asian Affairs, Phillips Talbot, on April 11, 1962, "it would be misunderstood in the Arab world to our detriment."[13] And indeed, al-

though the Israeli operation of March 16, 1962, was confined to the demilitarized zone and had been preceded by several Syrian violations of
the cease-fire, the administration, on March 28, 1962, introduced to the
United Nations Security Council a resolution condemning the Israeli attack as a "flagrant violation of the cease-fire provision of the Security
Council's resolution of July 15, 1948"[14] without alluding to earlier Syrian provocations.

A final demonstration of this initial compatibility between the two administrations concerns the highly charged, emotion-laden issue of
Jerusalem. Fully committed to the policy of the Truman Administration,
which had refused to recognize the Israeli decision of December 11,
1949, to move Israel's capital to Jerusalem, the Eisenhower Administration reacted sharply and angrily to any Israeli action designed to further
consolidate and institutionalize the status of Jerusalem as its capital in
defiance of the United Nations General Assembly's partition resolution
of November 29, 1947, which envisioned Jerusalem as an international-
ized city (this resolution was reaffirmed on December 12, 1949, when
the General Assembly, in the wake of the Israeli decision, called for the
internationalization of Jerusalem). And indeed, frustrated and exasperated, Secretary Dulles strongly criticized the Israeli decision of July 12,
1953, to transfer its Foreign Ministry from Tel-Aviv to Jerusalem. Viewing the move as "inconsistent with UN resolutions," and as an added
source of regional tension, he imposed a boycott of all official Foreign
Ministry functions and proceedings in Jerusalem.[15]

Eight years later, the 1947 plan to establish an international regime in
Jerusalem had faded into the background. Nevertheless, the Kennedy
Administration expressed grave concern when Israel disclosed its intention to hold a military parade in Jerusalem on its independence day, on
April 20, 1961. Maintaining that the parade would violate the 1949 Israeli-Jordanian Armistice Agreement (according to which Jerusalem was
to become "a restricted armaments area"), the administration fully supported the Jordanian position and repeatedly urged Israel to avoid "any
act of military provocation." Ultimately, on April 11, 1961, the U.S.
voted for a Security Council resolution that urged Israel to comply with
the decision of the Mixed Armistice Commission, which determined
that the Israeli rehearsals for the parade violated the 1948 Armistice
Agreement and called upon Israel to avoid further violations.

The American effort proved abortive. Despite the administration's determined drive and strong rhetoric, Israel opted to stage the military pa-

rade as scheduled. Although the administration refrained from specific punitive measures, it condemned the Israeli behavior, and issued an irreconcilable statement according to which "the status of Jerusalem is a matter of United Nations concern and no member of the United Nations should take any action to prejudice the United Nations interest in this question . . . or to [seek a solution] through fait accompli to the exclusion of international interest."[16]

The above examples were by no means isolated episodes. Rather, they constitute but three facets in a broad picture of basic compatibility between the policies pursued respectively by the Eisenhower and Kennedy Administrations. Indeed, contrary to the widespread belief that the election of John F. Kennedy as president precipitated a profound change in the American posture toward Israel, the picture that emerges from a review of the decade 1953–1962 is one of basic convergence between some of President Eisenhower's early premises and preferences and those adhered to by his successor in the White House. To the extent that the two presidents differed, it was largely on the tactical rather than the strategic level, namely, in their respective assessments of the most appropriate means for effectively promoting American national interests in the region. Specifically, in the same way that the initial Middle East strategy of the Eisenhower Administration had been predicated upon the desire to solicit Egypt's support for and participation in Washington's containment endeavors, so did the Kennedy Administration embark, in early 1961, on a major effort to improve relations with President Nasser and the UAR. Indeed, in the same way that the Eisenhower entourage had been motivated, in 1953, by the conviction that "the West must be more forthright in helping Egypt, through such means as buying its cotton and providing military and financial assistance,"[17] so did the Kennedy Administration launch, in late 1961, a multifaceted initiative designed "to open a new chapter in US relations with [the UAR]."[18]

Convinced that, in view of President Nasser's "desire not to become too dependent on the USSR," American diplomacy was provided with an exquisite opportunity to exert "some restraining influence on UAR policies by creating a vested interest on Nasser's part in good relations with the US,"[19] the administration moved apace to vastly increase the level of economic assistance to the UAR (particularly the PL-480 surplus wheat program) without making it contingent upon any specific political preconditions. As Robert Komer of the National Security Council further elaborated in a message sent to the President on December 8, 1961:

A somewhat more forthcoming policy towards Nasser—a policy of limited objectives but one which will set us on the path toward a more constructive relationship resembling that of the pre-1955 period, [will] break the vicious circle of aloofness in US-UAR relations which has persisted since the Aswan Dam fiasco.[20]

It is true that in the initial thinking of President Eisenhower, the role assigned to Egypt as a leading and pivotal component in the broadly based regional security alliance, which the administration sought to forge for the purpose of effectively blocking Soviet penetration and encroachment, was far more significant and far-reaching when juxtaposed with the modest expectations, on the basis of which American policy toward the UAR in the early 1960s was shaped and delineated. Thus, whereas the Eisenhower Administration, in 1953, sought "closer ties with Egypt in the military and economic spheres" and was even prepared "to consider making the Egyptian Army a real force in the world,"[21] President Kennedy was much more circumspect in inaugurating his accommodative posture toward Cairo. In his view, this conciliatory approach was intended to constrain and restrain President Nasser "by inducing him to turn his revolutionary fervor inward toward the settlement of Egypt's chronic weaknesses" rather than as an impetus for comprehensively and dramatically changing the direction of the UAR's behavior both regionally and globally.[22] In Komer's words:

> Let us remember that Nasser could cause us a lot more trouble if he were actively hostile—in Libya, North Africa, Sudan, Syria, or on Suez transit and Middle East oil, to mention but a few instances. Thus, perhaps our greatest gains would be negative; we would not get a great deal from Nasser, but at least we might restrain him from doing a lot of things we don't like.[23]

Indeed, while President Kennedy and his entourage did not believe that a major increase in the level of economic assistance to the UAR could fundamentally modify President Nasser's "basic positions on international issues," they expected such carrots as the PL-480 wheat program "to reduce the violence," with which these positions were expressed and promoted.[24] Thus, in October 1961, the administration announced its decision to provide the UAR with $432 million of PL-480 assistance over the next three years, as well as $20 million in stabilization credits and $51 million in development loans. Furthermore, during Kennedy's thousand days in the White House, American grain shipments accounted for more than 30 percent of the UAR's entire supply of wheat and wheat flour.[25]

For all these differences in context and scope, it is clear that the Kennedy foreign policy machinery adopted the same accommodative premises from which American policy toward Egypt had been delineated during Eisenhower's first term. Fully committed to the logic and premises of the strategy of reciprocity that had characterized the preliminary approach of the Eisenhower Presidency toward Egypt, the Kennedy Administration strongly believed that the unilateral initiation of an accommodative course vis-à-vis the UAR would ultimately bear fruit by encouraging President Nasser to reciprocate in kind and—at the very least—avoid "taking actions which would upset us."[26] It also assumed that the dramatic increase of American aid would divert President Nasser "from international relations to internal problems and economic development," while strengthening the relative position of the pro-Western faction within the leadership of the UAR at the expense of the pro-Soviet group.[27] In addition, the administration was acutely aware of the risks involved in the unmitigated pursuit of coercive diplomacy. Convinced that any effort "to exert unilateral pressure on Nasser" as a means of forcing him to instantly and drastically reorient his entire foreign and defense policy "would most likely undo the limited progress already made in improving US-UAR relations" and thus force the UAR into adopting intransigent and "extreme Arab positions,"[28] the President was clearly predisposed to assign priority, in the formulation of American policy toward the UAR, to reassuring and conciliatory measures at the expense of more forceful and assertive bargaining devices and tools.

Here, then, lies the essence of President Kennedy's bargaining approach toward the UAR (as well as toward Israel). Rather than relying upon the premises of coercive diplomacy as his principal bargaining vehicle, the President predicated his tactical behavior toward the UAR upon the belief that by increasing the level of economic assistance, American diplomacy would be provided with a more effective "leverage to restrain [President Nasser] to some extent." By virtue of becoming increasingly dependent upon American assistance, President Kennedy surmised, the UAR would be gradually integrated into a framework of moderation and restraint, unwilling to risk the interruption of the much-needed Western aid in an era of continued tension between Cairo and Moscow. It was hoped that the pursuit of a strategy of reciprocity toward the UAR would "lead to increased US influence over Nasser,"[29] thus creating a self-imposed "deterrent to radical behavior on Nasser's part, both internally and abroad."[30] In the words of Robert Komer:

> Are there not areas where we can cooperate, thus providing [Nasser] with Western support if he runs afoul eventually of the Soviets? . . . One of the key things we have to offer is assistance in economic development. *In turn, however, we must let Nasser know that we expect a compensatory quid pro quo in a less antagonistic policy on his part.*[31]

One week before his death, despite President Nasser's refusal to implement the terms of the April 1963 disengagement agreement in Yemen, which called for a phased withdrawal of foreign troops from Yemen (and despite Nasser's continued effort to threaten the very existence of the monarchies in Jordan and Saudi Arabia, as well as his flirtation with China, Cuba, and the Vietcong), President Kennedy was still refusing to deviate from the basic accommodative premises of his initial strategy toward the UAR. Although his last letter to President Nasser was permeated with concern over the UAR's failure to honor its pledge to disengage from Yemen, this growing disillusionment and exasperation did not lead the American President to reassess his basic approach toward the UAR (although he attempted, during 1963, to accompany it with increased support to President Nasser's main regional conservative opponents). Maintaining that the suspension of aid to the UAR "would limit American leverage in dealing with Nasser," Kennedy remained convinced that—as was the case in the aftermath of the American decision to withdraw the promised assistance for constructing the Aswan Dam—the adoption of a coercive course by the U.S. was bound to make Nasser defiant and recalcitrant. Specifically, the President predicted that, faced with a punitive posture, the leader of the UAR would "behave even more irresponsibly, perhaps gambling—as he had in 1956—or threatening to interfere with the free flow of shipping and oil."[32]

Even though the escalating war in Yemen demonstrated that it was "unrealistic to expect radical leaders who attained power riding the crest of anticolonial revolution to show the restraint and maturity demanded by true statesmanship,"[33] the President refused to abandon or modify his preconceived posture toward progressive revolutionary forces and regimes in the Arab world, or to reconsider his decision of December 19, 1962, to recognize the Yemen Arab Republic, which was strongly supported by the UAR. Irrevocably committed to his initial policy of nonintervention in Yemen, President Kennedy continued to believe that "the

Yemeni revolutionaries were inspired by nationalist and reformist tendencies and not by Communist dogmas."[34]

In addition, Kennedy's foreign policy elite was considerably more nuanced and far less rigid and dichotomous than Eisenhower's entourage, thus further reinforcing the administration's willingness to seek an improvement in the U.S. relations with the UAR despite President Nasser's unabated pan-Arab ambitions. Convinced that Nasser's alienation from the U.S. could be traced to President Eisenhower's excessive preoccupation with the Cold War, President Kennedy was predisposed to decouple American relations with the nonaligned world from the plethora of East-West predicaments, tensions, and anxieties in which they were embedded. Instead, he saw the need to side with, rather than against, "a good deal of the political turbulence" in the third world and thus to address a broad complex of regional issues and problems, including "the quarrels over boundaries, the tensions involved in lifting . . . economies from stagnation, [and] the cross-pressures of nationalism,"[35] on their own ideographic and intrinsic terms and merits and without applying to them the yardstick of the omnivorous, global Soviet-American rivalry. Kennedy, when still in the Senate, on March 23, 1960, comprehensively articulated this perspective:

> We tended to deal with [this area] exclusively in the context of the East-West struggle. The issues of nationalism, of economic development and local political squabbles, have been discussed by our policy-makers as being of secondary importance. . . . We have given our support to regimes instead of to people. . . . The question is not whether we should recognize the form of Arab nationalism, but how can we help to channel it along constructive lines.[36]

Clearly, Kennedy's undiminished desire—both as U.S. Senator and as President—to link American diplomacy to the resurgent forces of Arab nationalism in the hope of channeling them into a benign and constructive process of economic development (which derived from his basic approach to third-world nationalism), outweighed the traditional American objective of confronting Communist or pro-Communist forces wherever a threat arose without addressing their social root-causes and appeal. As a result, the President remained oblivious to such developments as the possibility that the republican regime in Yemen (which was backed and supported by the UAR) could become a springboard for Soviet penetration and encroachment, thus posing a serious threat to the stability of such traditional conservative allies as Saudi Arabia. As Gerges points out:

> . . . to Kennedy, the United States should talk to Egypt and other non-aligned states beyond the vocabulary of the Cold War. It should supply them with the essential requirements for development; bread and butter should replace threats and gunboat diplomacy. . . . Nonalignment was no longer an evil to be combated, but a positive idea that could have advantages for the United States in many developing states.[37]

President Kennedy's belief in the effectiveness of the strategy of reciprocity, combined with his conviction that influence could be gained by inducements and dependence, was not confined to the constrained parameters of American relations with the UAR. Rather, it can be thought of as the conceptual lens through which the strategic dynamics of the American-Israeli dyad (as well as of other regional crises and conflicts) during the period 1961–1962 could be elucidated. Specifically, while the Kennedy Administration continued to support most policies of the Eisenhower Presidency (including the insistence on "a significant unilateral concession by Israel," as a precondition for progress along the Arab-Israeli front[38]), these positions were now integrated into a considerably more accommodative framework than the one initially formulated by President Eisenhower and Secretary Dulles, a framework closely patterned on the logic and basic premises of the strategy of reciprocity. Thus, while President Kennedy did not change fundamentally the preliminary policy objectives of his predecessor within the American-Israeli framework, he was predisposed to set aside deterrence and coercive diplomacy and instead to focus on the less threatening strategy of reciprocity as his central bargaining tool vis-à-vis Israel. In doing so, the President was motivated by the same set of calculations that prompted him to predicate the U.S. relations with the UAR upon accommodative premises, and that evolved around the belief that the pursuit of an accommodative course toward Israel, which would "help in meeting Israel's security needs," would "permit Israel to take a little less rigid attitude toward the risks [inherent in the renewed effort to resolve] the refugee problem."[39]

In fact, these two frameworks may well have been inextricably linked to each other by virtue of President Kennedy's belief that the offering to Israel of significant incentives and inducements was the necessary condition for the consolidation of a sufficient base of support for his equally accommodative course toward the UAR. In this respect, the compensation of Israel was viewed as a prerequisite for meeting the domestic constraint, namely, for enabling the administration to win legitimacy and broad support for its overall regional approach.

Beyond his tactical calculations and considerations, President Kennedy—who was convinced that Israel could be induced to make concessions only from a position of relative strength—applied to the American-Israeli framework the very same cluster of assumptions and derivative policy lines that characterized his attitude toward the UAR, and that underscored the need to reassure Prime Minister Ben-Gurion by responding to Israel's security problems in the hope that Jerusalem would reciprocate by softening its posture on such core issues as the refugee question. As Rusonic observes, contrary to the prevailing interpretation that the Hawk sale "resulted simply from lobby pressures," the evidence suggests that President Kennedy hoped that "closer US-Israel relations would at once deter Arab attacks on Israel and bolster Israel's security confidence to the point where preemption/retaliation and use of nuclear weapons would be rejected."[40]

Thus, whereas President Eisenhower attempted initially to coerce Israel into acquiescence, his successor abandoned the stick in favor of the carrot in the hope that the supply of arms to Israel would reduce Israel's feelings of vulnerability and insecurity while increasing American influence and leverage on its behavior. Furthermore, while Eisenhower's policymakers had originally believed that the incorporation of reassuring measures into their policy toward Israel would alienate the Arab world and thus jeopardize their entire regional design, President Kennedy's approach was far less dichotomous, being predicated upon the assumption that American diplomacy could "maintain good relations with both Israel and the Arabs."[41]

Faced with a turbulent regional landscape, in which some of the major actors in the Middle East were already deeply committed to a pro-Soviet posture, the administration had little to fear in terms of the likely repercussions of its apparent tilt toward Israel. Indeed, in deciding to reverse its traditional arms sales posture, the Kennedy Presidency clearly recognized that providing arms to Israel was unlikely to rupture relations with conservative Arab regimes which were deeply concerned with Arab radicalism, and had nowhere else to turn even if the U.S. drew closer to Israel.[42]

In seeking "a limited accommodation with Nasser," the Kennedy Administration did not expect any immediate and "specific political commitments in return for expanded US interest and assistance."[43] Instead,

it defined its objectives in broad terms, hoping to increase its overall influence on President Nasser's behavior and ultimately exert "a restraining influence on UAR policies."[44]

By comparison, in pursuing the strategy of reciprocity toward Israel,
Washington envisaged a far more concrete and tangible linkage between
two central facets of its strategy, namely, its arms-sale policy and its approach for resolving, or at least mitigating, the dilemma of the Palestinian refugees. It did not insist, however, on a simultaneous tradeoff between the initial inducement offered to Israel (the sale of the Hawk
anti-aircraft missiles), and the expected reciprocal Israeli move (acceptance of the Johnson Plan). Thus, fully committed to the belief (embedded in the strategy of reciprocity, which it consistently pursued) that the
offering of a significant inducement to Israel would provide the impetus
for a mutually beneficial dialogue, with Israel becoming increasingly prepared to voluntarily reciprocate by softening its position regarding the
parameters of a settlement of the Palestinian predicament, the administration did not even attempt to incorporate into its policy less amorphous
and more binding forms of linkage between the carrot provided and the
compensation expected. Indeed, while Israel was expected, in return for
American support, "to practice self-restraint not only toward its neighbors but toward US policy elsewhere in the region," these expectations
never comprised a set of preconditions for aid.[45]

In President Kennedy's words, which clearly elucidate the essence of
his reciprocal bargaining strategy:

> We have to concern ourselves with the whole Middle East. On [the] ques-
> tions of water, of the UN role and reprisals, of refugees and of missiles. . . .
> *We are asking the cooperation of Israel in the same way that we are cooperating with Is-*
> *rael to help meet its needs.* . . . I think it is quite clear that in case of an invasion,
> the United States would come to the support of Israel. . . . Also, the United
> States is helping Israel economically. We would like now to see if we can
> make some progress on refugees and maintain our friendship with Israel
> without constantly cutting across our interests in the Middle East. When Is-
> rael takes actions in these matters, we hope it will understand our problems
> as well as its own.[46]

It was this innate reluctance to cross the threshold between the desired
and the required and thus to base American bargaining behavior on the
notion of a built-in, automatic, and concurrent mutuality between the
American action and the Israeli reaction, which contributed to the ultimate failure of the American effort to promote a settlement of the high-

ly complex, emotion-laden issue of the Palestinian refugees. Indeed, the fact that the U.S. was now prepared to reward Israel *in advance* for the flexibility it was expected to demonstrate in the course of the approaching bargaining over the Johnson Plan could, in itself, by no means guarantee that Israel would indeed agree to lend even a qualified and partial support for the enterprise.

While the President's basic support of the Israeli position in its Water Dispute with Syria and Jordan can also be interpreted as an integral part of his strategy of reciprocity, the decision to sell Hawk missiles to Israel was at the core of his bargaining approach. While the literature on the Kennedy era and Israel abounds with interpretations that depict the Hawk sale as a major watershed in the political and strategic history of the American-Israeli relationship, an analysis of the documentary evidence suggests otherwise: that in considering the issue, the President and his advisers were less concerned with the broad strategic ramifications of the deal than with its expected tactical implications on Israel's mode of conduct in the Palestinian zone. Indeed, as soon as President Kennedy accepted the assessment of the Defense Intelligence Agency (DIA), which asserted that there was "a valid military basis for Israel's concern and for the selection of the Hawk as an item of key importance in [the Israeli] military posture,"[47] and that "in a strictly air defense sense, Israel does have considerable vulnerability to air attack,"[48] his attention shifted from the theoretical and strategic to the concrete and tactical. By viewing the sale as a potentially stabilizing measure designed to "strengthen the weak link in Israel's defenses and thereby reduce any temptation Israel may have to take preemptive action,"[49] and at the same time "help to deter an attack against Israel by modern aircraft being supplied to Egypt by the Soviet Union,"[50] the administration focused, in the summer of 1962, on the terms of the linkage it sought to establish between the Hawk sale and the promotion of certain core objectives in the Arab-Israeli sphere.

Although the specific timing of the decision to sell the Hawk missiles to Israel was largely determined by developments in the Palestinian sphere, the administration could not remain oblivious to Israel's growing sense of vulnerability in view of the spate of intelligence reports (reinforced by President Nasser's announcement of July 21, 1962) indicating that the UAR was engaged in an accelerated effort (with the participation of German scientists) to develop a surface-to-surface missile. While analysts at the DIA concluded that the UAR's missile program was still in an embryonic phase in the summer of 1962, the administration feared that President Nasser's proclamation that the newly developed surface-to-surface missile was capable of "hitting any target South of Beirut" could become a precipitant for Israel to preempt. In this respect, the Hawk decision of August 1962 reflected—in no small measure—Washington's desire to allay Israel's fears and thus to stabilize a situation permeated with tension.[51]

Ultimately, it was this effort to link the sale to an Israeli gesture on the Palestinian front rather than the question as to whether to abandon its traditional policy of refusing to sell Israel sophisticated weapons systems that increasingly preoccupied the Kennedy Administration during the period immediately preceding its announcement of the Hawk decision. With the vision of Israel as a strategic asset of the U.S. increasingly permeating the thinking of American diplomacy during the years that followed the Jordanian Crisis of 1958, what was left for the Kennedy Administration was to activate these preexisting mutual interests in the hope that the Hawk sale would set in motion a mutually beneficial and reassuring process of conflict resolution in the Arab-Israeli zone.[52]

The desire to use the administration's revised arms sale policy as an inducement for Israel to reciprocate by softening its position regarding the parameters of an acceptable Palestinian settlement originated in President Kennedy's strong conviction that "the impoverished and tragic existence [of the Palestinian refugees] in makeshift camps near Israel's borders offers a constant source of national antagonism, economic chaos, and Communist exploitation of human misery."[53]

As for the means of comprehensively resolving the problem, Kennedy—both as Senator and as President—insisted that the principles of repatriation, resettlement, and compensation should be the essential components of any American or multilateral initiative. As Senator Kennedy pointed out in his February 24, 1957, address:

> Let those refugees be repatriated to Israel at the earliest practical date who are sincerely willing to live at peace with their neighbors, to accept the Israeli Government with an attitude of *civitatus filia*. Those who would prefer to remain in Arab jurisdiction should be resettled in areas under control of governments willing to help their Arab brothers, if assisted and enabled to earn their own living, make permanent homes, and live in peace and dignity. The refugee camps should be closed. Those who suffered actual losses of property or bank accounts in flight should be compensated by Israel. New water utilization and arable land projects should be instituted to assist their resettlement in Arab countries.[54]

Four years later, these principles resurfaced in a considerably more operational form as the three major tenets of the administration's intensive drive to resolve the refugee issue under the auspices of the Palestine Conciliation Commission (PCC). As Kennedy asserted in his message of May 11, 1961, to President Nasser:

> The United States, as a member of the Palestine Conciliation Commission, takes seriously the task entrusted to the Commission by the United Nations. We are determined to use our influence to assure that the Commission intensify its efforts to promote progress toward a just and peaceful solution. . . . It is my sincere hope that all the parties directly concerned will cooperate fully with whatever program is undertaken by the Commission so that the best interests and welfare of all the Arab refugees of Palestine may be protected and advanced.[55]

Whereas the Eisenhower Administration became increasingly convinced, during its second term in office, that any effort to tackle, head-on, the refugee problem was doomed to failure and bound to further exacerbate a situation already fraught with tension and permeated with irreconcilable cleavage on the Arab-Israeli front, the Kennedy Administration embarked—shortly after its inauguration—on a determined and multifaceted drive, designed to promote a Palestinian settlement as a prerequisite to an overall Arab-Israeli settlement. Closely patterned on the traditional parameters of American diplomacy as articulated by Senator Kennedy in his February 24, 1957, address, the initiative was based on the belief that "a genuine Israeli move to accept the principle of repatriation of Arab refugees was both feasible and absolutely essential."[56] As Secretary of State Dean Rusk further asserted:

> The Arabs were forced out of Palestine, have no desire to remain where they are, and were never regarded as other than refugees by the countries in which they now reside. In any case, unless a move is made with respect to repatriation, progress on the refugee question is not likely and this is the central issue at the moment.[57]

On May 30, 1961, three weeks after he had already informed the leaders of the UAR, Saudi Arabia, and Jordan of his plan to reactivate the PCC by supporting the appointment of a special representative who would operate under its auspices and guidelines, President Kennedy—in the course of his meeting with Prime Minister Ben-Gurion—advised him of his determination to seek a settlement to the Palestinian predicament which would incorporate the principles of repatriation, compensation and "resettlement in the Arab countries or elsewhere."[58]

Notwithstanding Ben-Gurion's conviction that "any commission

would be likely to fail in this effort," and that "until there is peace between Israel and the Arabs I don't see much chance of success,"[59] the
Kennedy Administration remained fully committed to its Palestinian initiative and, in August 1961, persuaded Joseph Johnson, President of the
Carnegie Endowment for International Peace (who was a personal
friend of Secretary Rusk), to become the special representative of the
PCC. While operating under the formal auspices of the PCC, Johnson—a former member of the Department of State—"spent more time
negotiating with US officials than with Israel or the Arab states."[60] Believing that only the United States was in a position to underwrite the financial burden of a settlement and exert effective pressure upon Israel,
he worked closely with both the White House and the Bureau of Near
Eastern Affairs in the Department of State.

The initial outcome of these consultations (as well as Johnson's two
trips to the Middle East) was the formulation of a plan—defined as a
pilot project—which sought to repatriate "a relatively small number of
refugees."[61] Although Israel was highly skeptical of the plan—fearing
that in the absence of adequate safeguards a large number of refugees
would seek repatriation—Johnson remained irrevocably committed to
the principle of repatriation as an integral tenet of his overall design,
maintaining that Israel should "consider taking back 100,000–150,000
Arab [refugees] if the Arab countries are cooperating in resettlement of
the remainder . . . and there is assurance of generous United States support in meeting costs of repatriating and settlement in Israel."[62]

In early August 1962, oblivious to the Israeli claim that the repatriation of at least 100,000 Palestinian refugees was bound to create a major
security predicament, Joseph Johnson submitted to the White House the
final draft of his plan, which outlined the procedures for implementing
the principles of repatriation and compensation. It was expected that
"after quiet approval by the US . . . the special representative [Johnson]
would personally deliver the text of the proposal to the Arab host governments and Israel."[63] Although President Kennedy thought "that neither the Arabs nor the Israelis would accept the plan," he ultimately gave
it his endorsement.[64]

It is precisely at this crucial juncture (which also coincided with a
spate of Israeli statements expressing profound concern over the UAR's
missile program), and in an effort to secure Israel's acquiescence,[65] that
the President resorted to the strategy of reciprocity as his central bargaining vehicle vis-à-vis Prime Minister Ben-Gurion. Notwithstanding
Johnson's willingness to consider "the threat of sanctions [against] Israel

if it rejected a fair proposal that the Arabs have accepted,"[66] President Kennedy opted to predicate his attempt to influence the Israeli approach toward the Johnson Plan upon the accommodative premises of the strategy of reciprocity rather than upon the less benign principles of the strategies of deterrence and coercion. Thus, while Secretary Rusk continuously looked upon—as Secretary Dulles had initially done—"a significant unilateral concession by Israel on the key element of repatriation" as the panacea for "breaking the ever more dangerous Arab-Israeli impasse,"[67] President Kennedy's attitude was closely patterned on his belief that Israel had to be induced, rather than coerced, into acceptance of the Johnson Plan.

Convinced that the only means of softening the Israeli opposition to several key components in the plan was an advance compensation of such magnitude as to fundamentally alter its threat perceptions and risk calculations, the President looked upon the sale of the Hawk missiles to Israel as a reassuring, confidence-building measure which—as such— was bound to entice the Israeli Prime Minister to adopt a more pragmatic and accommodative posture in the Palestinian zone. Indeed, in view of the undiminished Israeli desire to purchase from the U.S. the Hawk missiles, and the growing conviction of the Pentagon that there was "a valid military basis for [Israel's] concern and for [its] selection of the Hawk as an item of key importance in [its] military posture,"[68] it was only natural for President Kennedy to look upon this weapon system as the optimal carrot and hence as the essential accommodative tenet in the strategy of reciprocity he sought to implement within the confines of the American-Israeli framework.

Believing that without tangible evidence of American support for the risks it was called upon to take Israel was bound to adopt a defiant and recalcitrant attitude toward the Johnson Plan, the President decided in August 1962 to modify the traditional American posture on arms sales to Israel in the hope of establishing an inextricable, built-in linkage between the Hawk sale and the Palestinian predicament. In defiance of the position of the Department of State, however, he did not insist on a simultaneous linkage between the two issues, nor did he seek to make the Hawk deal contingent upon a prior Israeli acceptance of the Johnson Plan. While the timing of the Hawk decision coincided with the completion of the Johnson mission and reflected primarily the President's belief that even a qualified Israeli endorsement of the plan would accelerate progress by modifying Arab perceptions and positions on the parameters of a Palestinian settlement,[69] it was originally dictated by un-

folding developments on the American-Israeli scene, and particularly by
the renewed and vigorous Israeli effort to overcome the long-standing
American opposition to sell the Hawk missile. This effort culminated in
Prime Minister Ben-Gurion's message of June 24, 1962, in which he
pleaded with President Kennedy to reconsider his approach. In Ben-
Gurion's emotion-laden words:

> I am bound to say to my deep regret that . . . thoughts of total aggression
> are not absent from the minds of some of the Arab rulers of our region.
> The propaganda campaign which they conduct against us . . . does not
> differ much from the ill-famed and ill-fated Nazi propaganda. . . . For
> these reasons it is of utmost importance to provide the Israeli Defense
> Forces with sufficient deterrent strength which will prevent our neighbors
> from making war.[70]

For all of Ben-Gurion's rhetoric and passionate words, it was the
Palestinian predicament rather than the balance of military capabilities
that largely preoccupied the Kennedy policy elite during the summer of
1962, when the desire to inject new life and direction into the Johnson
mission and thus to provide the administration with a broadened margin
of maneuverability vis-à-vis Jordan, the UAR, Lebanon, and Syria dominated the thinking and behavior of the Kennedy entourage. From the
numerous memoranda and reports it is evident that the Hawk sale was
inextricably linked to the Johnson mission as the initial inducement expected to precipitate a more conciliatory Israeli attitude toward the initiative. Most revealing was the message sent on August 9, 1962, by Assistant Secretary Talbot, to the President's Deputy Special Counsel Meir
Feldman on the eve of his departure to Israel. Outlining the Department
of State's perspective and preferences, Talbot advocated a concurrent
tradeoff between the Hawk sale and Israel's acceptance of the Johnson
Plan. As he advised Feldman,

> our resolve on the quid pro quo is firm and remains firm. The deal would
> have to be (a) Hawks, subject to an Israel-UAR arms limitation, (b) assur-
> ance of financial help in meeting Israel's contributions to refugee com-
> pensation and in reintegration of refugees who are repatriated . . . , in ex-
> change for Ben-Gurion's pledge of cooperation in Johnson's plan,
> including establishment of procedures for prompt and equitable bearing
> of compensation claims submitted by returning refugees. . . . Unless [Ben-
> Gurion] is convinced we are not bluffing about withholding [the Hawk
> missiles] if he does not cooperate on the Johnson plan, he will be the more

likely to feel he can risk non-cooperation in, or sabotage of, the refugee plan. Ben-Gurion is a hard bargainer and can be dealt with successfully only on the basis of hard bargaining.[71]

For all this advocacy of a bargaining strategy which consisted of a simultaneous quid pro quo, the strategy that finally emerged was predicated upon the premise of an expected symmetry rather than upon the notion of linkage between the carrot provided to Israel, and its reciprocal move vis-à-vis the Johnson Plan. Thus in his message to the President of August 10, 1962, while Feldman acknowledged the need to link the Hawk sale to the Johnson Plan, he objected to Talbot's idea that the Hawk sale be made contingent, as a formal precondition, upon Israel's endorsement of the Johnson Plan, as well as upon the conclusion of an arms limitation agreement between Israel and the UAR. Convinced that it was "highly unlikely that Nasser would agree to any such limitation,"[72] Feldman's recommendations, from which the American approach was ultimately derived, were closely patterned on the logic and premises of the strategy of expected (rather than required) reciprocity between the Hawk sale and the Johnson Plan. Thus, while supporting a softer and more amorphous form of linkage than the one envisaged by Assistant Secretary Talbot, it is clear that the President's Deputy Special Counsel was motivated by a desire to promote a Palestinian settlement along the lines of the Johnson Plan rather than by considerations based upon or even indirectly related to the special relationship paradigm. Cold and unsentimental strategic considerations and calculations rather than feelings of sympathy and empathy toward Israel and its security needs and concerns determined his behavior, with the Hawk missile perceived as merely the bait designed to lure Israel into cooperating with, or at least acquiescing in, the Johnson initiative, rather than as the main objective sought by the architects of American diplomacy. In Feldman's own words:

> The only chance the [Johnson] plan has for success is to accompany it with notice to Ben-Gurion that we will guarantee the security of Israel and provide Hawk missiles. . . . We should not, in the meantime, defer for too long our offer to Ben-Gurion, for *I should like to be in the position of notifying him that we will provide Hawks at the time we request his acquiescence in the Johnson plan*.[73]

Five days later, in his letter to the Israeli Prime Minister informing him of Feldman's impending visit, President Kennedy directly linked the

Hawk missiles and the Johnson Plan as two matters "of prime importance to Israel's security and well-being as well as to the improvement in the atmosphere in the Near East and in prospects for peace." Urging Ben-Gurion "to find . . . the basis for an understanding [concerning the Johnson Plan]," the President—alluding to the inducement which his special emissary was authorized to offer Israel—promised "that the security and economic stability of Israel [will] not be endangered in the process of resolving the Arab refugee problem."[74]

On the same day, during a White House conference on the Johnson Plan, and faced with the President's skepticism regarding the prospects of convincing Israel to accept the principle of repatriation, Feldman reiterated his belief that the Johnson Plan should be linked to the Hawk sale, adding that "if we could tie in the Hawk, [the Johnson Plan] might work." And although President Kennedy did inquire, in the course of the meeting, about the "threats [which] we have on the Israelis and Arabs to get them to accept [the Johnson Plan]," the discussion drifted back to the question of carrots rather than sticks, with Feldman asserting that "we must be prepared to tie in security guarantees [to Israel] with the Johnson Plan, but [should] tell Ben-Gurion *ahead of time* he gets the Hawks."[75]

And indeed, in his August 19, 1962, meeting with Prime Minister Ben-Gurion, Feldman quickly moved to implement his preferred stratagem of expected reciprocity. At first, the carrot was duly offered to the astonished Israeli leadership. "The President had determined," he announced, "that the Hawk missile would be made available to Israel." Then, the conversation shifted to the expected Israeli part of the equation, with the American envoy urging Israel to cooperate "in good faith" with the Johnson Plan. Seeking to reassure the skeptical Prime Minister, Feldman repeatedly asserted that the plan did not call upon Israel to repatriate those refugees "who opt for repatriation" but merely "to examine such repatriation applications in good faith," and thus "to let the plan begin."[76]

Despite Feldman's initial optimism and impression that "Israel's leaders . . . have apparently not found in [the] Plan sufficient hazards to Israel to justify its immediate rejection,"[77] it became increasingly evident in subsequent weeks and months that Ben-Gurion and Meir remained highly suspicious of the Johnson Plan, unwilling to even marginally deviate from their preconceived conviction that it infringed upon Israel's sovereignty and posed an acute threat to basic Israeli security interests. Despite the carrot offered, the Israeli leadership remained irreconcilably committed to its initial belief that "even if the administrator of the [Johnson] plan was as pro-Israeli as possible, the pressures which the Arab governments were in a position to exercise . . . are such that half or more of the first group of refugees polled would opt for repatriation."[78] This continued Israeli reluctance to reassess its Palestinian posture keenly disappointed the administration, which had expected Israel to soften its opposition to the Johnson Plan and ultimately acquiesce in its implementation as a direct outcome of the Hawk sale. Thus faced with Ambassador Harman's assertion that the plan was "non-negotiable" and "totally unacceptable to the Government of Israel," Carl Kaysen, the President's Deputy Special Assistant for National Security Affairs, was uninhibited in articulating the premises upon which the administration's strategy of reciprocity had been originally delineated. As he pointed out in his October 2, 1962, conversation with the Israeli Ambassador:

> If the consequences of the Hawk transactions were such as to give the appearance that we had contributed to an increase in Israel's military capabilities without some quid pro-quo from Israel in the shape of an attempt on its part to contribute to conciliation of the refugee dispute or some other attempt to ease the Arab-Israel conflict, we would be put in a position which we could not and would not sustain.[79]

Two weeks later, in his conversation of October 17, 1962, with Mordechai Gazit, Minister of the Israeli Embassy in Washington, Robert Komer of the National Security Council was equally explicit and unequivocal in depicting the Hawk deal as the expected impetus for modifying the traditional Israeli operational code in the Palestinian sphere. Against the backdrop of this unprecedented demonstration of the American commitment to Israel's security, Komer argued, Israel's continued "inflexibility . . . and unwillingness . . . to take any risks against what [it] regards as only limited possibilities of any longer-run gains"[80] reflected a myopic, excessively cautious approach in the face of an exquisite opportunity to comprehensively resolve one of the root causes of the Arab-Israeli conundrum.

This perception of the Hawk sale as inherently and inextricably linked to a broad cluster of regional issues and as a major confidence-building measure for Israel which—as such—was bound to lead to a major reorientation of the Israeli modus operandi in the Palestinian sphere along more accommodative lines surfaced once again in the course of President Kennedy's meeting with Israeli Foreign Minister Golda Meir, which took place on December 27, 1962, in Palm Beach,

Florida. While still committed to the nonbinding premises of his strategy of reciprocity, the President was outspoken in reiterating his hope that
the Ben-Gurion Government would not remain oblivious to American
desires and predilections, and thus adjust its attitude toward the Johnson
Plan in view of the administration's willingness "to help meet [Israel's]
needs." As President Kennedy further elaborated:

> We have to concern ourselves with the whole Middle East. On these ques-
> tions—of water, of the UN role and reprisals, of refugees and of mis-
> siles—we are asking the cooperation of Israel in the same way that we are
> cooperating with Israel. . . . The United States is helping Israel. . . . We
> would like now to see if we can make some progress on the refugees [issue]
> and other interests in the Middle East. When Israel takes action in these
> matters, we hope it will understand our problem as well as its own.[81]

Despite the President's last-ditch effort to prevent the imminent collapse of Johnson's entire initiative, Israel refused to reconsider its approach toward "the refugee problem." Perceiving the refugee predicament as an intrinsic core issue and as an integral part of the overall Arab
design to destroy the Jewish state, Foreign Minister Meir maintained, in
her December 27, 1962, meeting with President Kennedy, that the acceptance of even "a very small number of Arabs" could pose a mortal
threat to Israel's security and well-being. In Meir's words:

> The question is this: even if Israel is to accept a very small number of
> Arabs, for what purposes would they be coming in? In the United Nations
> the Arabs repeat frankly and openly for hours and hours . . . that Israel
> has no right to exist and must disappear. . . . Israel knows about Arab plans
> to bring Arabs back to Israel and then to make an Algeria out of Israel.
> They would create difficulties within the country; then, when the Israeli
> Government would do what any state would have to do under the cir-
> cumstances, the Arab countries would come to the help of these return-
> ing Arab refugees.[82]

The Johnson Plan was thus sealed. Confronted with a defiant, uncompromising Israeli posture, which culminated in the unanimous decision of
the Israeli Government to reject—on September 16, 1962—the Johnson
Plan as "the worst of all plans dealing with the refugee question . . . lacking integrity and realism," and faced with an equally adamant Syrian opposition to the initiative (Syria argued that the Johnson Plan imposed
many restrictions upon the full implementation of the principle of repatriation), the administration was forced to *de facto* abandon the entire en-

terprise.[83] (the UAR and Jordan reacted to the initiative with skepticism). To paraphrase George, in the absence of perceived self-interest on the part of the side that is the target of the strategy of reciprocity, the strategy cannot expect "to elicit the hoped-for response."[84]

Indeed, for all his disenchantment and frustration with the Israeli unwillingness to accommodate its policy in the Palestinian sphere with Washington's expectations, President Kennedy did not attempt—in the aftermath of the suspension of the Johnson Plan—to reopen for further review the issue of the Hawk sale. Since the two matters had not been originally contingent upon one another, and since the linkage between them had never transcended the level of the amorphous, it is hardly surprising that they were ultimately destined for opposite fates: the Johnson Plan faded into the background as a transient and insignificant episode, while the Hawk deal was set for implementation. A letter Secretary Rusk wrote to Prime Minister Ben-Gurion on January 29, 1963, formally recognized the inevitable, acknowledging that the Johnson Plan "cannot be implemented," and that "we have no intention of trying to push it further with relevant parties."[85]

And although the Department of State still hoped, in subsequent months, to inject new life into the Johnson mission "by leaning hard on Israel . . . to change its position from rejection to acquiescence," Secretary Rusk's recommendation of March 28, 1963, to "engage our influence with . . . Israel" lest "our image of evenhandedness as between Israel and the Arabs will be tarnished and our effectiveness in dealing with the Arabs on other Arab-Israeli issues . . . will be impaired,"[86] was not converted into action.

Thus, contrary to the innate propensity of the Eisenhower Administration to predicate its actual bargaining approach toward Israel exclusively upon the logic and basic premises of the strategies of deterrence and coercion, with the carrot of multilateral territorial guarantees depicted as a long-term prospect, to be offered to Israel only after it had demonstrated flexibility and willingness to compromise and after the peacemaking process had been successfully completed, the Kennedy Administration—operating on the basis of considerably more optimistic premises—was predisposed to offer to Israel a major carrot without insisting on any concurrent reciprocal Israeli move, and without attempting to guarantee that the Hawk sale would be incorporated into a broader framework of mutually-beneficial or confidence-building measures.

Furthermore, although the administration became fully convinced that Israel had interpreted "the language of the plan in the blackest light" as a pretext and justification for "making an all-out effort to scuttle the plan," and that "having now received assurance of the Hawk missile [it] feels free to take a hard line in the hope of obtaining more benefits," it avoided any coercive measures vis-à-vis the Ben-Gurion Government. Confining his activity to the search of additional "means of reassuring Israel," the President decided to abandon whatever plans he had "to test out the depth of Israel's resolve."[87]

Could American diplomacy have been more successful had it attempted to link the two issues to one another by insisting on a concurrent tradeoff rather than expecting Israel to reciprocate for the Hawk sale? Although the purchase of the Hawk weapons system was a long-standing, much-desired Israeli objective that comprised a central part of its overall strategic thinking and planning, there can be no doubt that the cluster of questions integrated into the refugee problem constituted for Israel a highly charged, acutely sensitive complex of core existential issues. Convinced that the Palestinian refugees "would repatriate only with the support of [the] Egyptian army," and that "with repatriation, Nasser will send his army into Israel behind the refugees,"[88] Israel envisaged the implementation of the Johnson Plan—unless it was accompanied by a fundamental change in the basic Arab attitudes toward it—as a prelude to its destruction. As Prime Minister Ben-Gurion observed in his June 24, 1962, message to President Kennedy in alluding to the Johnson mission:

> Above all we are confronted with a unique security problem. It is not our democratic system, or our borders and independence alone which are threatened, but our very physical existence is at stake. What was done to six million of our brethren twenty years ago with the participation of Palestinian Arab leaders, among them the ex-Grand Mufti and his henchmen, could be done to the two million Jews of Israel . . . [89]

This perception of at least some of the facets incorporated into the Johnson Plan as posing a direct, immediate and mortal threat to Israel's very existence was converted into a formal Knesset resolution stipulating "that the Palestinian refugees should not be returned to Israeli territory [but] resettled in Arab countries."[90] It was therefore unlikely that, in the absence of a radical change in the basic structure of the Arab-Israeli conflict, any American compensation or inducement that entailed an Israeli acceptance of the Johnson Plan could have been of sufficient magnitude to lure Israel into acquiescence.

Thus, while the pursuit by the Kennedy Administration of a bargaining strategy consisting of a tradeoff between Israel's attitude toward the Johnson Plan and the Hawk sale would have undoubtedly aggravated Ben-Gurion's predicament by forcing upon him the necessity of choice, the ultimate strategic outcome would have most likely remained unchanged. And although Israel would have conceivably attempted to maintain a margin of ambiguity as well as a margin of maneuverability regarding the plan, in the final analysis it would not have compromised a basic tenet of its traditional Palestinian posture, which was viewed as inextricably linked not merely to Israel's security but to its very survival as an independent entity. In other words, with the balance of motivation and the intrinsic interests at stake favoring Israel, the administration ultimately remained empty-handed in its effort to entice Israel into acceptance of the Johnson Plan. With Israel having a far greater stake in the outcome than the U.S., it consistently and adamantly refused to adjust its Palestinian posture in accordance with Washington's preferences.

Although the administration did not, at any phase of its pursuit of the Johnson Plan, seriously attempt to replace its strategy of expected reciprocity with a more forceful approach based on a tradeoff, the failure of the carrot to moderate the Israeli approach toward the Johnson Plan did lead several officials to retrospectively reassess their strategy. Believing that the promise of a major inducement without any complementary, built-in demand as an integral part of the bargain enabled Israel to defy the President with impunity and thus contributed to Israel's recalcitrance, such policymakers as Assistant Secretary Talbot emerged from the episode with the conviction that in dealing with Israel, a "firm" line should be adopted. Such firmness, Talbot further elaborated, would force Israel to adopt more accommodative "fall-back positions." Convinced that because "Israel has recently obtained from us all that it now wants" Ben-Gurion could remain "adamant on the one issue on which we seek its reciprocal cooperation," he recommended that American diplomacy resort to a "determined" course in order to exert influence on Israel.[91]

It is indeed to the analysis of such an effort, albeit a brief and inconsequential one, to pursue a policy incorporating coercive or "firm" elements vis-à-vis Israel, that we will soon turn.

While the tenuous and ill-fated American effort to link the supply of the Hawk missile to Israel's acceptance of the Johnson Plan was explicit and direct, the question arises as to whether it was further reinforced or accompanied by other, more subtle forms of intended linkage, initiated by the administration in the hope of using the Hawk sale as an impetus for a major strategic tradeoff in the Arab-Israeli sphere. Specifically, was the Hawk missile perceived by President Kennedy as an adequate substitute for nuclear weapons, and did he try to link the sale to an Israeli pledge not to produce weapons grade material at the Dimona nuclear reactor?

Contrary to Spiegel's claim that the nuclear issue comprised an integral part of Meir Feldman's formal negotiating agenda in the course of his August 1962 bargaining with the Israeli leadership,[92] an analysis of the transcripts of his conversations with Ben-Gurion and Foreign Minister Meir unequivocally indicates that Feldman never referred to Israel's nuclear activities in Dimona in the entire course of his visit, nor did he seek to establish a quid pro quo between the Hawk sale and any facet of Israel's emerging nuclear posture.[93] And while the President, in his December 27, 1962, meeting with Meir, did address "Israel's atomic reactor," his remarks were general and did not entail any specific tradeoff or direct threat. "We would hope," he told Meir, "that Israel would give consideration to our problems on this atomic reactor." The President continued: "We are opposed to nuclear proliferation. Our interest here is not in prying into Israel's affairs, but we have to be concerned because of the overall situation in the Middle East."[94]

Although the Kennedy Administration, from its inception, was adamantly opposed to nuclear proliferation and hence continuously sought to place the Dimona nuclear reactor under some form of American control or supervision, it avoided—during the years 1961–1962—the use of blatant coercive and deterrence tactics vis-à-vis Prime Minister Ben-Gurion in trying to obtain assurances regarding the peaceful nature of the Dimona project. Indeed, while the President's involvement in the Israeli nuclear case constituted an integral part of his global nuclear agenda (which included intensive negotiations with the Soviet Union on a Partial Test Ban Treaty), he refrained—during this period—from exerting direct pressures upon the Israeli Government.[95]

A clear illustration of this noncoercive pattern is provided by the transcript of the May 30, 1961, meeting between Kennedy and Ben-Gurion. Although the nuclear issue was the first item to be comprehensively addressed by the two leaders, the discussion was relaxed and amicable, devoid of any tension or even a trace of irreconcilability and crisis. The fact that, on the very eve of the meeting, two American physicists (I. I. Rabi and Eugene Wigner) had visited Dimona and had given the President "a good report of it,"[96] contributed to the friendly atmosphere that prevailed during this American-Israeli summit. Therefore, while Prime Minister Ben-Gurion avoided any sweeping assurances concerning Israel's long-term intentions and objectives concerning Dimona, this omission did not seem to trouble the President, who was preoccupied with the immediate rather than with more remote contingencies and possibilities. Although Ben-Gurion pointedly stated, in referring to Dimona, that "we do not know what will happen in the future," and that "in three or four years we might have the need for a plant to process plutonium," the President remained unperturbed, merely restating his desire to prevent a nuclear arms race in the Middle East. "It is obvious," he added, "that the UAR would not permit Israel to go ahead in this field without getting into it itself."[97] Indeed, while the Israeli Prime Minister "did not explicitly exclude," in the course of the meeting, "a possible future [Israeli] interest in nuclear weapons," the President raised no questions "that went beyond what Ben-Gurion told him on his own. Instead, President Kennedy confined himself to making the American position on nonproliferation clear and thus did not even try to extract a promise "that Israel would not develop a nuclear capability in the future." Nor did he question Israel's need for two research reactors—"a small American reactor and a larger one of French design" that could potentially produce significant amounts of plutonium.[98]

For all the pressures that were exerted by the British Foreign Office upon the administration in early 1962 in the hope of inducing Washington into "working for the introduction of the International Atomic Energy Agency [IAEA] inspection system into the Near East countries,"[99] the administration remained, at least temporarily, committed to a strictly nonconfrontational posture vis-à-vis Israel. Rather than pressing for an international control of the Dimona site, it quietly sought Israel's consent for another inspection, to be conducted by American scientists (this visit took place in October 1962, and convinced the inspectors that the Dimona reactor was only for peaceful purposes). Faced with Prime Minister Ben-Gurion's claim that an international inspection system would violate Israel's sovereignty (as well as with his promise that Israel would not be the first to introduce nuclear weapons into the region), Washington decided to at least temporarily refrain from pursuing the IAEA option, insisting instead on inspections under the exclusive auspices of American scientists.

It was only in the spring of 1963 that this low-key and unobtrusive posture began to change. Confronted with a welter of reports and assessments indicating that the increasingly unstable situation in the Middle East "was likely to lead Israel to seek a nuclear deterrent to intimidate the Arabs and to prevent them from making trouble on the frontiers," that "the Dimona reactor is now in an advanced stage of construction . . . and does have potential capability of producing fuel for nuclear weapons," and that such an eventuality was bound to cause "substantial damage to the U.S. and Western position in the Arab world," the President, in March 1963, decided to accelerate his efforts to forestall "the development of advanced weapons in the Middle East."[100] Convinced that Israel's continued nuclear activity was liable to adversely affect vital American interests in the Middle East by raising suspicions in the Arab world that the U.S. was involved in the Dimona project and by precipitating a highly dangerous nuclear arms race in the region, President Kennedy decided to set aside his initial posture of friendly persuasion for the sake of pursuing a more assertive and forceful approach vis-à-vis the Israeli Government.[101] And indeed, the actual American policy that began to emerge in the American-Israeli zone in the spring of 1963—while still essentially patterned on the logic and premises of the bargaining strategy—increasingly incorporated the premises of deterrence and coercion while obfuscating or minimizing the reassurances contemplated. Believing that Israel "was the most determined proliferator after China," the President—who became acutely sensitive to the dangers of nuclear proliferation in the wake of the Cuban missile crisis—came to view the Israeli case as a test for American global nonproliferation policy.[102] Momentarily, at least, the Kennedy Presidency opted to assign priority to the cluster of coercive bargaining methods while downgrading and de-emphasizing the complex of more accommodative strategies vis-à-vis Israel.

Increasingly impatient and disenchanted with Israel's perceived tactics of evasion and procrastination concerning the future inspections of the Dimona reactor, the President—on several occasions in May and June 1963—adopted a bargaining style reminiscent of the first term of the Eisenhower Administration. Contrary to his innate predilection for the accommodative strategy of reciprocity, he temporarily resorted to uncompromising and harsh rhetoric as a means of securing Israel's acquiescence and cooperation. Focusing on the need to permit American scientists to continuously and comprehensively inspect the Dimona reactor, President Kennedy, in his message of May 18, 1963, to Prime Minister Ben-Gurion, demanded that Israel agree "to periodic visits to Dimona," and warned that Israel's development of a nuclear capability would have "disturbing effects" on world and regional stability. Kennedy wrote:

> I cannot imagine that the Arabs would refrain from turning to the Soviet Union for assistance if Israel were to develop nuclear weapons capability—with all the consequences this would hold. Development of a nuclear

weapons capability by Israel would almost certainly lead other larger countries, that have so far refrained from such development, to feel that they must follow suit. . . .

If it should be thought . . . that [the U.S.] Government was unable to obtain reliable information on a subject as vital to peace as the question of Israel's efforts in the nuclear field . . . then the American commitment to Israel's security would be seriously jeopardized in the public opinion in this country and in the West.[103]

One month later, in a letter initially drafted by the President on June 15, 1963 (but which, as a result of Prime-Minister Ben-Gurion's resignation on June 16, 1963, was actually delivered with minor modifications to his successor, Levi Eshkol, on July 5, 1963), Kennedy was even more forceful and irreconcilable. Viewing Ben-Gurion's willingness, which had been incorporated into his May 27, 1963, message to the President, to permit annual visits of American representatives to Dimona (as of late 1963 or early 1964) as "insufficient," the President insisted on "visits at intervals of six months." Indeed, in view of the unanimous conclusion of the American intelligence community that Ben-Gurion's terms—as outlined in his May 27, 1963, letter—"failed to meet our minimum requirements," the President insisted—in his strong letter of June 15, 1963—"that our scientists have access to all areas of the Dimona site and to any related part of the complex, such as fuel fabrication facilities or plutonium separation plant, and that sufficient time be allotted for a thorough examination." These visits, President Kennedy further demanded, "should be of a nature and on a schedule which will more nearly be in accord with international standards, thereby resolving all doubts as to the peaceful intent of the Dimona project."[104] In an effort to lend credence to these demands, the President concluded his message of June 15, 1963, with a thinly veiled threat:

Knowing that you fully appreciate the truly vital significance of this matter to the future well-being of Israel, to the United States and internationally, I am sure our carefully considered request will have your most sympathetic attention.[105]

Neither this message, nor the President's May 18, 1963, letter to the Israeli Prime Minister, made even an indirect reference to any potential compensation to Israel. Thus, although President Kennedy continued—in a number of internal discussions and meetings, which took place during the same period—to express undiminished support for the idea of a simultaneous tradeoff between an Israeli decision not to develop nuclear weapons and some form of a security guarantee to Israel, his concurrent messages to Israel focused exclusively on the steps and measures Israel was called upon to take, rather than on the American part of the equation.[106]

A clear illustration of this duality is provided by a review of the President's views, which was incorporated into a message sent by Assistant Secretary Talbot to the American Ambassador in the UAR, John S. Badeau, on May 20, 1963, two days after President Kennedy's strong letter to Prime Minister Ben-Gurion had been sent. While the message alluded to the Dimona reactor "as a reason for concern," it was permeated with empathy toward Israel's security predicament, and repeatedly underscored the need to compensate it for whatever concessions it would ultimately agree to make in the nuclear field. According to Assistant Secretary Talbot's report,

> . . . the president felt it important to give serious consideration to Israel's strong desire for a more specific security guarantee. He believes it is only through allaying Israel's fears about the long-range threat to its existence that leverage to forestall possible Israeli preventive warfare and to prevent proliferation of nuclear proliferation can be maintained.[107]

Similarly, on the same day that his second irreconcilable message to the Israeli Prime Minister was drafted (June 15, 1963), the President elaborated, in a conversation with CIA Director John McCone and his Middle East experts Robert Komer and Phillips Talbot, on the advantages inherent in his preferred bargaining strategy of a simultaneous quid pro quo. Implying that a security agreement with Israel would vastly reduce its margin of maneuverability in regional crises and would, therefore, practically ensure that Israel refrain from such military initiatives and moves as the occupation of the West Bank, President Kennedy asserted that such guarantees would be acceptable and perhaps even appealing, to President Nasser, and in any event would not jeopardize the administration's relations with the UAR. According to the memorandum of the conversation,

> the president said . . . that even a security guarantee to Israel was not without its attractions to Nasser, because if Jordan blew up, Nasser had only two options. He'd either have to stand aside or move in, but in the latter case he wasn't prepared sufficiently so he'd get licked. Thus it would be in Nasser's interest to have us give Israel a guarantee if this would lead the Israelis to agree not to move into Jordan. *So from our point of view we should*

give Israel reasonable assurances in return for their agreement not to move into Jordan or to develop nuclear weapons.[108]

This presidential predilection for a tradeoff incorporating reassuring measures to Israel as compensation (or substitute) for a decision to suspend its nuclear activities rather than for a strong coercive posture was echoed and reinforced by the National Security Council (but not by the Department of State). In numerous meetings, members of the NSC reiterated their belief in the bargaining strategy as the only viable means for progress. In the words of Robert Komer, which clearly illustrate the NSC support of this quid pro quo scenario: "Our hole card with Israel [is] its desire for a US security guarantee; if possible we should tie this to [an] Israeli agreement not to develop nuclear weapons."[109]

It was only in the aftermath of the abrupt resignation, on June 16, 1963, of Prime Minister Ben-Gurion, and against the backdrop of the expressed willingness of his successor Levi Eshkol (which was demonstrated in his August 19, 1963, message to President Kennedy), "to reach agreement on the future schedule of visits [to Dimona]" and "to move significantly in the direction of the president's demands," that this gap between intragovernmental and intergovernmental rhetoric and negotiating approaches was closed, with most coercive elements fading into the background of the American-Israeli dyad.[110]

With tension subsiding, the administration—during the period which immediately preceded the assassination of President Kennedy—concentrated (in its communications with the Israeli leadership) on the need to address *all* facets and components of its envisaged tradeoff between the suspension of Israel's nuclear program (or at least Israel's willingness to open the Dimona reactor to rigorous and continuous American inspection), and some form of American compensation. The question of the precise nature of this compensation rather than the status of the Dimona reactor increasingly preoccupied the President during the last months of his life.

Among the inducements the administration considered during the summer and fall of 1963, were security and territorial guarantees to Israel, and a commitment to provide it with advanced conventional weapons systems. These potential carrots were, in turn, integrated into and qualified by a broader and more ambitious scheme, which was designed to consolidate an intricate web of arms-limitation arrangements between Israel and the UAR.[111] (This search for arms-limitation arrangements in the Middle East culminated, in the summer of 1963, with the mission of John J. McCloy, the President's coordinator of disarmament activities, who sought in vain to induce Israel to agree to international supervision of the Dimona reactor in return for the UAR's willingness to freeze its missile program).

None of these ingredients of the bargaining strategy, which attempted to link a major Israeli concession in the nuclear field to a unilateral American conventional compensation, or to the establishment of a de facto regional arms control regime, were ever implemented. And although President Kennedy's letter of October 3, 1963, to Prime Minister Eshkol included "a most comprehensive expression of presidential commitment to Israel's security," it still fell short of the Israeli desire (incorporated in Prime Minister Ben-Gurion's letter of May 12, 1963, to President Kennedy) to extract from Washington a public bilateral security pact or "new deterrent weapons, including surface to surface missiles of the kinds that the Egyptians have" in exchange for "policy restraints on its nuclear program."[112]

The assassination of President Kennedy, who was acutely sensitive to the dangers inherent in nuclear proliferation, brought this intensive search for a multifaceted and viable arms limitation system to a halt. With President Johnson's attention diffused among many other global and regional issues and crises (such as, within the confines of the Middle East, the escalating water dispute between Israel and Syria and the continued military involvement of the UAR in Yemen), the entire complex of policy issues and potential linkages between the Dimona reactor and various unilateral or multilateral inducements and confidence-building measures faded into the background of the dyad.

Further aggravating a situation fraught with tension and uncertainty was President Nasser's irreconcilable opposition to any form of arms control arrangements with Israel. This reluctance, on the part of the UAR, to enter into a strategic dialogue incorporating specific confidence-building measures with Israel, deprived the administration of a potentially powerful leverage vis-à-vis Prime Minister Eshkol, and thus effectively sealed the fate of the "original idea to use [Nasser's acquiescence in] a nuclear missile scheme as the quid pro quo to sign up Israel."[113] Unable to set in motion any dynamic of regional conflict-reduction or to induce the parties to agree to even highly constrained and delimited forms of confidence-building measures, President Johnson, "who was much less sensitive to the issue of Israel's nuclear efforts" than was his predecessor,[114] ultimately opted to relegate the nuclear predicament to the periphery of the American-Israeli framework, while avoiding any blatant coercive measures vis-à-vis the Eshkol Government.

As to the idea of providing formal unilateral guarantees to Israel in exchange "for Israeli nuclear self-denial,"[115] it is clear that notwithstanding President Kennedy's support of a posture patterned on such a simultaneous tradeoff, it became increasingly clear, as the year 1963 approached its end, that the unwavering opposition of the Department of State to this bargaining strategy posed an insurmountable impediment to its implementation. Convinced that "a public guarantee" was bound "to undermine our even-handed Middle East policy, thus reducing our leverage on the Arabs to reduce Arab-Israeli tensions," while giving Israel "a blank check to be obstreperous in its Arab policy, confident that our guarantee would protect it from any adverse consequences of its actions," Secretary Rusk and the Department's Middle East experts vehemently warned the new President not to proceed beyond the general terms and parameters of his secret commitment to Israel, as outlined in his December 27, 1962, conversation with Foreign Minister Meir. Maintaining further that such guarantees "would invite the Soviets to offer similar guarantees to the Arabs"[116] and thus vastly complicate and aggravate a situation already fraught with tension and animosity in the Arab-Israeli zone "by bringing the Soviets back in, probably in a more permanent and damaging fashion,"[117] leading officials in the Department of State were relentless in their efforts to forestall or at least delay any executive initiative designed to implement a bargaining strategy incorporating formal security guarantees as its major incentive to Israel. As a Department of State paper entitled: "Israeli Security Guarantee," which was drafted on September 20, 1963, concluded: "The security arrangements Israel seeks with the United States would in our judgment harm our interests in the area and weaken rather than strengthen Israel's ultimate security."[118]

And indeed, distracted by a plethora of competing policy issues, President Johnson ultimately acquiesced in Secretary Rusk's position. However, while formal security guarantees would never be offered to Israel during the entire Johnson era, other inducements—including advanced conventional weapons systems—were provided. That these new inducements were not linked to, or contingent upon, any specific Israeli move or posture in either the nuclear field or the Palestinian sphere is, of course, quite a different matter.

V

Epilogue

For all the differences in style, bargaining approach, and perceptions of the region between the Eisenhower and Kennedy foreign policy elites, one central conclusion emerges from our review of American-Israeli relations between 1953 and 1962: the policy the Kennedy Administration pursued was patterned on at least some of the premises of Eisenhower's second term. And although the first major arms deal between Washington and Jerusalem, the Hawk sale, was concluded during the Kennedy era, the groundwork for this decision had been laid during Eisenhower's second term, as his administration, abandoning its earlier views, became increasingly predisposed to perceive Israel as a strategic asset. While President Kennedy was the one who ultimately converted the conceptual into a fully operational course of action, his decisions were deeply rooted in, and inextricably linked to the revised regional perceptions of his predecessor.

Against this backdrop of basic continuity in terms of the strategic visions of the Middle East, it is clear that President Kennedy's decision to sell arms to Israel was not predicated upon the logic and premises of the special relationship paradigm. Nor was it primarily motivated by a cluster of domestic (particularly electoral) considerations and pressures in defiance of the American national interest. Instead, as the preceding analysis sought to demonstrate, the Hawk decision quintessentially reflected the primacy of regional security considerations over ideological preferences and considerations, and was depicted by the administration as fully compatible with the President's *modus operandi* in the Middle East, and as one facet, which was fully incorporated into his overall strategy and bargaining approach.[1] Indeed, the offering of an inducement in the form of the Hawk missile by no means constituted an aberration or a major deviation from the administration's overall operational code in the Arab-Israeli zone. As we have already witnessed, this strategy of expected reciprocity, which was predicated upon the perception of the carrot (which is provided at the outset of the bargaining process) as a major impetus for a process of conflict-reduction and attitude-change was not confined to the American-Israeli dyad, but was fully implemented in the context of American relations with Egypt. In both instances, major incentives (economic or military) were offered in the hope of setting in motion a process of regional accommodation and as a means of increasing American influence and leverage upon the parties.

In other words, it was President Kennedy's innate optimism as well as irrevocable belief in the human capacity to set aside irreconcilable ideologies and dogmas for the sake of adopting a more accommodative and pragmatic attitude that was largely responsible for his decision to close the gap between the perceptual and the operational and thus to translate into congruent and derivative policy his vision of Israel as a strategic asset. While advocates of the special relationship paradigm had much more access to the Kennedy White House (as well as multiple channels of communication with the administration) than was the case during the Eisenhower era, this access did not invariably entail extended leverage or influence as strategic considerations continued, in the President's thinking, to downgrade and overshadow any competing cluster of predilections and preferences.

Despite such accomplishments of the pro-Israeli forces in the Congress as the Gruening Amendment to the 1961 Foreign Assistance Act, there is no evidence that the organizational representatives of the special relationship paradigm were even indirectly or marginally involved in the decision to sell the Hawk missile to Israel.[2] Derived from a complex of considerations and calculations linked inextricably to the national interest orientation, this decision therefore reflected the President's preconceived strategic preferences, proclivities, and expectations rather than the complex of domestic attitudes and beliefs patterned on the special relationship paradigm.

Furthermore, rather than constraining the administration by significantly restricting its margin of maneuverability and latitude of choice, the lobbying efforts of such Congressional supporters of Israel as Congressman Leonard Farbstein (D., N.Y.) and Senators Ernest Gruening (D., Alaska), Jacob K. Javits (R., N.Y.), Kenneth Keating (R., N.Y.), and Hubert H. Humphrey (D., Minnesota), occasionally infuriated the President and made him even more determined to persist in his accommodative posture toward President Nasser. Thus, confronted with the critical voices of Senators Javits and Humphrey, "who attacked the administration's allegedly pro-Nasser and pro-Arab policy," President Kennedy, in his White House staff meeting of May 1, 1963, toyed with the idea of "going straight to the Israelis themselves and telling them that these overly zealous Zionist attacks can be counter-productive."[3]

Six months later, in his conversation with the Minister of the Israeli Embassy in Washington, Mordechai Gazit, on November 21, 1963, Robert Komer of the National Security Council reported that the President was so incensed over the Gruening Amendment (according to which foreign aid, including agricultural sales, would be withheld from any country that was engaging in, or preparing for, aggressive military action against the United States or any country receiving American assistance), that he warned that this amendment (which had passed the Senate on November 7, 1963, by a vote of 65 to 13), would "make it very difficult for us to be as forthcoming with Israel in the refugee or other issues as we would otherwise like."[4]

The assassination of President Kennedy on the following day aborted any retaliatory measures against Israel and guaranteed that American policy would be continuously patterned on largely accommodative premises and on the logic of the strategy of reciprocity rather than on the assumptions of the strategies of coercion and deterrence. And indeed, the Johnson era witnessed an acceleration and intensification in the strategic ties between Washington and Jerusalem, which were not restricted any longer to the sale of strictly defensive weapons systems. Once the United States became committed to the preservation of the regional military balance, its decisions regarding the specific weapons systems to be supplied were merely the tactical and operational implementation of this strategic concern. This concern was further reinforced by growing sensitivity to Washington's signaling reputation. As Walt points out, "once the commitment was made . . . U.S. support for Israel was self-sustaining; like most overseas commitments, it became necessary for maintaining prestige and credibility."[5] Thus in 1965, for example, in view of the accelerated shipments of Soviet arms to Egypt and Syria, the Johnson Administration decided to approve the Israeli request for 210 M-48 Patton tanks.

Once again, then, it was the cluster of unsentimental global and regional strategic considerations rather than any feelings of empathy toward Israel that precipitated this sale. Similarly, in February 1966, motivated by a desire to balance the mounting Soviet military aid to Cairo, Damascus, and Baghdad, the President authorized the sale to Israel of 48 Skyhawk bombers, with 52 additional aircraft soon to follow. Maintaining that it could not remain oblivious "to the potentially destabilizing effect of massive Soviet sales of arms to the area,"[6] the Johnson Administration further reinforced the behavioral pattern that had been established by the Kennedy Administration in 1962, by seeking to balance Soviet shipments of arms to Egypt, Syria, and Iraq, as well as its own supply of arms to Jordan.

It is precisely this pattern—the conceptual origins of which were formed during the second term of the Eisenhower Presidency—that would, in subsequent years, become a recurrent component of the American-Israeli framework. Decoupled from its original bargaining context as an inducement for which Israel was expected to reciprocate by adopting more accommodative positions on such issues as its nuclear program or the Palestinian predicament, this cluster of balance-of-power linkages and considerations would increasingly dominate the thinking of successive administrations as an inevitable byproduct of the all-encompassing competition between East and West.

It is against the background of this superpower rivalry, as well as of the divisions that continuously permeated the region, that the image of Israel as a strategic asset to the U.S. and as a power whose mission was to assist Washington in its quest "to reduce Soviet influence"[7] would be further consolidated in future years and decades. That these objectives, which were derived from a bipolar-confrontational vision of the international system, were compatible with Israel's considerably more delimited and constrained perspective is, of course, quite a different matter and cannot be attributed to the impact of the premises of the special relationship paradigm. Thus, while the Kennedy era witnessed a growing convergence between the national interest orientation and the special interest paradigm, with the premises of the latter increasingly perceived as at least partially compatible with the strategic logic of containment and with American security interests in the region, it was the structural-realist complex of security concerns and objectives that continuously provided the main lens through which American policy toward Israel was shaped and delineated.

Similarly, although President Richard Nixon was occasionally faced with pressures exerted by the forces representing the special relationship paradigm (which demanded the sale of additional and more sophisticated weapons systems to Israel), his actual approach "to almost all practical issues" derived from "an unsentimental geopolitical analysis." In view of President Nixon's continued preoccupation with the global and regional balance of power, it is highly unlikely that considerations predicated upon the special relationship paradigm in themselves could have shaped his thinking and behavior. Instead, such calculations were subordinated to considerations patterned on the national interest paradigm, leading the President to ultimately advocate positions which were, as Henry Kissinger notes, "not so distant from ones others might take on the basis of ethnic politics." As Kissinger further observes:

> [Nixon] would make gestures to demonstrate . . . that he was free of the traditional influences that had constrained other Presidents. But at the end of the day, when confronted with the realities of power in the Middle East . . . he would pursue, in the national interest, the same strategy: to . . . . weaken the position of the Arab radicals, encourage Arab moderates, and assure Israel's security.[8]

Thus, notwithstanding the President's repeated assertions (which were reminiscent of the Eisenhower Presidency) that the Jewish vote "will have absolutely no . . . influence on [his] decisions," and that he was prepared "to pressure the Israelis to the extent required regardless of the domestic political consequences,"[9] the policies he actually pursued toward Israel and the region essentially converged with the premises of the special relationship orientation.

Thus, whereas President Eisenhower had predicated his initial Middle East strategy upon the conviction that the all-important objective of containment could best be promoted by an exclusive reliance on an Arab security system, his successors (and even Eisenhower himself during his second term)—operating in an altered regional landscape—adopted the view that Israel constituted an important link in any contemplated containment design.

For all their dominance and centrality in shaping the American approach, the factors related to the national interest paradigm did not unfold in a political and social vacuum. While the gap that had previously existed between the national interest orientation and the special relationship paradigm largely disappeared during the Kennedy Presidency, this growing compatibility could by no means guarantee that the relationship between Washington and Jerusalem would invariably remain harmonious and consensual, or that the administration would always emerge victorious—as had been the case in the crises of 1953 and 1956—from its encounters with the forces affiliated with the special relationship paradigm. In this respect, while the pressures exerted by the organizational proponents of the special relationship paradigm never resulted in any drastic transformation or reorientation of American policy in defiance of the administration's basic strategic premises and objectives, they repeatedly forced the architects of American foreign and defense policy to scale down, obfuscate, or altogether abandon certain punitive measures vis-à-vis Israel.

Although—during the entire period under consideration—the representatives of the special relationship paradigm did not for the most part play a dominant role in determining the very essence of the American posture toward Israel, and had but a marginal impact on the administration's basic approach toward such regional questions as the sale of arms to Arab states or American voting behavior in the UN Security Council on a variety of Middle East issues (including the Palestinian predicament and Israel's retaliatory raids), they did occasionally manage to constrain Washington's margin of maneuverability when it deviated sharply from the very core of the special relationship. And while these efforts were not always successful when viewed in themselves, they did help—in the aggregate—to clearly delineate the parameters within which American Middle East diplomacy could unfold and be implemented with equanimity. In performing this "delineating function" advocates of the special relationship paradigm benefited from the fact that broad segments of American opinion shared their objectives. Indeed, because the elements that merged into the special relationship paradigm reflected a widespread fund of goodwill toward Israel that was not restricted to the Jewish community, the backbone of the paradigm could effectively constrain the administration in such cases as the "reassessment crisis" of 1975 and the "superpower crisis" of 1977 without precipitating a major tilt in the basic premises and direction of American policy.[10]

Similarly, for all their intrinsic significance, the Congressional measures initiated by representatives of the special relationship paradigm, among them the Symington-Javits Resolution, the Ribicoff-Scott Amendment, the Case-Tydings declaration, the Jackson-Vanik Amendment and the Gruening Amendment, did not amount to a de facto repudiation of the administration's posture toward Israel. Combined with, and reinforced by, a series of appropriating measures, these legislative initiatives —which reflected a solid and broadly based infrastructure of domestic support—were designed to guarantee that American diplomacy toward Israel was not predicated exclusively upon coercive premises and tactics, and that the carrot of inducement was fully integrated into the administration's behavior.[11] And although American presidents did not always remain oblivious to such domestic factors as the Jewish vote, they did not altogether abandon the basic tenets of their operational code in the American-Israeli sphere but—at most—augmented them by more accommodative measures.

In the final analysis, and in terms of the strategies pursued, rather than the tactical devices and stratagems employed by American policymakers, it is therefore clear that cold and realistic calculations of the American national interest rather than idealistic notions and beliefs comprised, in the aggregate, the most powerful independent variable from which American policy in the Arab-Israeli sphere was continuously derived. In Organski's words:

> The record of foreign policy decisions with regard to the Middle East does not seem to support the conventional wisdom that the United States helps Israel because of the influence brought to bear on the executive branch by the leadership of the Jewish community. US policy decisions with respect to Israel have, in the main, been made by presidents and presidential foreign policy elites both by themselves and for reasons entirely their own. When the United States did not see Israel as supporting US interests in stemming the expansion of Soviet influence, it did not help Israel. . . . When US leaders . . . decided that Israel could be an asset in the US struggle with radical Arabs who were perceived as Soviet clients, they helped Israel. Jewish leaders and the Jewish community at large have been involved in a supportive role.[12]

And indeed, because Israel was increasingly perceived during the period that followed the Suez Crisis as an added bulwark against the forces of radicalism, the stage was set for American diplomacy to set its course upon the premises of integration and synthesis between the national interest orientation and the special relationship paradigm rather than upon the notions of exclusion and separation.

With the early Eisenhower legacy fading into the background, notions of convergence and compatibility progressively came to dominate the American-Israeli framework, outweighing and downgrading any residual visions of irreconcilability and cleavage between the two paradigms. It was this convergence between the strategic and the sentimental, between the realist and the utopian, and between the exogenous and the endogenous (a convergence becoming fully evident during the Kennedy era, and one patterned largely and primarily on the perception of Israel's military capability as an effective deterrent against the forces of militancy and radicalism), which made it exceedingly difficult for American diplomacy during the 1960s (and 1970s) to effectively pursue even a mild coercive course vis-à-vis Israel. Because a pro-Israeli posture could now be justified not only in emotional or idealistic terms but on strategic grounds as well, the way was now opened toward the consolidation of broadly based domestic support for Israel that would severely constrain the architects of American policy in the course of the 1970s and 1980s.

In this respect, the premises and legacies of the special relationship paradigm can be viewed as an added layer, which buttressed and further reinforced the complex of beliefs and assumptions deeply rooted in the strategic and operational environment rather than in the sentimental and affective realm. It is indeed this alliance between the tangible and the abstract, or between power and principle, that injected so much vigor and vitality into the American-Israeli alliance, transforming it from a transient convergence of certain interests and objectives into a more viable and durable bond encompassing a multifarious web of allegiances, ties, and sentiments. And it is indeed this combination of cognitive and affective components and caveats, derived respectively from the national interest paradigm and the special relationship orientation, that provided Israel with a viable and durable "safety net." That net transcended the idiosyncrasies and aspirations of successive administrations and ultimately doomed to failure any effort to redefine the basic rules of the game within the American-Israeli sphere.

It remains to be seen whether this "safety net" will be sufficiently broad and strong to fully absorb the strains that have intermittently dominated the American-Israeli framework since the end of the Cold War. Will the premises of the special relationship paradigm fade into the background under this altered regional strategic setting and against the backdrop of a revised Israeli agenda, no longer governed by a need for a broad range of security ties necessary to counter Soviet threats to the region? (Especially since the election of Benjamin Netanyahu as Prime Minister on May 29, 1996.) And will such a development provide Washington, at long last, with the necessary margin of maneuverability in order to accomplish an objective that has eluded the architects of American diplomacy for almost five decades, namely, the highly desirable objective of comprehensive peace in the turbulent Middle East? In other words: will the pendulum of American-Israeli relations swing back in the direction of the early 1950s, with the strategies of deterrence and coercion becoming once again the administration's chief bargaining tools in seeking to promote the goal of regional accommodation? And finally, will such a reliance on threatening or punitive methods ultimately prove more effective than was the case during Eisenhower's first term, when the pursuit of coercive diplomacy in its purest form made the Ben-Gurion Government recalcitrant and defiant rather than accommodative and conciliatory?

Although the legacy of the early 1950s appears remote in an era of multifaceted forms of strategic collaboration within the American-Israeli dyad, one should not remain oblivious to the process of continued erosion in some of the components that form the backbone of the special relationship paradigm. This erosion gained momentum in the mid 1990s and is increasingly threatening to convert what had originally been a cohesive and determined base of support into an alienated and ineffective entity. With the American Jewish community becoming increasingly fraught with disunity over such issues as Israel's legislative policy in matters that affect the Conservative and Reform communities in the U.S., the possibility that Israel will ultimately have to face the administration without such segments of its supportive infrastructure (which in the past has helped to constrain or abort numerous American initiatives and plans to which the Israeli Government was opposed), should not be discounted.[13]

The coming years will show whether or not the American-Israeli alliance has indeed exhausted its potential and usefulness and whether, more than forty years after it was shaped, it has started its descent into decline, erosion, and eventually oblivion. One can only hope that the facade of contentiousness and ambiguity will be lifted as the twenty-first century approaches.

Notes

Chapter 1: A Theoretical Framework and Objectives

1. For two interpretations of American-Israeli relations from the early 1990s, which differ fundamentally from one another in terms of their basic premises, hypotheses and conclusions, see David Schoenbaum, *The United States and the State of Israel* (New York: Oxford University Press, 1993), as juxtaposed with George Lenczowski, *American Presidents and the Middle East* (Durham: Duke University Press, 1990).

2. Secretary of State John Foster Dulles's statement of May 14, 1953. Memorandum of his conversation with Israeli Prime Minister David Ben-Gurion. *Foreign Relations of the United States: The Near and Middle East, 1952–1954*, part 1 (Washington D.C.: United States Government Printing Office, 1986): 39 (hereafter FRUS).

3. For illustrations of this line of argumentation see Mitchell G. Bard, *The Water's Edge and Beyond: Defining the Limits to Domestic Influence on United States Middle East Policy* (New Brunswick, NJ: Transaction Publishers, 1991), pp. 189–190; Steven L. Spiegel, *The Other Arab-Israeli Conflict: Making America's Middle East Policy, from Truman to Reagan* (Chicago: The University of Chicago Press, 1985), pp. 95–97; Ethan Nadelmann, "Setting the Stage: American Policy Toward the Middle East, 1961–1966," *International Journal of Middle East Studies* 14(1) (1982): 436–437; Mordechai Gazit, *President Kennedy's Policy Toward the Arab States and Israel: Analysis and Documents* (Tel-Aviv: The Shiloah Center, 1983), *passim*. Proponents of this "domestic politics" interpretation underscore the fact that President Kennedy's Cabinet included two Jews, Abraham Ribicoff and Arthur Goldberg, who had close ties with Israel. See Douglas Little, "From Even-Handed to Empty-Handed: Seeking Order in the Middle East," in Thomas G. Paterson, ed., *Kennedy's Quest for Victory: America's Foreign Policy, 1961–1963* (New York: Oxford University Press, 1989), p. 159; Stephen M. Walt, *The Origins of Alliances* (Ithaca: Cornell University Press, 1987), p. 250.

4. On the Sinai Campaign and the subsequent Suez Crisis see, for example, Yaacov Bar-Siman-Tov, *Israel, the Superpowers, and War in the Middle East* (New York: Praeger, 1987), pp. 27–83; Herman Finer, *Dulles Over Suez: The Theory and Practice of his Diplomacy* (Chicago: Quadrangle Books, 1964); Donald Neff, *Warriors at Suez* (New York: Simon and Schuster, 1981); Hugh Thomas, *The Suez Af-*

fair (Harmondsworth: Penguin Books, 1970); Kenneth Love, *Suez: The Twice-Fought War* (New York: McGraw-Hill, 1969); Robin Renwick, *Fighting With Allies: America and England at Peace and War* (New York: Times Books, 1996); Selwyn Ilan Troen and Moshe Shemesh, eds., *The Suez-Sinai Crisis, 1956: Retrospective and Reappraisal* (New York: Columbia University Press, 1990); William Roger Lewis and Roger Owen, eds., *Suez 1956: The Crisis and its Consequences* (Oxford: Clarendon Press, 1989). On the 1958 Lebanon Crisis see, for example, Alan Dowty, *Middle East Crisis: U.S. Decision-Making in 1958, 1970, and 1973* (Berkeley: University of California Press, 1984); Agnes G. Korbani, *U.S. Intervention in Lebanon, 1958 and 1982: Presidential Decisionmaking* (New York: Praeger, 1991); M. S. Agwani, ed., *The Lebanese Crisis, 1958* (New York: Asia Publishing House, 1965); Fahim I. Qubain, *Crisis in Lebanon* (Washington, D.C.: The Middle East Institute, 1961).

5. For a major exception, see Isaac Alteras, *Eisenhower and Israel: US-Israel Relations, 1953–1960* (Gainesville: University Press of Florida, 1993). Even this comprehensive book, however, is largely confined to the analysis of Eisenhower's first term. The period 1958–1960, during which the first indications of change in American policy toward Israel became evident, remains largely unexplored.

6. Douglas Little, "The Making of a Special Relationship: The United States and Israel, 1957–68," *International Journal of Middle East Studies* 25 (1993): 563.

7. For a definition of the "Israeli lobby" as distinguished from the "Jewish lobby" see Mitchell G. Bard, "The Influence of Ethnic Interest Groups on American Middle East Policy" in Eugene R. Wittkopf, ed., *The Domestic Sources of American Foreign Policy: Insights and Evidence*, second edition (New York: St. Martins Press, 1994), pp. 80–83; Bard, *The Water's Edge and Beyond*, pp. 267–287. See also Bernard Reich, *Securing the Covenant: United States-Israel Relations After the Cold War* (Westport: Praeger, 1995), pp. 71–76; Little, "The Making of a Special Relationship," p. 563; Edward Tivnan, *The Lobby: Jewish Political Power and American Foreign Policy* (New York: Simon and Schuster, 1987), *passim*.

8. Secretary Dulles's statement of May 14, 1953. Memorandum of his conversation with Israeli Prime Minister Ben-Gurion. FRUS 9, pt. 1: 39. See also an undated Department of State Paper entitled "Conclusion on [Dulles's] Trip [to the Middle East]." *The John Foster Dulles Papers*, Box 73, "Middle East" folder, Seeley Mudd Manuscript Library. Citations for the John Foster Dulles Papers are published with permission of Princeton University Libraries. For other illustrations of the same propensity, see Alteras, *Eisenhower and Israel*, pp. 32, 36.

9. For an earlier exposition of the national interest paradigm and the special relationship orientation, see Abraham Ben-Zvi, *The United States and Israel: The Limits of the Special Relationship* (New York: Columbia University Press, 1993), pp. 14–26. See also Arthur M. Schlesinger, Jr., *The Cycles of American History* (Boston: Houghton Mifflin, 1986), pp. 69–86; Robert Endicott Osgood, *Ideals and Self-Interest in America's Foreign Relations* (Chicago: The University of Chicago Press, 1953), *passim*.

10. Aaron S. Klieman, *Israel and the World After 40 Years* (New York: Pergamon-Brassey's, 1990), pp. 198–199; Reich, *Securing the Covenant*, p. 34; Lenczowski,

American Presidents and the Middle East, p. 31; Alteras, *Eisenhower and Israel*, p. 27; Schoenbaum, *The United States and the State of Israel*, pp. 84–85; William B. Quandt, *Peace Process: American Diplomacy and the Arab-Israeli Conflict Since 1967* (Washington, D.C.: The Brookings Institution, 1993), p. 1; Stephen D. Krasner, *Defending the National Interest: Raw Materials Investments and U.S. Foreign Policy* (Princeton: Princeton University Press, 1978), p. 13; Shibley Telhami, "Israeli Foreign Policy: A Realist Ideal-Type or a Breed of Its Own?" in Michael N. Barnett, ed., *Israel in Comparative Perspective: Challenging the Conventional Wisdom* (Albany: State University of New York Press, 1996), pp. 30–31; Alexander L. George and Richard Smoke, *Deterrence in American Foreign Policy: Theory and Practice* (New York: Columbia University Press, 1974), pp. 314–316; Richard Rosecrance, "Objectives of U.S. Middle East Policy," in Haim Shaked and Itamar Rabinovich, eds., *The Middle East and the United States: Perceptions and Policies* (New Brunswick, N.J.: Transaction Books, 1980), p. 31; Blema S. Steinberg, "American Foreign Policy in the Middle east: A Study in Changing Priorities," in Janice Gross Stein and David B. DeWitt, eds., *The Middle East at the Crossroads* (Oakville, Ontario: Mosaic Press, 1983), pp. 115–116; Wilson D. Miscamble, *George F. Kennan and the Making of American Foreign Policy, 1947–1950* (Princeton: Princeton University Press, 1992), p. 102.

11. William B. Quandt, *Decade of Decision: American Policy Toward the Arab-Israeli Conflict, 1967–1976* (Berkeley: University of California Press, 1977), p. 16. See also William J. Burns, *Economic Aid and American Policy Toward Egypt, 1955–1981* (Albany: State University of New York Press, 1985), p. 19; Ben-Zvi, *The Limits of the Special Relationship*, p. 16; Bernard Reich, *Quest for Peace: United States-Israel Relations and the Arab-Israeli Conflict* (New Brunswick, N.J.: Transaction Books, 1977), p. 365. Reich, *Securing the Covenant*, pp. 1–13; Bard, "The Influence of Ethnic Interest Groups," pp. 81–82; Alteras, *Eisenhower and Israel*, pp. 21, 35; Nadav Safran, *Israel: The Embattled Ally* (Cambridge: The Belknap Press of Harvard University Press, 1978), p. 572; Gabriel Sheffer, "The United States-Israeli 'Special Relationship,' " *The Jerusalem Journal of International Relations* 9(4) (December 1987): 37–39; A. F. K. Organski, *The $36 Billion Bargain: Strategy and Politics in US Assistance to Israel* (New York: Columbia University Press, 1990), p. 38; Charles Lipson, "American Support for Israel: History, Sources, Limits," *Israel Affairs* 2(3–4) (Spring/Summer 1996): 131–134. See also the essays in Menachem Kaufman, ed., *The American People and the Holy Land: Foundations of a Special Relationship* (Jerusalem: The Magnes Press, 1997).

12. Although the discussion in this work will exclusively focus on the specific contextual and regional attributes of the national interest paradigm and the special relationship orientation, this perspective should not overshadow the fact that, in terms of their premises and intrinsic logic, these orientations are indeed respectively patterned on two basic and divergent interpretations of human behavior, namely, the structural-realist theory and the constructivist approach. In its core assumptions, the national interest paradigm fully and quintessentially reflects the logic of the structural-realist theory of international behavior. Viewing the international system as inherently and endemically permeated with tension

and instability because states are not subject to one central authority, proponents of this theory are predisposed to define state behavior as an endless quest for security, which is exclusively determined by power considerations and calculations.

Against the backdrop of these acutely threatening conditions of international anarchy, national entities—according to this realist vision—repeatedly employ such strategies and methods as alliance formation and containment in order to increase their relative power and leverage in the constant struggle for survival or hegemony.

Contrary to this highly conflictual vision of the international arena, which presupposes a perennial preoccupation with the security dilemma and the strategic attributes of state behavior, the premises upon which the special relationship paradigm is delineated are patterned on a considerably more benign constructivist view of the world and of the processes that govern state behavior. According to this vision, state behavior is the cumulative outcome of certain formative social and cultural experiences, on the basis of which shared identities, affinities, norms, and domestic structures are formed. In other words, it is not the "objective" conditions of international anarchy that invariably and automatically shape state behavior, but rather the specific cognitive and normative attributes of the social structure in which a given political entity is embedded, and which ultimately delineate and define the range of the legitimate and the viable behavioral patterns in the international arena.

Chapter 2 of this work, which deals with American policy toward Israel during the period 1953–1956, will attempt to expose and elucidate the initial incompatibility between the national interest paradigm and the special relationship orientation, while chapter 4, which deals with American policy toward Israel during the years 1961–1962, will seek to explain the reasons for the growing compatibility between them (despite the irreconcilable gap that continued to exist in terms of their respective premises).

On the general debate between proponents of structural-realist and constructivist theories of international behavior, see, for example, Zeev Maoz, *National Choices and International Processes* (Cambridge: Cambridge University Press, 1990), pp. 543, 548; Leon V. Sigal, *Fighting to a Finish: The Politics of War Termination in the United States and Japan, 1945* (Ithaca: Cornell University Press, 1988), pp. 12–14; Samuel P. Huntington, *American Politics: The Promise of Disharmony* (Cambridge: Harvard University Press, 1981), *passim;* Alexander Wendt and Daniel Friedheim, "Hierarchy Under Anarchy: Informal Empire and the East German State," *International Organization* 49(4) (Autumn 1995): 692; Alexander Wendt, "Constructing International Politics," *International Security* 20(1) (Summer 1995): 71–81; Alexander Wendt, "Anarchy is What States Make of It: The Social Construction of Power Politics," *International Organization* 46(2) (Spring 1992): 422–425, *passim;* Charles A. Kupchan and Clifford A. Kupchan, "The Promise of Collective Security," *International Security* 20(1) (Summer 1995): 59–61; John Mearsheimer, "The False Promise of International Institutions," *International Security* 19(3) (Winter 1994/95): 9–11; Charles L. Glaser, "Realists as Optimists: Cooperation as Self-Help," *International Security* 19(3) (Winter 1994/95): 53–56;

John Lewis Gaddis, "History, Theory, and Common Ground," *International Security* 22(1) (Summer 1997): 80; Stephen H. Haber, David M. Kennedy, and Stephen D. Krasner, "Brothers Under the Skin: Diplomatic History and International Relations," *International Security* 22(1) (Summer 1997): 37; Kenneth Waltz, *Theory of International Politics* (Reading: Addison-Wesley, 1979), *passim;* Markus Fischer, "Feudal Europe, 800–1300: Communal Discourse and Conflictual Practices," *International Organization* 46(2) (Spring 1992): 428–434; John H. Herz, *Political Realism and Political Idealism* (Chicago: The University of Chicago Press, 1951), *passim;* Peter M. Haas, "Introduction: Epistemic Communities and International Policy Coordination," *International Organization* 46(1) (Winter 1992): 1–2.

13. Michael J. Cohen, *Truman and Israel* (Berkeley: University of California Press, 1990), *passim;* Reich, *Quest for Peace*, p. 365. See also Bernard Reich, *The United States and Israel: Influence in the Special Relationship* (New York: Praeger, 1984), pp. 256–259; Safran, *The Embattled Ally*, p. 572; Walt, *The Origins of Alliances*, pp. 256–259; Seth P. Tillman, *The United States in the Middle East: Interests and Obstacles* (Bloomington: Indiana University Press, 1982), pp. 54–55; Ben-Zvi, *The Limits of the Special Relationship*, pp. 14–20; Bruce J. Evensen, *Truman, Palestine and the Press: Shaping the Conventional Wisdom at the Beginning of the Cold War* (Westport: Greenwood Press, 1992), pp. 151–167.

14. Ben-Zvi, *The Limits of the Special Relationship*, p. 16. See also Quandt, *Decade of Decisions*, p. 14; Bernard Reich, "Reassessing the United States-Israeli Special Relationship," *Israel Affairs* 1(1) (Autumn 1994): 66–68; Schoenbaum, *The United States and the State of Israel*, pp. 79–80; George W. Ball and Douglas B. Ball, *The Passionate Attachment: America's Involvement with Israel, 1947 to the Present* (New York: Norton, 1992), p. 203; Mitchell G. Bard and Daniel Pipes, "How Special is the U.S.-Israel Relationship?" *Middle East Quarterly* 6(2) (June 1997): 46.

15. Alteras, *Eisenhower and Israel*, pp. 102–103. See also Isaiah L. Kenen, *Israel's Defense Line: Her Friends and Foes in Washington* (Buffalo: Prometheus Books, 1981), pp. 102–103; Ben-Zvi, *The Limits of the Special Relationship*, pp. 44–45; Organski, *The $36 Billion Bargain*, p. 27.

16. Alexander L. George, "Knowledge and Statecraft: The Challenge for Political Science and History," *International Security* 22(1) (Summer 1997): 48; Alexander L. George and Richard Smoke, "Deterrence and Foreign Policy," *World Politics* 41(2) (January 1989): 18; Paul Gordon Lauren, "Theories of Bargaining with Threat of Force: Deterrence and Coercive Diplomacy," in Paul Gordon Lauren, ed., *Diplomacy: New Approaches in History, Theory and Policy* (New York: The Free Press, 1979), pp. 198–200; Robert Jervis, "Deterrence Theory Revisited," *World Politics* 31(2) (January 1979): 292–296. For a specific effort to integrate concepts from crisis theory into the American-Israeli dyad, see Ben-Zvi, *The Limits of the Special Relationship*, pp. 2–13.

17. The term "intramural crises of alliances" is taken from Coral Bell, "Crisis Diplomacy," in Lawrence Martin, ed., *Strategic Thought in the Nuclear Age* (London: Heinemann, 1979), p. 159.

18. Alexander L. George, "Strategies for Facilitating Cooperation," in

Alexander L. George, Philip J. Farley, and Alexander Dallin, eds., *U.S.-Soviet Security Cooperation: Achievements, Failures, Lessons* (New York: Oxford University Press, 1988), p. 693. See also Robert Axelrod, *The Evolution of Cooperation* (New York: Basic Books, 1984), *passim.*

19. Glenn H. Snyder and Paul Diesing, *Conflict Among Nations: Bargaining, Decision-Making and System Structure in International Crises* (Princeton: Princeton University Press, 1977), p. 7. See also Michael Brecher, "Toward a Theory of International Crisis Behavior," *International Studies Quarterly* 21(1) (March 1977): 41; Charles F. Hermann, "International Crisis as a Situational Variable," in James N. Rosenau, ed., *International Politics and Foreign Policy* (New York: The Free Press, 1969), p. 414. For a pioneering analysis of the dynamics of non-violent alliance crises, see Richard E. Neustadt, *Alliance Politics* (New York: Columbia University Press, 1970).

20. Zeev Maoz, *Paradoxes of War: On the Art of National Self-Entrapment* (Boston: Unwin Hyman, 1990), p. 66; Frank C. Zagare, *The Dynamics of Deterrence* (Chicago: The University of Chicago Press, 1992), p. 7; Shai Feldman, *Israeli Nuclear Deterrence: A Strategy for the 1980s* (New York: Columbia University Press, 1982), p. 30.

21. Alexander L. George, "Coercive Diplomacy: Definition and Characteristics," in Alexander L. George and William E. Simons, eds., *The Limits of Coercive Diplomacy*, 2nd edition (Boulder: Westview Press, 1994), pp. 7–10. See also Maoz, *Paradoxes of War*, pp. 65–71; Thomas C. Schelling, *Arms and Influence* (New Haven: Yale University Press, 1966), pp. 72–79; Lauren, "Theories of Bargaining," p. 192; Patrick M. Morgan, *Deterrence: A Conceptual Analysis* (Beverly Hills: Sage Library of Social Science, 1983), pp. 25–43; Jervis, "Deterrence Theory Revisited," pp. 289–324; *passim;* Yair Evron, *War and Intervention in Lebanon: The Israeli-Syrian Deterrence Dialogue* (London: Croom Helm, 1987), pp. 177–179; Jonathan Shimshoni, *Israel and Conventional Deterrence: Border Warfare from 1953 and 1970* (Ithaca: Cornell University Press, 1988); Gordon A. Craig and Alexander L. George, *Force and Statecraft: Diplomatic Problems of Our Time*, 2nd edition (New York: Oxford University Press, 1994), pp. 172–173; Frank C. Zagare and D. Mark Kilgour, "Asymmetric Deterrence," *International Studies Quarterly* 37(1) (March 1993): 1–2.

22. Klaus Knorr, "International Economic Leverage and Its Uses," in Klaus Knorr and Frank N. Trager, eds., *Economic Issues and National Security* (Lawrence: University of Kansas Press, 1977), pp. 193–196. See also Ben-Zvi, *The Limits of the Special Relationship*, p. 3; Lisa L. Martin, *Coercive Cooperation: Explaining Multilateral Economic Sanctions* (Princeton: Princeton University Press, 1992), pp. 4–6; Hiroshi Kimura, "The Russian Way of Negotiating," *International Negotiation* 1(3) (1996): 370–373.

23. George, "Coercive Diplomacy," p. 7. See also Schelling, *Arms and Influence*, pp. 72, 77.

24. Morgan, *Deterrence*, pp. 25–43; Evron, *War and Intervention in Lebanon*, p. 177.

25. Morgan, *Deterrence*, pp. 25–32; Evron, *War and Intervention in Lebanon*, p. 177.

26. Richard Ned Lebow and Janice Gross Stein, *When Does Deterrence Succeed*

and How Do We Know (Ottawa: Canadian Institute for International Peace and Security, Occasional Paper No. 8, February 1990), p. 5.

27. Shimshoni, *Israel and Conventional Deterrence*, pp. 62–122; Mordechai Bar-On, *The Gates of Gaza: Israel's Road to Suez and Back, 1955–1957* (New York: St. Martin's Griffin, 1994), *passim*. See also, for an analysis of the strategy of retaliation and reprisals, George, "Coercive Diplomacy," p. 8.

28. Lauren, "Theories of Bargaining," p. 193; Benjamin Miller, "Great Powers and Regional Peacemaking: Patterns of the Middle East and Beyond," *The Journal of Strategic Studies* 20(1) (March 1997): 107.

29. Lauren, "Theories of Bargaining," pp. 193–194; Jervis, "Deterrence Theory Revisited," p. 306; Shimshoni, *Israel and Conventional Deterrence*, p. 6; Charles Lockhart, *Bargaining in International Conflicts* (New York: Columbia University Press, 1979), p. 119.

30. Jervis, "Deterrence Theory Revisited," pp. 314–315. See also Robert Jervis, "Rational Deterrence: Theory and Evidence," *World Politics* 41(2) (January 1989): 192; Alexander L. George and William E. Simons, "Findings and Conclusions," in *The Limits of Coercive Diplomacy*, p. 279; Paul Huth and Bruce M. Russett, "Testing Deterrence Theory: Rigor Makes a Difference," *World Politics* 42(4) (April 1990): 492; Paul Huth, *Extended Deterrence and the Prevention of War* (New Haven: Yale University Press, 1988), *passim*.

31. George and Simons, "Findings and Conclusions," pp. 281–282; Jervis, "Deterrence Theory Revisited," pp. 314–315; Ben-Zvi, *The Limits of the Special Relationship*, p. 4; Saadia Touval, "Coercive Mediation on the Road to Dayton," *International Negotiation* 1(3) (1996): 566–568.

32. George and Simons, "Findings and Conclusions," p. 284.

33. Snyder and Diesing, *Conflict Among Nations*, p. 184.

34. George and Simons, "Findings and Conclusions," p. 283. See also George, "Coercive Diplomacy," p. 9; Snyder and Diesing, *Conflict Among Nations*, p. 198; Ole R. Holsti, "Theories of Crisis Decision-Making," in *Diplomacy*, p. 145. The following sources, which seek to explain this apparent paradox, comprise a representative sample of the theoretical and empirical literature on economic sanctions: Michael Mastanduno, "Strategies of Economic Containment: U.S. Trade Relations with the Soviet Union," *World Politics* 37(4) (July 1985): 504–505; Klaus Knorr, "Is International Coercion Waning or Rising?" *International Security* 1(4) (Spring 1977): 102–103; Abraham Ben-Zvi, *The Illusion of Deterrence: The Roosevelt Presidency and the Origins of the Pacific War* (Boulder: Westview Press, Studies in International Politics, 1987), pp. 31–65; Scott D. Sagen, "From Deterrence to Coercion to War: The Road to Pearl Harbor," in *The Limits of Coercive Diplomacy*, pp. 58–85; Margaret P. Doxey, *Economic Sanctions and International Enforcement* (New York: Oxford University Press, 1980), *passim*.

35. James Barber, "Economic Sanctions as a Policy Instrument," *International Affairs* 55(3) (July 1979): 376. See also James N. Rosenau, *The Scientific Study of Foreign Policy* (New York: Nichols, 1980), p. 509; Martin, *Coercive Cooperation*, p. 5; Roger Fisher, *Basic Negotiating Strategy* (New York: Harper and Row, 1969), pp. 110–127; Jonathan Kirshner, "The Microfoundations of Economic Sanc-

tions," *Security Studies* 6(3) (Spring 1997): 33–34; Richard Stuart Olson, "Economic Coercion in World Politics: With a Focus on North-South Relations," *World Politics* 31(4) (July 1979): 490; Lisa Martin, "Credibility, Costs, and Institutions: Cooperation on Economic Sanctions," *World Politics* 45(3) (April 1993): 406–409.

36. Richard Ned Lebow, "Misconceptions in American Strategic Assessment," *Political Science Quarterly* 97(2) (Summer 1982): 196. See also Louis Kriesberg, *International Conflct Resolution: The U.S.-USSR and Middle East Cases* (New Haven: Yale University Press, 1992), pp. 114–115; Barry E. Carter, *International Economic Sanctions* (Cambridge: Cambridge University Press, 1988), pp. 9–30.

37. Steven Rosen, "War, Power and the Willingness to Suffer," in Bruce M. Russett, ed., *Peace, War, and Numbers* (Beverly Hills: Sage, 1972), p. 168.

For additional examples of the weaknesses inherent in the pursuit of a pure and unmitigated strategy of economic sanctions, see Johan Galtung, "On the Effects of International Economic Sanctions with Examples from the Case of Rhodesia," *World Politics* 19(3) (April 1967): 398; Jarrold D. Green, "Strategies for Evading Economic Sanctions," in Miroslav Nincic and Peter Wallensteen, eds., *Dilemmas of Economic Coercion in World Politics* (New York: Praeger, 1983), pp. 62–63; Sidney Weintraub, "Current Theory," in Sidney Weintraub, ed., *Economic Coercion and U.S. Foreign Policy: Implications of Case Studies from the Johnson Administration* (Boulder: Westview Press, 1982), p. 10; Gary Clyde Hufbauer and Jeffrey J. Schott, *Economic Sanctions Reconsidered: History and Current Policy* (Washington, D.C.: Institute for International Economics, 1982), pp. 315–323; Robin Renwick, *Economic Sanctions* (Cambridge: Center for International Affairs, Harvard University, 1981), *passim;* Margaret P. Doxey, *Economic Sanctions in Contemporary Perspective* (New York: St. Martin's Press, 1987), *passim;* Gil Merom, "Democracy, Dependency, and Destabilization: The Shaking of Allende's Regime," *Political Science Quarterly* 105(1) (Spring 1990): 77–78; M.S. Daudi and M.S. Dajani, *Economic Sanctions: Ideals and Experience* (London: Routledge and Kegan Paul, 1983), p. 49; H. Harrison Wagner, "Economic Interdependence, Bargaining Power, and Political Influence," *International Organization* 42(3) (Summer 1988): 474.

38. Knorr, "International Economic Leverage," p. 108. See also Mastanduno, "Strategies of Economic Containment," p. 503; Barber, "Economic Sanctions as a Policy Instrument," p. 370; Robert D. Putnam, "Diplomacy and Domestic Politics: The Logic of Two-Level Games," *International Organization* 42(3) (Summer 1988): 434; Andrew Moravcsik, "Integrating International and Domestic Theories of International Bargaining," in Peter B. Evans, Harold K. Jacobson, and Robert D. Putnam, eds., *Double-Edged Diplomacy: International Bargaining and Domestic Politics* (Berkeley: University of California Press, 1993), pp. 7–9; Martin Patchen, *Resolving Disputes Between Nations: Coercion or Conciliation?* (Durham: Duke University Press, 1988), p. 304; Anna P. Schreiber, "Economic Sanctions as an Instrument of Foreign Policy: U.S. Economic Measures Against Cuba and the Dominican Republic," *World Politics* 35(3) (April 1973): 404; Jacob Bercovitch and James W. Lamare, "The Process of International Mediation: An

Analysis of the Determinants of Successful and Unsuccessful Outcomes," *Australian Journal of Political Science* 28(1) (1993): 299–300.

39. George and Simons, "Findings and Conclusions," p. 277. See also Jervis, "Deterrence Theory Revisited" p. 305; Jervis, "Rational Deterrence," p. 198; Ben-Zvi, *The Illusion of Deterrence*, pp. 52–53; Ben-Zvi, *The Limits of the Special Relationship*, p. 6; Zeev Maoz, "Power, Capabilities, and Paradoxical Conflict Outcomes," *World Politics* 41(2) (January 1989): 243; Rosen, "War, Power and the Willingness to Suffer," p. 48.

40. George and Simons, "Findings and Conclusions," p. 275. See also George, "Strategies for Facilitating Cooperation," p. 704; Robert Jervis, "War and Misperception," *Journal of Interdisciplinary History* 18(4) (Spring 1988): 679; Jonathan G. Utley, *Going to War with Japan, 1937–1944* (Knoxville: University of Tennessee Press, 1985), pp. 175–180; Patrick M. Morgan, "Examples of Strategic Surprise in the Far East," in Klaus Knorr and Patrick M. Morgan, eds., *Strategic Military Surprises: Incentives and Opportunities* (New Brunswick, NJ.: Transaction Books, 1984), p. 49; Ariel Levite, *Intelligence and Strategic Surprises* (New York: Columbia University Press, 1987), pp. 39–94; Roberta Wohlstetter, *Pearl Harbor: Warning and Decision* (Stanford: Stanford University Press, 1962), *passim;* Sagen, "The Road to Pearl Harbor," p. 81; Russell F. Weigley, "The Role of the War Department and the Army," in Dorothy Borg and Shumpei Okamoto, eds., *Pearl Harbor as History: Japanese-American Relations, 1931–1941* (New York: Columbia University Press, 1974), p. 185; James W. Morley, ed., *The Fateful Choice: Japan's Advance into Southeast Asia, 1939–1941* (New York: Columbia University Press, 1980), p. 245; Michael A. Barnhart, *Japan Prepares for Total War* (Ithaca: Cornell University Press, 1987), pp. 230–231; Maoz, *Paradoxes of War*, pp. 67, 96–97.

41. George and Simons, "Findings and Conclusions," pp. 275–276.

42. Ibid., p. 276.

43. Ibid.

44. George, "Strategies for Facilitating Cooperation," p. 693. See also David A. Baldwin, "The Power of Positive Sanctions," *World Politics* 23(1) (October 1971): 23, 31; David A. Baldwin, "Power Analysis and World Politics: New Tendencies versus Old Tendencies," *World Politics* 31(2) (January 1979): 192; Martin, *Coercive Cooperation*, p. 31. For an early analysis of the concept of mutuality, see Ernest B. Haas, *Beyond the Nation State: Functionalism and International Organization* (Stanford: Stanford University Press, 1964), *passim.*

45. George, "Strategies for Facilitating Cooperation," p. 693.

46. Fred H. Lawson, "Positive Sanctions and the Management of International Conflict: Five Middle Eastern Cases," *International Journal* 40(4) (Autumn 1985): 628–629; David A. Baldwin, "The Power of Positive Sanctions," *World Politics* 23(1) (October 1971): 23, 31; Kenneth A. Oye, "Explaining Cooperation Under Anarchy: Hypotheses and Strategies," in Kenneth A. Oye, ed., *Cooperation Under Anarchy* (Princeton: Princeton University Press, 1986), pp. 1–24; Jacob Bercovitch and Allison Houston, "The Study of International Mediation: Theoretical Issues and Empirical Evidence," in Jacob Bercovitch, ed., *Resolving Inter-*

national Conflicts: The Theory and Practice of Mediation (Boulder: Lynne Rienner Publishers, 1996), p. 30; Martin, *Coercive Cooperation*, pp. 31–32. See also the analysis of a related concept: "innovative bargaining" in Fred Charles Iklé, *How Nations Negotiate* (New York: Harper and Row, 1964), *passim*.

47. George, "Strategies for Facilitating Cooperation," p. 693. See also Patchen, *Resolving Disputes Between Nations*, p. 280; Janice Gross Stein, "Reassurance in International Conflict Management," *Political Studies Quarterly* 106(3) (Fall 1991): 431–435; Axelrod, *The Evolution of Cooperation, passim;* Brian Mandell, "The Limits of Mediation: Lessons from the Syria-Israel Experience, 1974–1994," in *Resolving International Conflicts*, pp. 129–144; William P. Smith, "Effectiveness of the Biased Mediator," *Negotiation Journal* 1(4) (October 1985): 367.

48. George, "Strategies for Facilitating Cooperation," p. 693. Italics original. See also Richard Ned Lebow, "The Deterrence Deadlock: Is There a Way Out?" in Robert Jervis, Richard Ned Lebow, and Janice Gross Stein, eds., *Psychology and Deterrence* (Baltimore: The Johns Hopkins University Press, 1985), p. 194; Janice Gross Stein, "The Political Economy of Security Agreements: The Linked Costs of Failure at Camp David," in *Double-Edged Diplomacy*, pp. 86–87; Russell J. Leng, "Influence Techniques Among Nations," in Philip E. Tetlock, ed., *Behavior, Society, and International Conflict*, Vol. 3 (New York: Oxford University Press, 1993), pp. 606–607; Janice Gross Stein, "Deterrence and Reassurance," in Paul Stern, Jo. L. Husbands, Robert Axelrod, Robert Jervis, and Charles Tilly, eds., *Behavior, Society, and Nuclear War* (New York: Oxford University Press, 1991), pp. 8–72, *passim*.

49. For the term "psychological environment" see Michael Brecher, *The Foreign Policy System of Israel: Setting, Images, Process* (New Haven: Yale University Press, 1972), pp. 3–5. See also Axelrod, *The Evolution of Cooperation, passim*; George, "Strategies for Facilitating Cooperation," p. 707.

50. Stein, "Deterrence and Reassurance," p. 86.

51. Ibid., pp. 86–87. See also Stein, "Reassurance in International Conflict Management," pp. 449–451; Robert Jervis, *The Logic of Images in International Relations* (Princeton: Princeton University Press, 1970), pp. 3–4; Zeev Maoz and Dan Felsenthal, "Self-Binding Commitments, the Inducement of Trust, Social Choice, and the Theory of International Cooperation," *International Studies Quarterly* 31(2) (Autumn 1987): 177–200; Martin, *Coercive Cooperation*, pp. 25–35; Charles E. Osgood, *An Alternative to War or Surrender* (Urbana: University of Illinois Press, 1962), p. 137; Patchen, *Resolving Disputes Between Nations*, pp. 285–290.

52. George, "Strategies of Facilitating Cooperation," pp. 693–694, 706–707; Little, "The Making of a Special Relationship," pp. 567–569.

53. Thomas Princen, *Intermediaries in International Conflict* (Princeton: Princeton University Press, 1992), pp. 27–28. Italics in original. See also the distinction between the distributive and integrative types of bargaining in Princen, *Intermediaries in International Conflict*, pp. 35–36.

54. Glenn H. Snyder, "The Security Dilemma in Alliance Politics," *World Politics* 36(1) (April 1984): 466.

55. George, "Strategies for Facilitating Cooperation," p. 695. As George

points out, the strategy of negative linkage "bears a resemblance to . . . coercive diplomacy." See also Robert O. Keohane, "Reciprocity in International Relations," *International Organization* 40(1) (Winter 1986): 1–27, *passim*.

56. For an analysis of "background images" see Snyder and Diesing, *Conflict Among Nations*, pp. 291–310.

57. For the term "operational environment" see Brecher, " *The Foreign Policy System of Israel*," pp. 6–8.

58. For an analysis of the process of frame change in the context of the 1938 Munich Crisis see Barbara Farnham, "Roosevelt and the Munich Crisis: Insights from Prospect Theory," *Political Psychology* 13(2) (June 1992): 205–235.

59. Snyder and Diesing, *Conflict Among Nations*, pp. 291–294.

60. Ibid. See also Stein, "Reassurance in International Conflict Management," p. 451.

61. Regarding the historical parameters of the work, it should be pointed out that in terms of its basic approach to the Middle East and Israel, the Eisenhower Administration largely followed the policies pursued by the Truman Administration in the aftermath of its decision to recognize Israel. The reason for concentrating exclusively on the Eisenhower period is that during most of Truman's tenure as president the Middle East remained peripheral to American thinking.It had been outweighed and downgraded by developments and crises in other regions (such as the Korean Peninsula), which posed a more acute and direct menace to American interests. It was only during the first term of the Eisenhower Administration, and against the backdrop of a growing Soviet threat to Western strongholds in the region, that the Middle East came to increasingly preoccupy the thinking of the President and his Secretary of State because it was linked to the global Soviet effort to disrupt the balance of power and pose a threat to core Western interests.

Chapter 2: The United States and Israel, 1953–1956: Divergence Dominates

1. Secretary Dulles's remarks of March 28, 1956. Memorandum of his conversation with Eisenhower. FRUS 15: 422.

2. Ibid. See also George, "Coercive Diplomacy," p. 8; Richard Ned Lebow and Janice Gross Stein, *We All Lost the Cold War* (Princeton: Princeton University Press, 1994), p. 324.

3. Jervis, "Rational Deterrence," pp. 198–199. See also Uri Bialer, *Between East and West: Israel's Foreign Policy Orientation, 1948–1956* (Cambridge: Cambridge University Press, 1990), p. 270; Alteras, *Eisenhower and Israel*, p. 115.

4. Quoted from the Department of State Memorandum of Conversation, April 8, 1953. FRUS 9, pt. 1: 1167–1169. Italics added. See also Sharett's memorandum of this conversation dated April 21, 1953. *Israeli State Archives* (hereafter ISA), Foreign Ministry Files, Box 2479/11:2, as well as Sharett's report of his conversation with Assistant Secretary Byroade to Prime Minister David Ben-Gurion, which was sent from Buenos Aires on April 17, 1953. ISA, Foreign Min-

istry Files, Box 4621/B: 2–4. For a detailed review of the meeting, see Gabriel Sheffer, *Moshe Sharett: Biography of a Political Moderate* (Oxford: Clarendon Press, 1996), p. 663.

5. George, "Strategies for Facilitating Cooperation," p. 695.

6. In the course of his April 8, 1953, meeting with Byroade, Sharett indicated that Israel "would be willing to provide an arrangement for a free passage across southern Israel to connect Egypt with Jordan . . . [and] would grant free port facilities at Haifa for the use of Jordan and other Arab states," but these proposals fell short of Byroade's expectations and persistent demand that Israel withdraw from territories which were "acquired [in the 1948 Arab-Israeli War] by force of arms." Quoted from FRUS 9, pt. 1: 1168–1169.

7. Ibid., p. 1168. See also Sheffer, *Moshe Sharett*, p. 665.

8. Secretary Dulles's remarks of November 21, 1955. Memorandum of his conversation with Sharett. FRUS 14: 793.

9. Sharett's remarks of November 21, 1955. Memorandum of his conversation with Sharett. Ibid., p. 794.

10. Dulles's remarks of November 21, 1955. Ibid., p. 795. Italics added.

11. Sharett's remarks of November 21, 1955. Ibid., p. 795. Italics added. See also Schoenbaum, *The United States and the State of Israel*, p. 101.

12. Memorandum from Byroade to Dulles on June 3, 1954. FRUS 9, pt. 1: 572. Italics added. See also Deon Geldenhuys, *Isolated States: A Comparative Analysis* (Cambridge: Cambridge University Press, 1990), *passim*.

13. Benjamin Miller, *When Opponents Cooperate: Great Power Conflict and Collaboration in World Politics* (Ann Arbor: The University of Michigan Press, 1995), pp. 33–55; 125–171; Abraham Ben-Zvi, "The Management of Superpower Conflict in the Middle East," in Steven L. Spiegel, Mark H. Heller, and Jacob Goldberg, eds., *The Soviet-American Competition in the Middle East* (Lexington, MA: Lexington Books, 1988), pp. 344–353; Janice Gross Stein, "Proxy Wars—How Superpowers End Them: The Diplomacy of War Termination in the Middle East," *International Journal* 35(3) (Summer 1980): 479–481; Alexander L. George, "Political Crises," in Joseph S. Nye, Jr., ed., *The Making of America's Soviet Policy* (New Haven: Yale University Press, 1984), p. 150; Lebow and Stein, *We All Lost the Cold War*, pp. 324–325.

14. Abraham Ben-Zvi, *The American Approach to Superpower Collaboration in the Middle East, 1973–1986* (Boulder: Westview Press, 1986), p. 11. For alternative definitions of this foreign policy orientation see: William O. Chittick, Keith R. Billingsley, and Rick Travis, "A Three-Dimensional Model of American Foreign Policy Beliefs," *International Studies Quarterly* 39(1) (March 1995): 313–331; Ole R. Holsti, "Public Opinion and Foreign Policy: Challenges to the Almond-Lippmann Consensus," *International Studies Quarterly* 36(2) (June 1992): 439–466; Ole R. Holsti, "Public Opinion and Foreign Policy: Attitudes Structures of Opinion Leaders After the Cold War," in *The Domestic Sources of American Foreign Policy*, pp. 36–55; Ole R. Holsti, "The Three-Headed Eagle: The United States and System Change," *International Studies Quarterly* 23(3) (September 1979): 343; Daniel Yergin, *Shattered Peace: The Origins of the Cold War and the National Security State*

(Boston: Houghton Mifflin, 1977), p. 11; Alexander Dallin and Gail W. Lapidus, "Reagan and the Russians: United States Policy Toward the Soviet Union and Eastern Europe," in Kenneth A. Oye, Robert J. Lieber, and Donald Rothschild, eds., *Eagle Defiant: US Foreign Policy in the 1980s* (Boston: Little, Brown, 1982), p. 206; William Schneider, "Conservatism, Not Interventionism: Trends in Foreign Policy Opinion, 1974–1984," in *Eagle Defiant*, p. 50; Eugene R. Wittkopf, *Faces of Internationalism: Public Opinion and American Foreign Policy* (Durham: Duke University Press, 1990), p. 9; Eugene R. Wittkopf, "On the Foreign Policy Beliefs of the American People: A Critique and Some Evidence," *International Studies Quarterly* 30(4) (December 1986): 426; James N. Rosenau and Ole R. Holsti, "U.S. Leadership in a Shrinking World: The Breakdown of Consensus and the Emergence of Conflicting Belief Systems," *World Politics* 35(3) (April 1983): 377–378.

15. Ben-Zvi, *The Limits of the Special Relationship*, p. 30; Yergin, *Shattered Peace*, p. 196; Holsti, "The Three-headed Eagle," p. 34. See also Robert L. Beisner, "1898 and 1968: The Anti-Imperialism and the Doves," *Political Science Quarterly* 95(2) (June 1970): 211; Jack Snyder, "Introduction," in Robert Jervis and Jack Snyder, eds., *Dominos and Bandwagons: Strategic Beliefs and Great Power Competition in the Eurasian Rimland* (New York: Oxford University Press, 1991), p. 3; Robert J. Lieber, *No Common Power: Understanding International Relations* (New York: Harper Collins, 1995), pp. 49–55.

16. Robert Dallek, *The American Style of Foreign Policy: Cultural Politics and Foreign Affairs* (New York: Oxford University Press, 1983), p. 191; Corall Bell, *Negotiations from Strength: A Study in the Politics of Power* (New York: Knopf, 1963), pp. 6–7. See also Shibley Telhami, *Power and Leadership in International Bargaining: The Path to the Camp David Accords* (New York: Columbia University Press, 1990), p. 53.

17. Spiegel, *The Other Arab-Israeli Conflict*, p. 58.

18. Raymond Garthoff, *Detente and Confrontation: American-Soviet Relations from Nixon to Reagan* (Washington, DC.: The Brookings Institution, 1985), p. 674; Dowty, *Middle East Crisis*, p. 57.

19. Dulles's remarks of May 11, 1953. Memorandum of the conversation which took place at the American Embassy in Cairo. FRUS 9, pt. 1: 13–15. See also Ben-Zvi, *The Limits of the Special Relationship*, p. 31; Organski, *The $36 Billion Bargain*, p. 27.

20. Bialer, *Between East and West*, p. 265; Klieman, *Israel and the World*, p. 200; Henry Kissinger, *Diplomacy* (New York: Simon and Schuster, 1994), p. 525; Peter L. Hahn, *The United States, Great Britain, and Egypt, 1945–1956: Strategy and Diplomacy in the Early Cold War* (Chapel Hill: The University of North Carolina Press, 1991), p. 180. While Egypt consistently refused to directly or indirectly participate in this envisaged multilateral alliance, the Northern tier states became, between 1954 and 1955, gradually integrated into this regional design. Thus on April 2, 1954, a defense treaty between Turkey and Pakistan was signed. On February 24, 1955, this treaty was augmented and reinforced by a security pact between Turkey and Iraq. On April 4, 1955, Britain joined this pact while the U.S., which did not want to become associated with the British colonial legacy, decided to sell arms to Iraq without formally joining the pact. However, the fact

that Egypt remained vehemently opposed to the very notion of a regional security system allied with the Western powers doomed the prospects of establishing a broadly based and effective alliance. See Steven Z. Freiberger, *Dawn Over Suez: The Rise of American Power in the Middle East* (Chicago: Ivan Dee, 1992), pp. 84–105; Miles Copeland, *The Game of Nations: The Amorality of Power Politics* (London: Weidenfeld and Nicolson, 1969), pp. 128–129.

21. Spiegel, *The Other Arab-Israeli Conflict*, p. 56. See also Robert J. McMahon, *The Cold War on the Periphery: The United States, India, and Pakistan* (New York: Columbia University Press, 1994), p. 152; Andrew and Leslie Cockburn, *Dangerous Liaison: The Inside Story of the U.S.-Israeli Covert Relationship* (London: The Bodley Head, 1992), pp. 68–69; Fred I. Greenstein, *The Hidden-Hand Presidency: Eisenhower as President* (New York: Basic Books, 1982), p. 71.

22. Dulles's radio address of June 1, 1953. Quoted from the verbatim record of his address, in which he summarized his trip to the Middle East. *Dulles Papers*, Box 73, "Middle East" folder. See also John S. Badeau, *The American Approach to the Arab World* (New York: Harper, 1968), p. 21.

23. Michael J. Cohen, *Fighting World War Three From the Middle East: Allied Contingency Plans, 1945–1954* (London: Frank Cass, 1997), p. 137. See also, on the role assigned to the Abu Sueir air base in American strategic planning during the period 1948–1954, ibid., pp. 132, 135–136, 328.

24. Ibid., pp. 320, 323. See also Bialer, *Between East and West*, pp. 262, 273; Spiegel, *The Other Arab-Israeli Conflict*, p. 61; Organski, *The $36 Billion Bargain*, p. 27, and Burton, I. Kaufman, *The Arab Middle East and the United States: Inter-Arab Rivalry and Superpower Diplomacy* (New York: Twayne, 1996), pp. 17–18. On the specific terms and conditions of the April 1954 arms deal between the U.S. and Iraq see the message, which was sent on April 19, 1954, by Secretary Dulles to American Ambassador in Baghdad, Burton Y. Berry. FRUS 9, part 2: 2381–2383.

25. See Department of State Position Paper, May 7, 1953—one of a series of position papers on regional problems prepared for the briefing book for Secretary Dulles's trip to the Middle East and South Asia. FRUS 9, pt. 1: 1215. See also the national intelligence estimate, August 18, 1953. FRUS 9, pt. 1: 1290; Lipson, "American Support for Israel," p. 139; Sheffer, *Moshe Sharett*, p. 659.

26. Dulles's statement of May 15, 1953. Quoted by David W. Lesch, *Syria and the United States: Eisenhower's Cold War in the Middle East* (Boulder: Westview Press, 1992), p. 32. See also Alteras, *Eisenhower and Israel*, p. 21; Efraim Karsh and Martin Navias, "Israeli Nuclear Weapons and Middle East Peace," *Israel Affairs* 2(1) (Autumn 1995): 88; Organski, *The $36 Billion Bargain*, p. 27; Spiegel, *The Other Arab-Israeli Conflict*, p. 57; Kaufman, *The Arab Middle East and the United States*, p. 26; Kissinger, *Diplomacy*, p. 527; Walt, *The Origin of Alliances*, p. 158.

27. Quoted from Byroade's address of April 9, 1954, before the Dayton World Affairs Council. *Dulles Papers*, Box 73, "Middle East" folder: 4. See also Alteras, *Eisenhower and Israel*, p. 21; John C. Campbell, *Defense of the Middle East: Problems of American Policy* (New York: Praeger, 1960), p. 47; Organski, *The $36 Billion Bargain*, p. 27; Kaufman, *The Arab Middle East and the United States*, p. 18.

28. Dulles's remarks at the 147th Meeting of the National Security Council, June 1, 1953. FRUS 9, pt. 1: 384. Italics added. See also Mordechai Gazit, "Israeli Military Procurement from the United States," in Gabriel Sheffer, ed., *Dynamics of Dependence: U.S.-Israeli Relations* (Boulder: Westview Press, 1987), p. 90; Moshe Sharett, *Personal Diary*, Vol. 3, 1955 (Hebrew) (Tel-Aviv: Ma'ariv Book Guild, 1978), p. 794; Klieman, *Israel and the World*, p. 200; Lipson, "American Support for Israel," p. 139; Abba Eban, *Personal Witness: Israel Through My Eyes* (New York: Putnam, 1992), p. 233.

29. Teddy Kollek, *For Jerusalem: A Life* (London: Weidenfeld and Nicolson, 1978), p. 97. See also Bialer, *Between East and West*, p. 261; Uri Bialer, "Facts and Pacts: Ben-Gurion and Israel's International Orientation, 1948–1956," in Ronald W. Zweig, ed., *David Ben-Gurion: Politics and Leadership in Israel* (London: Frank Cass, 1991), p. 223; Klieman, *Israel and the World*, pp. 189–197; Ben-Zvi, *The Limits of the Special Relationship*, p. 9. On the Israeli decision of July 2, 1950, to support the American course in Korea, see Yehoshua Freundlich, ed., *Documents on the Foreign Policy of Israel*, 5, 1950 (Jerusalem: Israel State Archives, 1988): 419 (editorial note).

30. See the report, which was sent on August 24, 1953, by Israeli Ambassador in Washington, Abba Eban, to Sharett, in Yemima Rosenthal, ed., *Documents on the Foreign Policy of Israel*, 8, 1953 (Jerusalem: Israel State Archives, 1995): 603. See also Sharett's message of August 25, 1953, to the Israeli Delegation to the United Nations in New York, in *Documents on the Foreign Policy of Israel*, 8: 607. In opposing India's participation at the conference, the U.S. argued that only the parties that fought in Korea should be represented at the Korean Conference. On the other hand, Britain, France, the Asian bloc, the Soviet Union and most Arab states supported India's participation on the ground that since the conference was organized under the auspices of the U.N., it could not prevent any member state that wished to attend the conference from doing so. See *Documents on the Foreign Policy of Israel*,8, editorial notes: 599–600; 603–604; 607.

31. Dulles's remarks of April 10, 1956. Memorandum of his conversation with a group of Congressional leaders. FRUS 15: 506. Italics added. See also Bard, *The Water's Edge and Beyond*, p. 285; Bialer, *Between East and West*, pp. 208–209. On the policy implications of these premises within the framework of the American-Egyptian dyad, and particularly on the administration's desire to sell arms to Egypt, see the memorandum entitled: "Military Assistance to Egypt," which was submitted on September 28, 1954, by Deputy Assistant Secretary of State for Near Eastern, South Asian, and African Affairs, John D. Jernegan. FRUS 9, pt. 2: 2305–2306.

32. Bialer, *Between East and West*, pp. 230–231; 270, 273. See also Kissinger, *Diplomacy*, p. 527; Leopold Yehuda Laufer, "U.S. Aid to Israel: Problems and Perspectives," in *Dynamics of Dependence*, pp. 130–131; Sharett, *Personal Diary*, 3: 794; Hahn, *The U.S., Great Britain, and Egypt*, pp. 184–185. On the secret CIA aid program to Egypt, see Barry Rubin, "America and the Egyptian Revolution, 1950–1957," *Political Science Quarterly* 97(1) (Spring 1982): 80–82; Copeland, *The Game of Nations*, pp. 144–150.

33. Department of State Position Paper, May 7, 1953. FRUS 9, pt. 1: 1216–1217. See also Dulles's remarks of May 17, 1953, to a group of American businessmen, clergymen, and university presidents in Lebanon. FRUS 9, pt. 1: 83. According to the memorandum of the conversation, the Secretary alluded to the two paradigms as incompatible with one another. Whereas the special relationship paradigm represented the sectorial, partisan, and parochial, the national interest orientation—which was the only source from which American policy was shaped and delineated—represented the "general good" and the vital interests the administration was determined to defend. As Dulles pointed out: "There is not the slightest tendency for the present administration to be pro-Jewish, since it is not under any obligation whatsoever to [promote] Jewish interests. What the administration must do is what is good for the United States" (FRUS 9, pt. 1: 83). For a similar statement by Byroade, see his remarks of September 23, 1953, to Eban. ISA, Foreign Ministry Files, Box 2403/13. Dulles's assertion that "the U.S. would not become an Israeli prisoner" is quoted by Sheffer, *Moshe Sharett*, p. 659.

Despite this continued propensity to ignore, or set aside, the premises upon which the special relationship paradigm was shaped and to view it as inherently incompatible with the national interest orientation, Candidate Eisenhower was nevertheless unequivocal in his pledge to provide Israel with political and economic support. See the message from Eban to the United States Division of the Israeli Foreign Ministry on March 7, 1953. In *Documents on the Foreign Policy of Israel*, 8: 185. The message alludes to Eisenhower's strong pro-Israeli statement of October 24, 1952.

34. Dulles's remarks of May 14, 1953. Memorandum of his conversation with Ben-Gurion. FRUS 9, pt. 1: 39. See also Dulles's radio address of June 1, 1953. *Dulles Papers*, Box 71, "Israel" folder: 6. See also Burns, *Economic Aid and American Policy*, p. 21; Tivnan, *The Lobby*, p. 36; Sheffer, *Moshe Sharett*, pp. 666–667; Matthew F. Holland, *America and Egypt from Roosevelt to Eisenhower* (Westport: Praeger, 1996), p. 42.

This new order of priorities and the Administration's desire to pursue, in the Middle East, an accommodative posture toward the Arab world at the expense of Israel, was fully recognized by the Israeli leadership as early as March 8, 1953. In his meeting with Ben-Gurion, which was held on that date, Sharett remarked that "almost all the information which we received [from Washington] indicates that the administration is seeking to appease the Arabs, with Israel depicted as an obstacle to an American-Arab rapprochement." Memorandum of Sharett's meeting with Ben-Gurion, of March 8, 1953. *Documents on the Foreign Policy of Israel*, 8: 208–209.

35. Byroade's remarks of June 9, 1953. Memorandum of his conversation with Eban. FRUS 9, pt. 1; 1235–1236. Italics added. See also, for similar statements, Dulles's remarks to Eban in their October 8, 1953, meeting, in FRUS 9, pt. 1: 341; Dulles's remarks to Syrian Ambassador in Washington, Farid Zeineddine in their December 28, 1953, meeting in FRUS 9, pt. 1: 1467; A report on American-Israeli relations during the period September 1953-February 1954,

prepared by the staff of the Israeli Embassy in Washington on February 22, 1954, in ISA, Foreign Ministry Files, Box 2480/2: 2–4; a semiannual report, prepared by the staff of the Israeli Embassy in Washington on February 22, 1954, in ibid., Box 2480/2: 1–3; a memorandum entitled "The Arab-Israel Problem—Situation Report," drafted on November 22, 1953, by Byroade, in FRUS 9, pt. 1: 1694; the national intelligence estimate, August 18, 1953, in FRUS 9, pt. 1: 1290; the memorandum submitted by Israeli Military Attaché in Washington, Chaim Herzog, to Eban on February 2, 1953, in *Documents on the Foreign Policy of Israel*, 8: 84–85.

36. Alteras, *Eisenhower and Israel*, p. 21. See also Sharett's memorandum of February 5, 1954. ISA, Foreign Ministry Files, Box 2403/19/A; Klieman, *Israel and the World*, p. 194; Badeau, *The American Approach to the Arab World*, p. 21; Spiegel, *The Other Arab-Israeli Conflict*, p. 66. The Baghdad Pact initiative was the multilateral security design, which was contemplated by the US and Britain, and which included—at its peak—Turkey, Iraq, Iran, Pakistan, and Britain.

37. Alteras, *Eisenhower and Israel*, p. 143. This citation is from Dulles's press conference of October 4, 1955. In this statement, the Secretary alluded to the major Israeli retaliatory raid on Gaza, on the night of February 28, 1955, which exposed serious vulnerabilities in the Egyptian army and military equipment. See also Shimshoni, *Israel and Conventional Deterrence*, pp. 79–80.

38. Dulles's remarks to Sharett of October 30, 1955. Quoted by Bialer, *Between East and West*, p. 273. See also the memorandum dated March 6, 1953, by Ester Herlitz, the First Secretary in the Israeli Embassy in Washington, summarizing the Embassy's activities in February 1953, in ISA, Foreign Ministry Files, Box 2460/8/B: 2; the memorandum dated May 25, 1954, by Herlitz, in ISA, Box 2463/18; Michael B. Oren, *Origins of the Second Arab-Israel War: Egypt, Israel, and the Great Powers: 1952–1956* (London: Frank Cass, 1992), p. 109; Spiegel, *The Other Arab-Israeli Conflict*, pp. 63–66; Ben-Zvi, *The Limits of the Special Relationship*, pp. 50–51.

39. William Roger Louis, "Dulles, Suez, and the British," in Richard H. Immerman, ed., *John Foster Dulles and the Diplomacy of the Cold War* (Princeton: Princeton University Press, 1990), p. 143. See also Telhami, *Power and Leadership in International Bargaining*, p. 53.

40. Dulles's remarks of May 11, 1953. Memorandum of the conversation between Dulles and the Egyptian Minister for Foreign Affairs, Mahmoud Fawzi. FRUS 9, pt. 1: 7. See also Eban's remarks of September 8, 1953, during a consultation with senior members of the Foreign Ministry. *Documents on the Foreign Policy of Israel*, 8: 622–623.

41. Quoted from Byroade's remarks of October 8, 1953, to Eban. See memorandum of the conversation in FRUS 9, pt. 1: 1341. For another illustration, see Dulles's remarks of December 28, 1953, to Zeineddine. FRUS 9, pt. 1: 1467. See also Sharett's remarks of March 8, 1953, during his meeting with Ben-Gurion. *Documents on the Foreign Policy of Israel*, 8: p. 193.

42. Dulles's remarks. Memorandum of his conversation with Senator Walter F. George (D, GA.), on October 21, 1955. *Dulles Papers*, Box 5, "Subject Series"

folder: 1. See also the memorandum "American-Israeli relations," of August 4, 1953, by the Israeli Embassy in Washington. Section 14 indicates that the new American accommodative posture toward the Arab world was clearly diagnosed by Israeli diplomacy. *Documents on the Foreign Policy of Israel*, 8: 559.

43. Nixon's remarks are quoted from the memorandum of his conversation with Attorney General Herbert Brownell, Jr., and Treasury Secretary George M. Humphrey, of October 21, 1955. *Dulles Papers*, Box 10, "Subject Series" folder: 1. See also Badeau, *The American Approach to the Arab World*, p. 21; Hahn, *The U.S., Great Britain, and Egypt*, pp. 208–209.

44. Dulles's statement of April 23, 1956. Memorandum of his conversation with a group of Republican Senators. *Dulles Papers*, Box 10, "Subject Series" folder: 2. For an almost identical statement, which alluded to "Zionist pressures for substantial arms to Israel" as a "liability" because of the "broader and very important issues involved" see Dulles's remarks of April 1, 1956, as quoted from the memorandum of his conversation with British Ambassador to the U.S., Sir Roger Makins. FRUS 15: 439. See also Kaufman, *The Arab Middle East and the United States*, pp. 20–22. On the American inability to overcome the barriers of ethnocentric thinking in approaching the Middle East, see Raymond Cohen, *Negotiating Across Cultures: Communication Obstacles in International Diplomacy* (Washington, D.C.: United States Institute of Peace Press, 1991), pp. 38–40.

45. Dulles's remarks of October 3, 1955. Memorandum of his conversation with the British Chancellor of the Exchequer, Harold Macmillan. FRUS 14: 543. See also Sharett, *Personal Diary*, 5 (1955): 1267; Kissinger, *Diplomacy*, p. 529.

46. Dulles's remarks of March 28, 1956. Memorandum of his conversation with Eban. FRUS 15: 405. On Israel's political miscalculations in planning the Sinai Campaign see Zeev Schiff, "A Farewell to Shimon Peres," *Ha'aretz* (Hebrew), June 21, 1996, p. 13.

47. Dulles's remarks of January 11, 1956. Memorandum of his conversation at the White House with Eisenhower and Robert B. Anderson. The meeting took place on the eve of Anderson's peace mission to the Middle East as the President's special envoy. *Dulles Papers*, Box 10, "Subject Series" folder: 3. See also the memorandum of the conversation of January 27, 1953, between Byroade and Eban. The memorandum was drafted on February 4, 1953. ISA, Foreign Ministry Files, Box 2403/18/A: 1–2. See also Organski, *The $36 Billion Bargain*, p. 31; Reich, *Securing the Covenant*, p. 27; Spiegel, *The Other Arab-Israeli Conflict*, p. 63; Hahn, *The U.S., Great Britain, and Egypt*, p. 188.

48. Quoted from a message sent on November 22, 1954, by Dulles to several American ambassadors in the region. FRUS 9, pt. 1: 1696. See also Sharett's remarks of March 8, 1953, during his meeting with Ben-Gurion. *Documents on the Foreign Policy of Israel*, 8: 190–196.

49. The Water Crisis of October 1953 among Israel, Syria, and the UN originated in the Israeli plan to divert the Upper Jordan river at B'not Ya'acov bridge as the starting point of the plan to transport to the arid Negev. The immediate goal was to use the 270-meter drop in the Jordan flow just beyond the bridge and to use that power to pump water into a diversion canal to the south. For techni-

cal and budgetary reasons, it was decided that the location of the diversion project would be inside the demilitarized zone between Israel and Syria. In view of
the Syrian protests that immediately greeted the work, the Acting Chairman of
the Israeli-Syrian Mixed Armistice Commission, General Roy Tillotson, decided to transfer the issue to his superior, General Vagn Bennike, Chief of Staff of
the United Nations Truce Supervision Organization (UNTSO). On September
23, 1953, General Bennike ruled that since part of the work had been carried
out on Syrian-owned land in the demilitarized zone, Israel had to refrain from
any additional work in the area. Israel's refusal to comply with this decision,
combined with Syria's complaint to the Security Council, prompted the Eisenhower Administration, in October 1953, to resort to a policy of economic sanctions vis-à-vis Israel. For a detailed review of the crisis, see Ben-Zvi, *The Limits of
the Special Relationship*, pp. 29–48. See also Aryeh Shalev, *Cooperation Under the Shadow of Conflict: The Israeli-Syrian Armistice Regime, 1949–1955* (Hebrew) (Tel-Aviv:
Ma'arachot, 1989), pp. 253–268; Yaacov Bar-Siman-Tov, "The Power of Economic Sanctions: The B'not Ya'acov Bridge, 1953" (Hebrew), *Ma'arachot* 291
(January 1984): 46; Nissim Bar-Yaacov, *The Israeli-Syrian Armistice: Problems of Implementation, 1949–1966* (Jerusalem: The Magnes Press, 1967), pp. 118–120;
Michael Brecher, *Decisions in Israel's Foreign Policy* (New Haven: Yale University
Press, 1975), pp. 173–191.

50. Princen, *Intermediaries in International Conflict*, p. 32. See also the memorandum of the conversation of October 25, 1953, between Dulles and Eban. FRUS
9, pt. 1: 1321–1323; Byroade's memorandum of July 1953, to Dulles, entitled
"Israel's Request for a Funding Loan." FRUS 9, pt. 1: 1252–1253; Schoenbaum, *The United States and the State of Israel*, p. 97.

51. Quoted from a position paper, prepared in the Bureau of Near Eastern,
South Asian, and African Affairs, November 23, 1953. FRUS 9, pt. 1: 1409. The
paper was entitled: "Trends in Israel Policy Toward the Arabs."

52. Dulles's words of April 21, 1954. Quoted from his conversation with
Eisenhower by Alteras, *Eisenhower and Israel*, p. 92. See also Shimshoni, *Israel and
Conventional Deterrence*, pp. 62–121; Amir Oren, "Post Oslo, Post Mortem,"
Ha'aretz, March 1, 1996, p. 17.

53. Quoted from the November 23, 1953, Department of State Position
Paper. FRUS 9, pt. 1: 1407–1408. See also Alteras, *Eisenhower and Israel*, pp.
92–93; Shimshoni, *Israel and Conventional Deterrence*, pp. 62–63; Gideon Rafael,
Destination Peace: Three Decades of Israeli Foreign Policy (New York: Stein and Day,
1981), p. 33. In a strongly worded aide-mémoire, sent by Dulles to Sharett on
February 16, 1953, eight months before the massive Qibya raid took place, the
Secretary of State defined the parameters of the American approach toward the
issue of Israeli retaliatory raids. In the message, Dulles wrote:

"The Government of the United States inquires . . . whether it is to assume
that the Government of Israel will continue to disregard friendly counsel on this
score and to take matters into its own hands. The Government of the United
States considers retaliatory raids to be a grave danger to the stability and security of the region and if they are not expressly and clearly abandoned, it must

reserve the right to take appropriate action under the Tri-Partite Declaration of 1950 and possibly under the procedures of the United States." Quoted from an aide-mémoire of February 16, 1953, by Dulles to Sharett. *Documents on the Foreign Policy of Israel*, 8: 151.

54. Dulles's remarks of October 8, 1953. Memorandum of his conversation with Eban. FRUS 9, pt. 1: 1341. Dulles's highly critical remarks were reported by Eban on the same day to Sharett. In his message, Eban recommended that the Israeli Government "might wish to reconsider its current practice . . . of securing short-term objectives in [border] disputes without regard [for] world opinion." Quoted from Eban's message of October 8, 1953, to Sharett. *Documents on the Foreign Policy of Israel*, 8: 726.

55. Memorandum, "Representation to Israel on Arab-Israel Border Incidents," from Byroade to Dulles on April 7, 1954. FRUS 9, pt. 1: 1502–1503.

56. Memorandum, "Israel's Request to Purchase American Jet Aircraft," submitted by Byroade to Dulles on June 3, 1954. FRUS 9, pt. 1: 1572–1573. See also Barry Rubin, *Secrets of State: The State Department and the Struggle Over U. S. Foreign Policy* (New York: Oxford University Press, 1985), p. 89; Shimshoni, *Israel and Conventional Deterrence*, pp. 62–63; Mordechai Bar-On, *The Gates of Gaza, passim;* Amir Oren, "Post Oslo, Post Mortem," p. 17.

57. Memorandum from Dulles on April 10, 1954. FRUS 9, pt. 1: 1508. See also Raymond Cohen, *Culture and Conflict in Egyptian-Israeli Relations: A Dialogue of the Deaf* (Bloomington: Indiana University Press, 1990), p. 4.

58. Shimshoni, *Israel and Conventional Deterrence*, p. 86. See also Netanel Lorch, "David Ben-Gurion and the Sinai Campaign, 1956," in *Politics and Leadership in Israel*, p. 293.

59. Selwyn Ilan Troen, "The Sinai Campaign as a 'War of No Alternative': Ben-Gurion's View of the Israel-Egyptian Conflict," in *The Suez-Sinai Crisis, 1956*, p. 181. See also Shimshoni, *Israel and Conventional Deterrence*, p. 86; Benny Morris, *Israel's Borders Wars, 1949–1956* (Oxford: Clarendon Press, 1993), chapter 11; Lorch, "Ben-Gurion and the Sinai Campaign," pp. 293–301; Moshe Dayan, *Diary of the Sinai Campaign* (New York: Harper and Row, 1957), pp. 73–75; David Ben-Gurion, *The Restored State of Israel* (Hebrew) (Tel-Aviv: Am Oved, 1969), p. 526; Maoz, *Paradoxes of War*, p. 56; Avner Yaniv, *Deterrence Without the Bomb: The Politics of Israeli Strategy* (Lexington: Lexington Books, 1987), p. 65; Schoenbaum, *The United States and the State of Israel*, p. 130; Baruch Kimmerling, "The Rise of the Third Israeli Kingdom," *Ha'aretz*, August 16, 1996, p. 11; Eli Lieberman, "What Makes Deterrence Work? Lessons from the Egyptian-Israeli Enduring Rivalry," *Security Studies* 4(4) (Summer 1995): 893; Cohen, *Culture and Conflict*, pp. 92–93.

60. Moshe Dayan, *The Story of My Life* (New York: William Morrow, 1976), pp. 180–181. See also Shabtai Teveth, *Moshe Dayan* (London: Weidenfeld and Nicolson, 1972), p. 242; Safran, *Israel: The Embattled Ally*, p. 227; Shimshoni, *Israel and Conventional Deterrence*, p. 120; Mordechai Bar-On, "The Influence of Political Considerations on Operational Planning in the Sinai Campaign," in *The Suez-Sinai Crisis, 1956*, p. 197.

61. Shimshoni, *Israel and Conventional Deterrence*, p. 120. The reference to the prospects of "the liquidation of Israel" is quoted from Ben-Gurion, *The Restored State*, p. 526. In his diary entry of September 25, 1956, Ben-Gurion similarly states that Nasser is trying "to liquidate us. " See Selwyn Ilan Troen, ed., "Ben-Gurion's Diary: The Suez-Sinai Campaign," in *The Suez-Sinai Crisis, 1956*, p. 299. An earlier manifestation of this Israeli determination to challenge the American order of priorities in the Middle East and to abort Washington's efforts to solicit Egypt's goodwill and support, was its initiation of a series of covert actions against Western installations in Egypt in 1954. These actions—which were exposed by the Egyptian authorities—were designed to portray Egypt as an unstable, anti-Western state that could not become a reliable ally. It is interesting to note that the possibility that Israel would defy American pressure and embark on a collision course with the Eisenhower Administration was fully recognized by Ben-Gurion as early as March 8, 1953. In his meeting with Sharett, the Prime Minister observed that "it is very likely that we shall have to challenge [the U. S.] and do the opposite of what [the administration] desires. " Quoted in *Documents on the Foreign Policy of Israel*, 8: 207. See also p. 208. On the development of Israel's offensive military doctrine, see Ariel Levite, *Offense and Defense in Israeli Military Doctrine* (Boulder: Westview Press, 1989), pp. 46–57. On the likely ramifications of a potential American-Israeli arms deal concerning Israel's margin of maneuverability, see Zaki Shalom, *David Ben-Gurion, The State of Israel and the Arab World, 1949–1956* (in Hebrew) (Sede Boker: The Ben-Gurion Research Center, 1995), p. 167.

62. Uri Bialer, "Israel's Global Foreign Policy, 1948–1956," in Laurence J. Silberstein, ed. , *New Perspectives on Israeli History: The Early Years of the State* (New York: New York University Press, 1991), p. 237. On the threat to militarily intervene, see Sharett, *Personal Diary*, 4 (1955): 926. See also Shalom, *Ben-Gurion*, p. 169; Cohen, *Culture and Conflict*, p. 93.

63. Gad Barzilai, *Wars, International Conflicts, and Political Order: A Jewish Democracy in the Middle East* (Albany: State University of New York Press, 1996), p. 29. See also Bar-Siman-Tov, *Israel, the Superpowers, and the War in the Middle East*, p. 49; Elmo H. Hutchison, *Violent Truce: A Military Observer Looks at the Arab-Israeli Conflict, 1951–1955* (New York: Devin-Adair, 1956), *passim*. On the theoretical implications of the Israeli strategy, see Robert Jervis, "Political Implications of Loss Aversion," *Political Psychology* 13(2) (June 1992): 189–199; Princen, *Intermediaries in International Conflict*, pp. 33.

64. Dulles's words. Quoted from his October 21, 1955, conversation with Senator Walter F. George. *Dulles Papers*, Box 5, "Subject Series" folder: 1. For a similar expression of concern, see the memorandum of July 6, 1956, by Dulles's special assistant, Francis H. Russell, to Dulles. In this message, Russell observed that "the danger of an outbreak between the Israelis and the Arabs during the next six months will stem principally from the Israeli Government. " FRUS 15: 787.

65. Dulles's statement of April 23, 1956. Memorandum of the conversation between Dulles and a group of Republican Senators. *Dulles Papers*, Box 10, "Subject Series" folder: 2. Despite the strong opposition of the President and the De-

partment of State to a major Israeli military operation against Egypt, elements in the CIA and the Pentagon quietly supported an attempt to topple the Nasser regime. See Oren, *Origins of the Second Arab-Israeli War*, p. 133.

66. Quoted from the message of March 1, 1956, from the American Ambassador to Israel, Edward B. Lawson, to the Department of State. The Ambassador's assessment is based on his conversations with Ben-Gurion and Sharett. FRUS 15: 272. See also pp. 270–271.

67. Dulles's remarks of October 20, 1955. Memorandum of the 262nd meeting of the National Security Council. FRUS 14: 622. See also Gazit, "Israeli Military Procurement," p. 90. Similarly, in his press conference of March 7, 1956, Eisenhower explained the administration's refusal to supply arms to Israel in terms of the demographic asymmetry between Israel and its neighbors. As he pointed out: "We do not believe that it is possible to assure peace in that area by rushing some arms to a nation that at most can absorb only that amount that 1. 7 million people can absorb whereas, on the other side, there are some 40 million people. " (Quoted by Gazit, "Israeli Military Procurement," p. 91). Notwithstanding this consistent position, the President, on a number of occasions, expressed skepticism concerning the basic premises of this posture. For example, in his telephone conversation of March 1, 1956, with Undersecretary of State, Herbert Hoover Jr., Eisenhower stated that "he was a little worried that perhaps we were being too tough with the Israelis with respect to arms. " However, he ultimately accepted the position of the Department of State, which argued that "any indication of a departure from our present position might seriously jeopardize our ability to bring the two parties together. " Memorandum of the conversation of March 1, 1956, between Eisenhower and Undersecretary Hoover. FRUS 15: 260–261.

68. Prime Minister Sharett's remarks. Memorandum of his October 26, 1955, conversation with Dulles, which took place in Geneva. The memorandum was sent by Dulles to the Department of State. FRUS 14: 657. See also Sheffer, *Moshe Sharett*, p. 865.

69. Dulles's remarks. Memorandum of his October 26, 1955, conversation with Prime Minister Sharett. FRUS 14: 659. Sharett served as prime minister until November 2, 1955.

70. Sharett, *Personal Diary*, 2 (1954): 466. In his message to Eisenhower, of March 28, 1956, Dulles underscored the need to prevent an Israeli preemptive strike against Egypt or "a planned deterioration towards such a war. " Dulles further asserted that despite the recent Egyptian tilt toward Moscow, the administration should avoid any drastic retaliatory measures "so that the Egyptian leader would not be able to say that he was forced by the US into even closer relations with the Kremlin. " Determined to maintain a margin of maneuverability vis-à-vis Egypt, the Secretary remained adamant in his opposition to the Israeli request for arms, maintaining that American diplomacy should be continuously predicated upon "the notion of evenhandedness" (Quoted by Sheffer, *Moshe Sharett*, p. 863).

71. Quoted from Dulles's letter of February 6, 1956, to members of the

House of Representatives, *Dulles Papers*, Box 101, "Congress" folder. On the theoretical implications of this failure of the administration's coercive strategy see Patchen, *Resolving Disputes Between Nations*, p. 304; Richard Smoke, *War: Controlling Escalation* (Cambridge: Harvard University Press, 1977), *passim*.

72. Dulles's remarks. Memorandum of the conversation of November 21, 1955, between Dulles and Sharett. FRUS 14: 794. See also Eban, *Personal Witness*, p. 234; Kimmerling, "The Rise of the Third Israeli Kingdom," p. 11. In his meeting of March 27, 1953, with Ben-Gurion, Sharett pointed out that, in the administration's thinking, the very willingness of the Arabs to enter into peace negotiations with Israel "should be reciprocated by an Israeli gesture regarding the terms of an agreement. " Quoted in *Documents on the Foreign Policy of Israel*, 8: 252.

73. Byroade's remarks. Memorandum of the conversation of April 8, 1953, with Sharett. FRUS 9, pt. 1: 1166–1167. See also Alteras, *Eisenhower and Israel*, p. 90; Eban, *Personal Witness*, p. 234.

74. Byroade's remarks. Memorandum of his May 5, 1954, conversation with Eban. FRUS 9, pt. 1: 1544. Unlike several other tenets of the administration's approach, which reflected the thinking of Eisenhower and Dulles, the demand that Israel restrict the level of Jewish immigration had also been a consistent component in Truman's policy. See, for example, the statement of policy toward the Arab states and Israel, drafted by the National Security Council on April 24, 1952. FRUS 9, pt. 1: 225.

75. Quoted from a memorandum of September 29, 1953, by Byroade; Alteras, *Eisenhower and Israel*, p. 91; Sheffer, *Moshe Sharett*, p. 627.

76. Quoted from a Department of State Position Paper, May 7, 1953. FRUS 9, pt. 1: 1215. See also, for similar statements, Dulles's remarks to Lebanon's President, Camile Shamoun, of May 16, 1953. Quoted from a memorandum of conversation between Dulles and Shamoun, May 16, 1953. FRUS 9, pt. 1: 58. See also Lipson, "American Support for Israel," p. 139; Sheffer, *Moshe Sharett*, p. 627.

77. Byroade's remarks of June 9, 1953. Memorandum of his conversation with Eban. FRUS 9, pt. 1: 1235. See also Byroade's remarks to Eban on September 25, 1953. FRUS 9, pt. 1: 1323.

78. Quoted from Byroade's address of May 1, 1954, in Philadelphia, before the American Council of Judaism. ISA, Foreign Ministry Files, Box 2414/28: 4. See also Byroade's remarks to a group of Jewish leaders of April 30, 1954. ISA, Foreign Ministry Files, Box 2414/28:5. See also Alteras, *Eisenhower and Israel*, p. 106; Spiegel, *The Other Arab-Israeli Conflict*, p. 63; Sheffer, *Moshe Sharett*, p. 731.

79. Quoted from Byroade's address of May 1, 1954. ISA, Foreign Ministry Files, Box 2414/28: 4. See also Byroade's remarks to a group of Jewish leaders, of April 30, 1954. ISA, Foreign Ministry Files, Box 2480/3: 1–3. In his November 22, 1954, message to several American ambassadors in the Middle East, Dulles similarly alluded to "the insistence of Israel on a special role as the center of a world-wide 'nation' of Jewry as one of the main obstacles in attaining the objective of peace. " FRUS 9, pt. 1: 1696.

80. Byroade's remarks, May 7, 1954. Quoted by Sheffer, *Moshe Sharett*, p. 735.
81. Byroade's remarks, April 30, 1954. Memorandum of his meeting with representatives of the American Zionist Committee for Public Affairs. ISA, Foreign Ministry Files, Box 2480/3: 2. See also the memorandum of the conversation of June 9, 1953, between Byroade and Eban. FRUS 9, pt. 1: 1235.
82. Quoted from a document: "Palestine Settlement," drafted by the Department of State and the British Foreign Office on July 14, 1955, which outlined the Alpha Plan. FRUS 14: 312. See also Freiberger, *Dawn Over Suez*, pp. 110–123; Oren, *Origins of the Second Arab-Israeli War*, p. 114; Bar-On, *The Gates of Gaza*, p. 86; Alteras, *Eisenhower and Israel*, p. 129; Schoenbaum, *The United States and the State of Israel*, p. 101; Rubin, "America and the Egyptian Revolution," p. 86; Eban, *Personal Witness*, p. 246; Evelyn Shuckburgh, *Descent to Suez: Diaries, 1951–56* (New York: Norton, 1987), pp. 256–257, 266.
83. Dulles's remarks of November 21, 1955. Memorandum of his conversation with Sharett. FRUS 14: 793–794. See also Sheffer, *Moshe Sharett*, pp. 844–845; Eliahu Elath, *Through the Mist of Time: Reminiscences* (Jerusalem: Yad Izhak Ben-Zvi, 1996), pp. 66–75; Bar-On, *The Gates of Gaza*, pp. 84–87. On November 2, 1955, Sharett's tenure as prime minister came to an end, and he continued to serve as foreign minister until his resignation from the Israeli Government on June 16, 1956.
84. Dulles's remarks of December 6, 1955. Memorandum of his conversation with Sharett. FRUS 14: 830. See also Sheffer, *Moshe Sharett*, pp. 798–799.
85. Dulles's remarks of January 27, 1955. Memorandum of his conversation with the main architect of the Alpha Plan, Sir Evelyn Shuckburgh. FRUS 14: 31. See also Lieberman, "What Makes Deterrence Work?," p. 896; Freiberger, *Dawn Over Suez*, pp. 117–123; Shuckburgh, *Descent to Suez*, pp. 240–242.
86. Quoted from Ben-Gurion's cable of December 4, 1955, to Sharett, who was then holding negotiations with members of the administration in Washington. Bar-On, *The Gates of Gaza*, p. 89. Ben-Gurion's reference to a settlement involving a unilateral Israeli concession as "suicidal" was made during his January 23, 1956, meeting with the American mediator Robert Anderson. FRUS 15: 52. The reference to the "severe complications" with the Western powers, which were expected to result from Israel's refusal to accept the basic premises of the Alpha Plan was made by Sharett on April 14, 1955. See Sharett, *Personal Diary*, 4, 1955, p. 935. See also Bialer, *Between East and West*, p. 269; Sheffer, *Moshe Sharett*, pp. 798, 845; Alteras, *Eisenhower and Israel*, p. 129. This Israeli determination to defy American pressure for unilateral Israeli territorial concessions was forcefully articulated as early as on March 27, 1953. In a meeting of that date between Ben-Gurion and Sharett, the Prime Minister asserted that "Israel will never compromise on the issues of Jerusalem, the Negev and the Galilee. . . . Any effort to change [Israel's] boundaries will require force. " See Ben-Gurion's remarks of March 27, 1953, in *Documents on the Foreign Policy of Israel*, 8: 255. As we have already witnessed (see note 4 above), Sharett expressed similar views in his April 8, 1954, conversation with Byroade.
87. Eban's words. Memorandum of his September 6, 1955, conversation

with Assistant Secretary of State for Near Eastern, South Asian, and African Affairs, George V. Allen. FRUS 14: 452.

88. Quoted from Ben-Gurion's address of May 14, 1955, by Bar-On, *The Gates of Gaza*, p. 90. See also Lieberman, "What Makes Deterrence Work?" p. 865; Oren, *Origins of the Second Arab-Israeli War*, p. 122; Shimon Shamir, "The Collapse of Project Alpha,"in *Suez 1956*, pp. 81–83; Freiberger, *Dawn Over Suez*, pp. 112–115. See also Shalom, *Ben-Gurion*, p. 121. In his message of November 21, 1955, to Dulles, Sharett—while using less combative rhetoric than Ben-Gurion did in his May 14, 1955, address—was equally uncompromising in his reference to the territorial components of the Alpha Plan. As he pointed out, "it is out of the question that Israel would concede any part of the Negev . . . " (quoted by Sheffer, *Moshe Sharett*, p. 844).

89. Dulles's remarks of May 12, 1955. Memorandum of his conversation with British Foreign Minister Harold Macmillan. FRUS 14: 185–186. In addition to this complex of tactical considerations, Dulles repeatedly argued that an American security guarantee to Israel required the prior ratification of the US Senate which, in his view, was unlikely. See, for example, Dulles's remarks on the subject on October 20, 1955, at the 262nd meeting of the National Security Council. FRUS 14: 622–623. It should be emphasized that Sharett remained irreconcilably opposed to Dulles's view that the guarantees should augment and reinforce a regional peace settlement rather than precede it. As he pointed out in his message of May 5, 1955, to Dulles, "if the [security] treaty is made contingent upon a prior settlement, there will be no treaty; and if the settlement is predicated upon one-sided concessions, there will be no settlement" (Quoted from Sharett's message of May 5, 1955, to Dulles. FRUS 14: 172). See also Shamir, "The Collapse of Project Alpha," in pp. 73–100, *passim;* Sheffer, *Moshe Sharett*, pp. 808–809.

90. David Tal, "The American-Israeli Security Treaty: Sequel or Means to the Relief of Israeli-Arab Tensions, 1954–55," *Middle Eastern Studies* 31(4) (October 1995): 842–843. See also Sheffer, *Moshe Sharett*, p. 787.

91. Shamir, "The Collapse of Project Alpha," p. 86. See also Hahn, *The U.S., Great Britain, and Egypt*, p. 193.

92. Saadia Touval, *The Peace Brokers: Mediators in the Arab-Israeli Conflict, 1948–1979* (Princeton: Princeton University Press, 1982), p. 125. Italics original. See also Shalom, *Ben-Gurion*, pp. 122, 126; Hahn, *The U. S., Great Britain, and Egypt*, pp. 194–199; Eban, *Personal Witness*, pp. 246–247.

On the role of the CIA in the inauguration of the Gamma Plan, see Wilbur Crane Eveland, *Ropes of Sand: America's Failure in the Middle East* (New York: Norton, 1980), pp. 148–149.

93. Touval, *The Peace Brokers*, p. 138. See also Frieberger, *Dawn Over Suez*, pp. 135–136; William Bragg Ewald, Jr., *Eisenhower as President: Critical Days, 1951–1960* (Englewood Cliffs: Prentice Hall, 1981), p. 194; David Ben-Gurion, *My Talks with Arab Leaders* (New York: Third Press, 1972), pp. 294–296.

94. Touval, *The Peace Brokers*, p. 133. See also Rubin, "America and the Egyptian Revolution," pp. 85–87; Rafael, *Destination Peace*, p. 51; Holland, *America and*

Egypt, pp. 79. 86. Another mediating effort initiated by the administration in the wake of the failure of the Anderson mission involved Ira Hirschmann—President Roosevelt's old adviser. It, too, failed to provide the impetus for progress. See Sheffer, *Moshe Sharett*, p. 816.

95. Touval, *The Peace Brokers*, pp. 125–126. See also Byroade's words. Memorandum prepared on November 22, 1954, entitled "The Arab-Israel Problem—Situation Report. " FRUS 9, pt. 1: 1694; Rafael, *Destination Peace*, p. 51.

96. Byroade's remarks. Memorandum of his conversation with Eban of June 9, 1953. FRUS 9, pt. 1: 1236. See also Alteras, *Eisenhower and Israel*, p. 152.

97. Sharett's words, April 8, 1953. Memorandum of his conversation with Byroade. FRUS 9, pt. 1: 1168. See also Alteras, *Eisenhower and Israel*, p. 152.

98. Dulles's remarks of January 11, 1956. Memorandum of the conversation which Dulles had with Eisenhower and the American envoy to the Middle East, Robert Anderson, *Dulles Papers*, Box 10, "Subject Series" folder: 3.

99. Ibid. See also the National Security Council Progress Report, May 17, 1956, on United States Objectives and Policies with respect to the Near East (NSC 5428), prepared by the Operations Coordinating Board. White House Office, Office of the Special Assistant for National Security Affairs: Records, 1952–1961; NSC Series Policy Papers Subseries, Box 12: NSC 5428, Near East [Deterrence of Arab-Israeli War]. The Dwight D. Eisenhower Library (hereafter DDE Library), Abilene, Kansas: 3–10.

100. Alteras, *Eisenhower and Israel*, p 148. See also Shimshoni, *Israel and Conventional Deterrence*, p. 55.

101. Quoted from the NSC Statement of Policy on United States Objectives and Policies with respect to the Near East (NSC 5428), July 13, 1954. Prepared by the Executive Secretary of the NSC. White House Office, Office of the Special Assistant for National Security Affairs: Records, 1952–1961; NSC Series, Policy Papers Subseries, Box 12: NSC 5428, Near East. DDE Library: 7.

102. Ibid., pp. 13–14.

103. Ibid., p. 11. For a detailed analysis of the punitive measures which the administration adopted vis-à-vis Israel in the course of this crisis episode, see Ben-Zvi, *The Limits of the Special Relationship*, pp. 69–74; Diane B. Kunz, *The Economic Diplomacy of the Suez Crisis* (Chapel Hill: The University of North Carolina Press, 1991), pp. 162–176.

104. Dulles's remarks of February 10, 1956. Memorandum of his conversation with Eban. FRUS 15: 166. See also Alteras, *Eisenhower and Israel*, pp. 99–101.

105. Dulles's remarks of March 2, 1956. Memorandum of his conversation with Eban. FRUS 15: 278.

106. Quoted from a personal letter sent by the American Ambassador in Egypt, Henry Byroade, to Dulles on February 23, 1956. *Dulles Papers*, Box 10, "Subject Series" folder: 2.

107. In May 1953, Nahum Goldmann was "recruited" by Byroade to promote the idea of a Jewish-Arab confederation along the lines of the 1947 partition plan. Three and a half years later, on October 30, 1956, the White House Chief of Staff, Sherman Adams, convinced Rabbi Abba Hillel Silver to assume

the role of liaison in an effort to persuade Ben-Gurion to stop the fighting in Sinai and "return immediately to [Israel's] own border" in return for an American declaration expressing the President's "deep admiration and friendship for Israel." On the Goldmann initiative see a report on Goldmann's meeting of May 5, 1953, with Byroade in *Documents on Israel's Foreign Policy*, 8: 339–341. On Rabbi Silver's mission, see Ben-Zvi, *The Limits of the Special Relationship*, p. 61. See also Alteras, *Eisenhower and Israel*, p. 86; Spiegel, *The Other Arab-Israeli Conflict*, p. 60; Organski, *The $36 Billion Bargain*, p. 31.

108. Alteras, *Eisenhower and Israel*, p. 101. See also Sharett, *Personal Diary*, 1, 1953–1954, p. 121.

109. Memorandum of a conversation at the White House on April 26, 1956, among Eisenhower, Dulles, and Rabbi Silver. *Dulles Papers*, Box 1, "General Correspondence" folder.

110. Ibid.

111. See, on the performance of the American Jewish leadership in the course of the Suez Crisis, Ben-Zvi, *The Limits of the Special Relationship*, pp. 61–74. This picture of disunity within the American Jewish leadership was not confined to the Suez Crisis. Thus, as early as on January 5, 1953, Eban reported to Ben-Gurion that the American Jewish leadership was sharply and bitterly divided over the issue of how to cope with the recent wave of blatant anti-Semitism then sweeping the Soviet Union and the Eastern bloc. See Eban's message of January 5, 1953, to Ben-Gurion. *Documents on the Foreign Policy of Israel*, 8: 5. Similarly, in the course of the October 1953 Water Crisis, while several Jewish leaders did voice concern over the coercive measures taken by the Eisenhower Administration, there was no softening in the American strategy. The main reason for this ineffectiveness was the behavior of such prominent Jewish leaders as Rabbi Silver, who were highly critical of various aspects of Israel's behavior in both this matter and other crises. See Sharett, *Personal Diary*, 1: 65; *Dulles Papers*, Box 67, "Bnai B'rith" folder; Eban's message of October 24, 1953, to Sharett, in *Documents on Israel's Foreign Policy*, 8: 807–808.

In his message of November 11, 1953, to Sharett, Eban complained about the highly critical attitude "of American Jewish leaders toward Israeli policy in the Arab-Israeli sphere." According to Eban's report, "practically all members of the Embassy's staff were continuously exposed to harsh criticism from many Jewish friends" over the conduct of Israel's foreign and defense policy on such issues as the Qibya raid and the water dispute with Syria and the UN. Quoted from Eban's message of November 11, 1953, to Sharett. *Documents on the Foreign Policy of Israel*, 8: 848.

112. Quoted from Nahum Goldmann's letter of November 7, 1956, to Ben-Gurion, by Brecher, *Decisions in Israel's Foreign Policy*, p. 287.

113. For illustrations, see Dulles's telephone conversation of February 13, 1957, with Congressman John M. Vorys. *Dulles Papers*, Box 6, "Telephone Conversations" folder: 1; Dulles's telephone conversation of February 16, 1957, with Senator William F. Knowland. *Dulles Papers*, Box 6, "Telephone Conversations" folder. See also Peter Golden, *Quiet Diplomat: A Biography of*

Max M. Fisher (New York: Cornwall Books, 1992), p. xvii; Bar-On, *The Gates of Gaza, passim.*

114. Quoted from Dulles's reply of February 6, 1956, to a joint letter from certain members of the House of Representatives. *Dulles Papers,* Box 101, "Congress" folder. See also Alteras, *Eisenhower and Israel,* pp. 174–175.

115. Brecher, *Decisions in Israel's Foreign Policy,* p. 196.

116. For an unconventional analysis of American diplomacy during the Suez Crisis see John Gerard Ruggie, "The False Premise of Realism," *International Security* 20(1) (Summer 1995): 63–64.

Chapter 3: The United States and Israel, 1957–1960: The Emergence of Strategic Convergence

1. NSC Statement of Policy on Long-Range US Policy Toward the Near East (NSC 5801), January 10, 1958. White House Office, Office of the Special Assistant for National Security Affairs: Records, 1952–1961; NSC Series, Policy Papers Subseries, Box 23: NSC 5801/1 - Policy Toward the Near East (2): 1.

2. Dulles's remarks. Memorandum of his October 29, 1957, conversation with Eban. FRUS 17, *The Arab-Israeli Dispute, 1957* (Washington, DC: United States Government Printing office, 1990): 783.

3. Spiegel, *The Other Arab-Israeli Conflict,* p. 90.

4. Dulles's remarks. Memorandum of his June 24, 1957, conversation with Israeli Finance Minister Levi Eshkol. FRUS 17: 783.

5. Dulles's remarks. Memorandum of his October 29, 1957, conversation with Eban. FRUS 17: 782.

6. Little, "The Making of the Special Relationship," p. 563.

7. George and Smoke, *Deterrence in American Foreign Policy,* pp. 310–311. See also Fawaz A. Gerges, *The Superpowers and the Middle East: Regional and International Politics, 1955–1967* (Boulder: Westview Press, 1994), pp. 85–86, 89; Keith Wheelock, *Nasser's New Egypt: A Critical Analysis* (New York: Praeger, 1959), p. 223. On the broader question of the American national style and the recurrent American inability to cope with divergent cultural and political backgrounds, see Stanley Hoffmann, *Gulliver's Troubles, or the Setting of American Foreign Policy* (New York: McGraw-Hill, 1968), *passim;* Charles A. Kupchan, "American Globalism in the Middle East: The Roots of Regional Security Policy," *Political Science Quarterly* 103(4) (Winter 1988–1989): 586.

8. Dulles's remarks. Memorandum of his August 6, 1957, meeting with Eban. FRUS 17: 706. Dulles presented the American plan for resolving the Arab-Israeli conflict (the Alpha Plan) on August 26, 1955.

9. Quoted from an oral history interview with Reverend Edward L. R. Elson of the National Presbyterian Church in Washington, of September 22, 1968 (Reverend Elson was interviewed by Paul Hopper). Columbia University Oral History Project, DDE Library: 255–256.

10. Dulles's telephone conversation of February 22, 1957, with Reverend Elson, *Dulles Papers,* Box 6, "Telephone Conversations" folder.

11. Dulles's belief that the basic premises of the special relationship paradigm were incompatible with the American national interest was repeatedly and forcefully articulated during the last phase of the Suez Crisis. For example, on the same day (February 22, 1957) in which Dulles's telephone conversation with Reverend Elson was held, the Secretary—in his telephone conversation with New York Protestant Church executive Dr. Rosewell Barnes—was equally harsh and irreconcilable in alluding to the activities of the representatives of the special relationship paradigm, and called upon non-Jewish religious leaders to mobilize their constituencies in support of the administration's Middle East policy. As the Secretary explained to Dr. Barnes:

"We needed very badly to get some more vocal support from the people other than the Jews and those very much influenced by Jews. We were really in an unfortunate position. There was no way in which the Protestant groups would be heard on an issue like this which might be very vitally affecting the future of the United Nations. . . . It was impossible to hold the line because we got no support from the Protestant elements of the country. All we got is a battering from the Jews. . . . Almost 90% of the mail was from Jews. Out of that percentage, 10% supported [the President] and 90% were against. The significant thing was that practically all the response was Jewish. There seemed to be no interest in this situation by others." (Quoted from Dulles's telephone conversation of February 22, 1957, with Dr. Rosewell Barnes, *Dulles Papers*, Box 6, "Telephone Conversations" folder: 1).

The activities which the major Jewish organizations initiated or sponsored at this stage of the Suez Crisis included a massive rally, on February 25, 1957, at Madison Square Garden. However, the American Jewish leadership was fraught with disunity throughout the crisis, a fact that contributed to the failure of its effort to redirect the course of American Middle East diplomacy. For evidence, see Eban, *Personal Witness*, p. 281; Ben-Zvi, *The Limits of the Special Relationship*, pp. 69–72; Nahum Goldmann, *The Autobiography of Nahum Goldmann: Sixty Years of Jewish Life* (New York: Holt, Rinehart and Winston, 1969), pp. 283–329, *passim*.

12. Quoted from Dulles's letter of July 31, 1958, to Reverend Elson. Ann Whitman File, DDE Diary Series, Box 34: DDE Dictations, July 1958. DDE Library: 1. Italics original.

13. Ibid.

14. Eisenhower's statement of November 23, 1956. Quoted by Spiegel, *The Other Arab-Israeli Conflict*, p. 84. For a similar statement, see Dulles's testimony of January 14, 1957, before the Senate Committee on Foreign Relations, in *The President's Proposal on the Middle East: Hearings Before the Committee on Foreign Relations and the Committee on Armed Services, United States, January–February 1957* (Washington: Government Printing Office, 1957), pp. 173–178.

15. Spiegel, *The Other Arab-Israeli Conflict*, p. 87.

16. Ibid., p. 86. See also Robert D. Schulzinger, "The Impact of Suez on United States Middle East Policy, 1957–1958," in *The Suez-Sinai Crisis, 1956*, p. 256.

17. Eban, *Personal Witness*, p. 289. See also Little, "The Making of a Special Relationship," p. 564.

18. Little, "The Making of a Special Relationship," p. 563.

19. Gerges, *The Superpowers and the Middle East*, pp. 80–81. See also Kenen, *Israel's Defense Line*, p. 140; George and Smoke, *Deterrence in American Foreign Policy*, pp. 329–331; Schulzinger, "The Impact of Suez," p. 256; Spiegel, *The Other Arab-Israeli Conflict*, p. 86; Seyom Brown, *The Faces of Power: Constancy and Change in United States Foreign Policy from Truman to Clinton* (New York: Columbia University Press, 1994), p. 100.

20. Schulzinger, "The Impact of Suez," p. 256; Walt, *The Origins of Alliances*, pp. 68–69; George and Smoke, *Deterrence in American Foreign Policy*, pp. 330–331; Burns, *Economic Aid and American Policy*, p. 110.

21. Little, "The Making of a Special Relationship," p. 565. See also Burns, *Economic Aid and American Policy*, pp. 110–111.

22. Eban, *Personal Witness*, p. 322.

23. Dulles's remarks of April 24, 1953. Memorandum of his conversation with Eban. FRUS 17: 104–105. See also Little, "The Making of a Special Relationship," p. 564.

24. Acting Secretary of State Christian A. Herter's remarks of May 2, 1957. Memorandum of his conversation with Eban. FRUS 17: 118. For a similar statement, which reflects Dulles's belief that the American and Israeli Governments now communicated "with more intimacy and confidence than . . . before [the Suez Crisis]," and that this growing confidence "was a basis for greater trust in the future," see the Secretary's remarks of August 6, 1957, from which the above citations were taken. FRUS 17: 703 (the remarks were made in a conversation with Eban). See also Rafael, *Destination Peace*, p. 124.

25. Dulles's words. Memorandum to Eisenhower on August 20, 1957.Quoted in Spiegel, *The Other Arab-Israeli Conflict*, p. 86. See also Schulzinger, "The Impact of Suez," p. 257; George and Smoke, *Deterrence in American Foreign Policy*, p. 333; Gerges, *The Superpowers and the Middle East*, p. 85.

26. Dowty, *Middle East Crisis*, p. 33. See also Gerges, *The Superpowers and the Middle East*, p. 86; George and Smoke, *Deterrence in American Foreign Policy*, p. 334; Lenczowski, *American Presidents and the Middle East*, pp. 54–56; Bonnie F. Saunders, *The United States and Arab Nationalism: The Syrian Case, 1953–1960* (Westport: Praeger, 1996), pp. 55–70.

27. Dulles's press release of September 7, 1957. Quoted by George and Smoke, *Deterrence in American Foreign Policy*, p. 334. See also Dowty, *Middle East Crisis*, pp. 33–34; Kupchan, "American Globalism in the Middle East," p. 594.

28. Dwight D. Eisenhower, *The White House Years: Waging Peace, 1956–1961* (New York: Doubleday, 1965), p. 199. See also Spiegel, *The Other Arab-Israeli Conflict*, p. 86; Lenczowski, *American Presidents and the Middle East*, pp. 55–56.

29. Dulles's remarks of August 30, 1957, to Senator William F. Knowland, in *Dulles Papers*, Box 1, "General Correspondence" folder: 1–2. For an earlier statement, which was permeated with empathy and sympathy toward Israel, see the memorandum of Dulles's conversation of August 6, 1957, with Eban. FRUS 17: 703.

30. Dulles's remarks of September 11, 1957, to Senator Mike Mansfield, in *Dulles Papers*, Box 1, "General Correspondence" folder: 2–3.

31. See, for example, Dulles's remarks to Eban in the course of their September 12, 1957, meeting. FRUS 17: 732. See also Little, "The Making of a Special Relationship," p. 565.

32. Dulles's remarks to Eban. Memorandum of his September 12, 1957, meeting with Eban. FRUS 17: 732.

33. Eisenhower's statement of September 13, 1957. Quoted by Little, "The Making of a Special Relationship," p. 565.

34. Dulles's remarks of September 12, 1957, to Eban. Memorandum of their meeting. FRUS 17: 731. See also Gerges, *The Superpowers and the Middle East*, p. 87.

35. See, for example, Eisenhower's message of September 12, 1957, to King Saud of Saudi Arabia. FRUS 17: 734. See also Organski, *The $36 Billion Bargain*, p. 31.

36. Dulles's remarks of October 29, 1957. Quoted from his conversation with the president of the International Bank for Reconstruction and Development. FRUS 17: 776–777. See also Gerges, *The Superpowers and the Middle East*, p. 87; Kupchan, "American Globalism in the Middle East," p. 590.

37. Rafael, *Destination Peace*, p. 124.

38. Dulles's remarks of December 5, 1957, to Iraqi Prime Minister Nuri al-Said. Memorandum of their meeting. FRUS 17: 844.

39. Ibid., pp. 844–845.

40. George and Smoke, *Deterrence in American Foreign Policy*, p. 334. See also Kenen, *Israel's Defense Line*, p. 140; Organski, *The $36 Billion Bargain*, p. 31; Gerges, *The Superpowers and the Middle East*, pp. 87–88; Spiegel, *The Other Arab-Israeli Conflict*, p. 87.

41. See the text of Dulles's November 12, 1957, message to Ben-Gurion. FRUS 17: 792. See also Little, "The Making of a Special Relationship," p. 365.

42. Dulles's address of August 26, 1955, before the Council on Foreign Relations. *Dulles Papers*, Box 95, "Selected Correspondence" folder: 1.

43. Little, "The Making of a Special Relationship," p. 565. Although the UAR was established in February 1958, this chapter—for the sake of continuity and coherence—uses the name "Egypt" (since part of the chapter deals with developments that took place before the establishment of the UAR). Contrary to the American belief that the UAR "was the product of a Communist conspiracy," the union was the product of purely inter-Arab considerations, and was accompanied by strong punitive measures against Communist leaders in Syria. See Kupchan, "American Globalism in the Middle East," p. 590.

44. Dulles's remarks of June 23, 1958. Memorandum of his meeting with a group of Congressional leaders. FRUS 11: *Lebanon and Jordan, 1958–1960* (Washington: United States Government Printing Office, 1992): 167. See also George and Smoke, *Deterrence in American Foreign Policy*, pp. 338–339; Dallek, *The*

172   3. U.S. and Israel, 1957–1960: Strategic Convergence

American Style of Foreign Policy, p. 204; Kupchan, "American Globalism in the Middle East," p. 590.

45. Dulles's address at the Pan American Union, June 25, 1958. *Dulles Papers*, Box 1: General Correspondence Files: 1. See also Little, "The Making of a Special Relationship," p. 565.

46. Dulles's remarks to United Nations Secretary General Dag Hammerskjöld, July 7, 1958. *Dulles Papers*, Box 1: General Correspondence Folder: 2–3.

47. George and Smoke, *Deterrence in American Foreign Policy*, p. 340; Gerges, *The Superpowers and the Middle East*, pp. 103–107; Lenczowski, *American Presidents and the Middle East*, pp. 59–60; Kupchan, "American Globalism in the Middle East," p. 593.

48. Dowty, *Middle East Crisis*, pp. 43–46. See also George and Smoke, *Deterrence in American Foreign Policy*, p. 345; Erika Alin, "U.S. Policy and Military Intervention in the 1958 Lebanon Crisis," in David W. Lesch, ed., *The Middle East and the United States: A Historical and Political Reassessment* (Boulder: Westview Press, 1996), pp. 152–158.

49. Dulles's statement of July 14, 1958. Memorandum of his meeting with Congressional leaders. FRUS 11: 219.

50. Eisenhower's statement of July 14, 1958. FRUS 11: 219–220. Gerges, *The Superpowers and the Middle East*, p. 117; Spiegel, *The Other Arab-Israeli Conflict*, p. 88; Dallek, *The American Style of Foreign Policy*, p. 204.

51. George and Smoke, *Deterrence in American Foreign Policy*, p. 348; Gerges, *The Superpowers and the Middle East*, pp. 116–117. See also Stephen E. Ambrose, "The Presidency and Foreign Policy," in *The Domestic Sources of American Foreign Policy*, p. 154.

52. Eisenhower's statement of July 14, 1958. Memorandum of his meeting with Congressional leaders. FRUS 11: 219. Although the President unequivocally supported the military intervention in Lebanon, Dulles was much more skeptical and circumspect, repeatedly alluding to the dangers inherent in a direct American engagement in the crisis. For example, in his May 13, 1958, conversation with the President, Dulles focused on the adverse implications "of the introduction of American forces" into Lebanon, maintaining that "once our forces were in, it would not be easy to establish a basis upon which they could retire and leave behind an acceptable situation," that the move "might create a wave of anti-Western feelings in the Arab world," and that "it was probable that oil pipelines would be cut in Syria . . . and that the Suez Canal would be closed to American and British shipping. " Dulles's remarks of May 13, 1958. Memorandum of his meeting with Eisenhower. FRUS 11: 47. Although these reservations were set aside by the President, they affected his decision not to intervene in the concurrent Jordanian Crisis, and underscored the need to rely upon "local influentials" in the effort to contain regional instability and radicalism. See also Dulles's remarks (which reflect his concern that "a military response by the West" to the intensifying crisis in Lebanon "would have the effect not of checking Nasserism but of strengthening it") to Lebanese Foreign Minister Charles Malik. Their meeting was held on June 15, 1958. FRUS 11: 131. See also Campbell, *The Defense of the Middle East*, p. 147.

53. Dulles's statement of July 14, 1958. Memorandum of his meeting with Congressional leaders. FRUS 11: 219. See also Gerges, *The Superpowers and the Middle East*, pp. 116–117; Brown, *Faces of Power*, p. 102.

54. Presidential Assistant Sherman Adams's words. Sherman Adams, *First-hand Report: The Story of the Eisenhower Administration* (New York: Harper, 1961), p. 293. See also George and Smoke, *Deterrence in American Foreign Policy*, pp. 353–354.

55. Gerges, *The Superpowers and the Middle East*, pp. 116, 152.

56. Dulles's remarks of July 16, 1958. Memorandum of his July 16, 1958, meeting with Eisenhower. Ann Whitman File, DDE Diary Series, Box 35: Staff Memos, July 1958: 1. On the Syrian decision to close its border with Jordan, see Dulles's remarks at the National Security Council meeting of August 7, 1958. Ann Whitman File, NSC Series, Box 10: 375th meeting of the NSC, DDE Library: 3.

57. Dulles's remarks of July 15, 1958. Quoted from a memorandum of his July 15, 1958, meeting with British Chargé d'Affaires in Washington, Lord Samuel Hood. John Foster Dulles: Papers, 1951–1959. JFD Chronological Series, Box 16: July 1958(1). DDE Library: 1.

58. Ibid., p. 2.

59. Eisenhower's remarks to Dulles. Quoted from a telephone conversation of July 15, 1958. Ann Whitman File, DDE Diary Series, Box 34: Telephone Calls, July 1958: 1. See also Dulles's remarks of July 23, 1958, in the course of his meeting with senior Department of State advisers. FRUS 11: 374–376.

60. Eisenhower's remarks to British Prime Minister Harold Macmillan. Quoted from the report of their July 14, 1958, telephone conversation. Ann Whitman File, DDE Dairy Series, Box 34: Telephone Calls, July 1958: 2. See also Eisenhower's remarks of July 23, 1958, in the course of his meeting with Dulles. FRUS 11: 377.

61. Dulles's remarks of July 14, 1958. Memorandum of his meeting with British Chargé d'Affaires Lord Hood. John Foster Dulles: Papers, 1951–1959. JFD Chronological Series, Box 16: July 1958(1): 1–2. See also Dulles's remarks, of July 19, 1958, to British Foreign Minister Selwyn Lloyd, in the Memorandum of their conversation. FRUS 11: 341.

62. Eisenhower's remarks of July 14, 1958. Memorandum of his conference with several cabinet members and military advisers. Ann Whitman File, DDE Diary Series, Box 35: Staff Memos, July 1958: 5.

63. Lenczowski, *American Presidents and the Middle East*, p. 62; Harold Macmillan, *Riding the Storm, 1956–1959* (London: Macmillan, 1971), pp. 512–528.

64. For a detailed review of the Soviet-Israeli crisis of July 1958, see the letter of August 5, 1958, from Ben-Gurion to Dulles, in FRUS 13, *Arab-Israeli Dispute; United Arab Republic; North Africa, 1958–1960* (Washington, DC: GPO, 1992): 86. See also the memorandum of the conversation of August 3, 1958, between Eban and Dulles. FRUS 11: 426–427.

65. Dulles's remarks of July 14, 1958. Memorandum of the President's conference with several cabinet members and military advisers. Ann Whitman File, DDE Diary Series, Box 35: Staff Memos, July 1958: 1. See also Dowty, *Middle*

East Crisis, p. 55; Gerges, *The Superpowers and the Middle East*, p. 116; Spiegel, *The Other Arab-Israeli Conflict*, p. 89.

66. Gerges, *The Superpowers and the Middle East*, pp. 116–117; Spiegel, *The Other Arab-Israeli Conflict*, p. 89.

67. For evidence, see Dulles's remarks of July 16, 1958. Memorandum of his July 16, 1958, meeting with Eisenhower. Ann Whitman File, DDE Diary Series, Box 35: Staff Memos, July 1958: 1, and Dulles's remarks to Eisenhower in the course of their July 19, 1958, telephone conversation. John Foster Dulles: Papers, 1951–1959. Telephone Calls Series, Box 12: Memorandum of Telephone Conversations, the White House, April 1, 1958, to July 31, 1958(1), DDE Library: 1.

68. Dulles's remarks of July 21, 1958. Memorandum of his conversation with Eban. FRUS 13: 72.

69. Ibid. For an early manifestation of this perception, see Herter's remarks of April 14, 1957, to British Ambassador in Washington, Sir Harold Caccia. Memorandum of conversation. FRUS 13: 93. See also Schoenbaum, *The United States and the State of Israel*, pp. 132–133.

70. Saadia Touval, *Domestic Dynamics of Change from Confrontation to Accommodation Politics* (Princeton: Princeton University Press, 1973), p. 17. See also Abraham Ben-Zvi, "Perception, Misperception and Surprise in the Yom Kippur War: A Look at the New Evidence," *The Journal of Conflict Studies* 15(2) (Fall 1995): 11.

71. Jervis, *The Logic of Images in International Relations*, p. 18.

72. See, on the cognitive dynamics of attitude-change and frame-change, Ben-Zvi, "Perception, Misperception and Surprise," p. 12. See also Farnham, "Roosevelt and the Munich Crisis," pp. 206–227; Daniel Kahneman and Amos Tversky, "On the Psychology of Prediction," *Psychological Review* 80(4) (1973): 241; Yehudit Auerbach, "Turning-Points Decisions: A Cognitive-Dissonance Analysis of Conflict Reduction in Israel-West German Relations," *Political Psychology* 7(3) (September 1986): 538–539; Daniel Kahneman, Paul Slovak, and Amos Tversky, *Judgment Under Uncertainty: Heuristics and Biases* (New York: Cambridge University Press, 1982), *passim*; Jack Levy, "Prospect Theory and International Relations: Theoretical Applications and Analytical Problems," *Political Psychology* 13(2) (June 1992): 294–296; Robert Jervis, "Political Implications of Loss Aversion," *Political Psychology* 13(2) (June 1992): 192–193.

73. "Factors Affecting US Policy Toward the Near East," memorandum submitted, on August 19, 1958, to the NSC by S. Everett Gleason, Acting Executive Secretary of the NSC Planning Board. White House Office, Office of the Special Assistant for National Security Affairs, 1952–1961; NSC Series, Policy Papers Subseries, Box 23: NSC 5801/1: Policy Toward the Near East (1), DDE Library: 6. Italics added. See also "Issues Arising Out of the Situation in the Near East," memorandum submitted, on July 29, 1958, to the NSC by James S. Lay, Jr., Executive Secretary of the NSC Planning Board, in ibid., p. 6. See also Dulles's remarks at the National Security Council meeting of July 24, 1958. Ann Whitman File, NSC Series, Box 10: 373rd meeting of the NSC, DDE Library:

5–6; James Lee Ray, *The Future of American-Israeli Relations: A Parting of the Ways?* (Lexington: The University Press of Kentucky, 1985), p. 14.

74. "Factors Affecting US Policy Toward the Near East," memorandum submitted, on August 19, 1958, to the NSC by S. Everett Gleason: 6.

75. Quoted from Dulles's letter to Ben-Gurion, August 1, 1958. FRUS 13: 78–79. See also Lesch, *Syria and the United States*, pp. 143–144.

76. Dulles's remarks of June 15, 1958. Memorandum of his conversation with Eisenhower. FRUS 11: 136.

77. Eisenhower's remarks of July 16, 1958. Memorandum of his conversation with Dulles. FRUS 11: 310. This view was shared by the Chairman of the Joint Chiefs of Staff, General Nathan F. Twining, who argued that the U.S. should collaborate with Israel and Turkey in a military offensive against Egypt and Syria.

78. Eisenhower's remarks of August 7, 1958, at the National Security Council meeting of August 7, 1958. Ann Whitman File, NSC Series, Box 10: 375th Meeting of the NSC, DDE Library: 4. See also Yossi Melman and Dan Raviv, *Friends in Deed: Inside the U.S.-Israel Alliance* (New York: Hyperion, 1994), pp. 88–89.

79. Dulles's remarks of August 8, 1958. Memorandum of his conversation with British Chargé d'Affaires Lord Hood. FRUS 11: 445.

80. Dulles's remarks of August 12, 1958. Memorandum of his conversation with British Foreign Minister Selwyn Lloyd. FRUS 11: 458. Italics added. For an illustration of the American willingness to consider a more active Israeli role in the Jordanian Crisis, see the memorandum of the meeting of July 14, 1958, between Dulles and the Chairman of the Joint Chiefs of Staff, General Twining. FRUS 11: 210. In the course of the meeting, General Twining alluded to the possibility of an Israeli preemptive move "into West Jordan" as part of a multilateral operation involving the U.S., Britain, Israel and Turkey. FRUS 11: 210. See also Gerges, *The Superpowers and the Middle East*, pp. 116–119.

81. Deputy Undersecretary Murphy's remarks of August 6, 1958. Memorandum (prepared on August 8) of his conversation with President Nasser. FRUS 11: 442.

82. Dulles's remarks. Memorandum of his conversation, of August 21, 1958, with Egyptian Foreign Minister Mahmoud Fawzi. FRUS 11: 507. For a similar deterrence threat, see Dulles's remarks to Soviet Foreign Minister Andrei A. Gromyko, which were made in their August 18, 1958, meeting. FRUS 11: 496–497.

83. Dulles's remarks of October 31, 1958. Memorandum of his conversation with British Ambassador Caccia. FRUS 11: 623.

84. Memorandum of August 22, 1958, by Assistant Secretary of State for Near Eastern and South Asian Affairs, William M. Rowntree, to Dulles. FRUS 13: 90. Similarly, in his August 1, 1958, message to Macmillan, Dulles observed that "up to now the Israelis certainly have been most helpful." FRUS 11: 420. See also Gabriel Sheffer, "Introduction: The United States and the 'Normal-

ization' of the Middle East and Israel," *Israel Affairs* 2(3–4) (Spring/Summer 1996): 5.

85. Dulles's remarks of October 2, 1958. Memorandum of his conversation with Israeli Foreign Minister Golda Meir. FRUS 13: 96.

86. Sheffer, "Introduction," p. 5; Melman and Raviv, *Friends in Deed*, pp. 88–89; Cockburn and Cockburn, *Dangerous Liaison*, pp. 69–70; Eveland, *Ropes of Sand*, p. 240; Ronen Bergman, "The Human Factor," *Ha'aretz*, November 15, 1996, weekly supplement, p. 50. For a review of the circumstances in which the initial ties between the CIA and members of the Israeli diplomatic and intelligence community were established in the early 1950s, see Kollek, *For Jerusalem*, pp. 98–101; Shmuel Cohen-Shany, *Paris Operation: Intelligence and Quiet Diplomacy in a New State* (Hebrew) (Tel-Aviv: Ramot, 1994), *passim*; Schoenbaum, *The United States and the State of Israel*, pp. 132–133; Bialer, *Between East and West*, p. 251. One of the major Israeli contributions in this context was the interception and transfer to the CIA of the full text of Nikita Khrushchev's speech, of February 1956, to the 20th Congress of the Soviet Communist party, which included a massive and unprecedented indictment of Stalin's crimes (see, for example, Schoenbaum, *The United States and the State of Israel*, p. 132).

87. Dulles's remarks of October 2, 1958. Memorandum of his conversation with Israeli Foreign Minister Golda Meir. FRUS 13: 96. See also the memorandum of the conversation of September 10, 1958, between Dulles and Eban. FRUS 13: 91–95. Unlike the situation which had existed between 1953 and July 1956, Israel had, in 1958, alternative sources of arms supply, including France and Britain. See also Little, "The Making of a Special Relationship," p. 566.

88. Dulles's remarks of October 2, 1958. Memorandum of his conversation with Meir. FRUS 13: 96. See also Ball and Ball, *The Passionate Attachment*, p. 51.

89. Eisenhower's remarks of March 10, 1960. Memorandum of his conversation with Ben-Gurion. FRUS 13: 288.

90. Statement of Assistant Secretary of State for Near Eastern and South Asian Affairs, G. Lewis Jones, February 16, 1959. Memorandum of his conversation with Israeli Ambassador Abraham Harman. FRUS 13: 266.

91. Dulles's statement of October 22, 1958, in *Dulles Papers*, Box 132, "Selected Correspondence: The Middle East, 1958" folder: 6. See also Douglas Little, "The Making of a Special relationship," p. 566. For an earlier reference by Dulles as to the need to concentrate on "peripheral areas in the Middle East" in view of the inability to retain influence in the heart of the Arab world, see his telephone conversation of August 23, 1958, with Undersecretary Herter. FRUS 11: 519.

92. Statement of Assistant Secretary of Defense for International Security Affairs Mansfield Sprague, August 8, 1958. Quoted by ibid., p. 566. See also Secretary of State Herter's remarks of September 29, 1959. Memorandum of his conversation with Meir. FRUS 13: 202.

93. Quoted from a memorandum which was sent on July 7, 1960, by Jones to Herter. FRUS 13: 344. See also Gazit, "Israeli Military Procurement," p. 93; Lipson, "American Support for Israel," p. 132.

94. Ben-Gurion's remarks of March 10, 1960. Memorandum of his conversation with Eisenhower. FRUS 13: 287. In the memorandum, which was submitted to Eisenhower on March 17, 1960, Herter summarized his March 13, 1960, meeting with Ben-Gurion without raising any objection to the Israeli request. White House Office, Office of the Staff Secretary, 1952–1961. International Series, Box 8: Israel (2): March–August, 1960. DDE Library: 1.

99. Herter's remarks of March 13, 1960, to Jones. Quoted from a memorandum of their meeting, which followed Herter's meeting with Ben-Gurion. FRUS 13: 299–300.

100. Herter's remarks of July 27, 1960. Memorandum of his meeting with Acting Assistant Secretary of State for Near Eastern and South Asian Affairs, Parker T. Hart, Director of the Office of Near Eastern Affairs, H. Armin Meyer, and Undersecretary of State for Political Affairs, T. Livingston Merchant. FRUS 13: 356.

101. Quoted from a letter which was sent on June 14, 1960, by Deputy Assistant of Defense for International Security Affairs, John A. Dabney, to Deputy Undersecretary of State for Political Affairs, Raymond A. Hare. FRUS 13: 337. See also Herter's remarks at his July 27, 1960, meeting with Acting Assistant Secretary Hart, Director of the Office of Near Eastern Affairs Meyer, and Merchant. FRUS 13: 356.

102. Meyer's remarks of July 27, 1960. Quoted in FRUS 13: 356–357. For similar arguments see Merchant's letter of July 15, 1960, to Herter. FRUS 13: 349–350.

103. Quoted from the July 27, 1960, memorandum drafted by Meyer. FRUS 13: 356.

104. Quoted from FRUS 13: 357.

105. For the text of Herter's letter of August 4, 1960, to Ben-Gurion, see FRUS 13: 358–361.

106. Ibid., p. 359. See also Gazit, "Israeli Military Procurement," p. 93; Michael Bar-Zohar, Ben-Gurion, III (Hebrew) (Tel-Aviv: Am Oved, 1975), p. 1320.

107. For a typical illustration of this line of reasoning in the context of the intragovernmental debate over the Hawk missiles issue see the memorandum of July 15, 1960, by Merchant to Herter. FRUS 13: 349–350. See also the memorandum of July 7, 1960, by Jones to Merchant. FRUS 13: 344–349; Badeau, The American Approach to the Arab World, p.23.

108. See Robert D. Kaplan, The Arabists: The Romance of An American Elite (New York: The Free Press, 1993), passim. For a major illustration of the role of the bureaucracy in the formation of American policy toward Israel, see the memorandum Byroade sent on May 5, 1954, to Dulles. FRUS 9, pt. 1: 1546–1547. See also Dulles's letter of July 27, 1954 to Louis Lipsky, Chairman of the American Zionist Committee for Public Affairs, in Dulles Papers, Box 82, "General Correspondence" folder.

109. For a similar illustration of the role of the bureaucracy in inducing President Franklin D. Roosevelt and Secretary of State Cordell Hull to adopt, in

1940 and 1941, an increasingly coercive policy toward Japan despite their recognition of the dangers of escalation inherent in such a course, see Ben-Zvi, *The Illusion of Deterrence, passim*. Eisenhower's attitude toward Israel and the policy he advocated, as manifested in his remarks of March 1, 1956, to Undersecretary of State Herbert Hoover, Jr., closely resembled President Roosevelt's initial approach toward Japan (which was never implemented). For evidence concerning Eisenhower, see *Dulles Papers*, Box 10, "Subject Series" folder (Undersecretary Hoover's memorandum to Dulles, March 1, 1956).

110. Telhami, *Power and Leadership in International Bargaining*, p. 117.

111. Quoted from a Staff Study on the Near East, drafted on January 16, 1958, as a supplement to NSC 5801, by the Department of State. White House office, Office of the Special Assistant for National Security Affairs: Records, 1952–1961; NSC Series, Policy Papers Subseries, Box 23: NSC 5801/1, Policy Toward the Near East (2): 16.

112. "US Policy Toward the Near East," memorandum of June 17, 1960, to the NSC by James S. Lay, Jr. White House Office, Office of the Special Assistant for National Security Affairs, Records: 1952–1961; NSC Series, Policy Papers Subseries, Box 291, NSC 6011: The Near East: 16.

113. Yaniv, *Deterrence Without the Bomb*, pp. 104–105. See also Amikam Nachmani, "The Politics of Water in the Middle East: The Current Situation, Imaginary and Practical Solutions," in Efraim Inbar, ed., *Regional Security Regimes: Israel and Its Neighbors* (Albany: State University of New York Press, 1995), p. 238.

114. Quoted from a briefing note, which was submitted on July 6, 1960, by James S. Lay, Jr. to the NSC. White House Office, Office of the Special Assistant for National Security Affairs, Records: 1952–1961; Special Assistants Series, Presidential Subseries, Box 5: Meetings with Presidents, 2 Vols., 1960: 3.

115. Dulles's remarks of October 3, 1955. Memorandum of his conversation with the British Chancellor of the Exchequer, Harold Macmillan. FRUS 14: 543.

116. Dulles's remarks of March 30, 1956. Memorandum of his conversation with Senator Walter F. George. *Dulles Papers*, Box 10, "Subject Series" folder: 1–2. See also Badeau, *The American Approach to the Arab World*, p. 21.

117. "Western European Dependence on Middle East Petroleum," memorandum submitted, on June 23, 1960, by James S. Lay, Jr. to the NSC. White House Office, Office of the Special Assistant for National Security Affairs: Records, 152–161, NSC Series, Policy Papers Subseries, Box 26: NSC 5820, Policy Toward the Near East (European Dependence on Middle East Oil) (1): 1–11. See also Ann Whitman File, NSC Series, Box 13: 460th Meeting of the NSC, September 21, 1960: 1–4.

118. Schoenbaum, *The United States and the State of Israel*, p. 127. See also Quandt's analysis of the American electoral cycle, and particularly of the President's *modus operandi* during his first year in office. William B. Quandt, *Camp David: Peacemaking and Politics* (Washington, DC.: The Brookings Institution, 1986), pp. 15–19.

119. George, "Coercive Diplomacy," p. 7.

120. For the term "benign neglect," see Blema S. Steinberg, "American Foreign Policy in the Middle East: A Study in Changing Priorities," in Janice Gross Stein and David B. DeWitt, eds., *The Middle East at the Crossroads* (Oakville, Ontario: Mosaic Press, 1983), pp. 115–116.

121. "U.S. Policy Toward the Near East," memorandum submitted, on June 17, 1960, to the NSC by James S. Lay, Jr. White House Office, Office of the Special Assistant for National Security Affairs, Records: 1952–1961; NSC Series, Policy Papers Subseries, Box 29, NSC 6011: The Near East: 18.

122. Ibid. See also Dulles's remarks of August 6, 1957, to Eban in the memorandum of the conversation. FRUS 17: 706. In addressing the search for peace in the Middle East, Dulles stated that "he had thought at one time that we might be able to find an overall solution to the Palestine problem." However, he added, the problems of the area were of such magnitude that he did not feel hopeful any longer "as to the prospects of an overall early settlement . . . ." Therefore, the Secretary concluded, "we must live with the problems on a crisis-to-crisis basis" (FRUS 17: 706).

123. Vice President Nixon's remarks of March 13, 1960. Memorandum of his conversation with Ben-Gurion. FRUS 13: 296.

124. Eisenhower's remarks of September 21, 1959. Memorandum of his conversation with Lebanese Prime Minister Rashid Karame. FRUS 11: 641.

125. Eisenhower's remarks of December 19, 1960. Memorandum of his meeting with several cabinet members and representatives of the intelligence community. White House Office, Office of the Staff Secretary, 1952–1961. International Series, Box 8, Israel (3): October 1960-January 1961, DDE Library: 3.

126. Quoted from Merchant's message of December 31, 1960, to American Ambassador in Israel, Ogden R. Reid. Ibid., p. 2. The message was also printed in FRUS 13: 399–400.

127. Herter's remarks of December 20, 1960. Memorandum of his conversation with Ambassador Harman. FRUS 13: 397.

128. Quoted from Merchant's message of December 31, 1960, to Ambassador Reid. White House Office, Office of the Staff Secretary, 1952–1961. International Series, Box 8, Israel (3): October 1960-January 1961: 2.

129. Ibid.

130. CIA Director Allen Dulles's remarks of December 19, 1960. Memorandum of the meeting Eisenhower held with several cabinet members and representatives of the intelligence community. White House Office, Office of the Staff Secretary, 1952–1961. International Series, Box 8, Israel (3): October 1960-January 1961: 2.

131. Memorandum which, on December 29, 1960, was sent by the Director of the Executive Secretariat in the Department of State, Walter J. Staessel, Jr., to Staff Secretary and Defense Liaison Officer to the President, Brigadier General Andrew J. Goodpaster. Ibid., p. 1. The fact that the nuclear issue surfaced only one month before the end of Eisenhower's second term evidently contributed to this low-profile approach. See Quandt, *Camp David*, pp. 13–15.

132. Avner Cohen, "Stumbling into Opacity: The United States, Israel, and the Atom, 1960–63," *Security Studies* 4(2) (Winter 1994–1995): 195–196. For a different interpretation see Shlomo Aronson, *The Politics and Strategy of Nuclear Weapons in the Middle East: Opacity, Theory, and Reality, 1960–1991: An Israeli Perspective* (Albany: State University of New York Press, 1992), pp. 71–72.

133. Eisenhower's remarks of December 19, 1960. International Series, Box 8, Israel (3): October 1960–January 1961: 2.

134. Quoted from the Department of State's press announcement of December 21, 1960. International Series, Box 8, Israel (3): October 1960-January 1961: 3.

135. For a comprehensive analysis of this strategy see Jervis, *The Logic of Images in International Relations*, pp. 179–187. See also Alexander L. George, "The Causal Nexus Between Cognitive Beliefs and Decision-Making Behavior: The 'Operational Code' Belief System," in Laurence S. Falkowski, ed., *Psychological Models in International Politics* (Boulder: Westview Press, 1979), pp. 101–102.

136. Reid's remarks of December 24, 1960. Memorandum of his conversation with Ben-Gurion, of December 24, 1960, to Herter. White House Office, Office of the Staff Secretary, 1952–1961. International Series, Box 8, Israel (3): October 1960–January 1961: 4. See also Aronson, *The Politics and Strategy*, p. 71.

137. Reid's remarks of December 24, 1960: 1. See also Cohen, "The United States, Israel, and the Atom," pp. 202–208; Seymour M. Hersh, *The Samson Options: Israel's Nuclear Arsenal and American Foreign Policy* (New York: Random House, 1991), pp. 62–69.

138. Rubin, *Secrets of State*, pp. 89–90.

139. Little, "The Making of a Special relationship," p. 567.

140. Quoted from Herter's letter of August 4, 1960, to Ben-Gurion. FRUS 13: 359.

141. On April 22, 1959, a group of pro-Israeli Senators met with Herter in an effort to persuade him to reconsider the decision to eliminate the line item of $7.5 million of grant aid to Israel from the Mutual Security Program. Herter, however, remained unmoved, and insisted that the decision "was not a political decision . . . and was based upon economic considerations." Quoted from the April 22, 1959, memorandum of the conversation. FRUS 13: 169. See also Kenen, *Israel's Defense Line*, p. 144.

142. Burns, *Economic Aid and American Policy*, pp. 20, 21.

143. Ibid., p. 21. See also Spiegel, *The Other Arab-Israeli Conflict*, p. 60; Stephen D. Isaacs, *Jews in American Politics* (Garden City: Doubleday, 1974), p. 152.

144. Burns, *Economic Aid and American Policy*, p. 118.

145. Kenen, *Israel's Defense Line*, p. 141; Spiegel, *The Other Arab-Israeli Conflict*, p. 90.

146. Kenen, *Israel's Defense Line*, p. 141. For several additional illustrations (albeit of a less specific nature) see Miles Copeland, *Without Cloak or Dagger* (New York: Simon and Schuster, 1974), pp. 52–53.

Chapter 4: The United States and Israel, 1961–1962:
Convergence Dominates

1. See, for example, Gazit, *President Kennedy's Policy Toward the Arab States and Israel*, pp. 33–35; Nadelmann, "American Policy Toward the Middle East, 1961–1966," pp. 436–437; Tivnan, *The Lobby*, pp. 52–53.

2. Kenen, *Israel's Defense Line*, p. 106; Sharett, *Personal Diary*, 1 (1953–1954): 292.

3. Dulles's remarks of February 10, 1956. Memorandum of his conversation with Eban. FRUS 15: 166.

4. Dulles's remarks of February 20, 1956. Memorandum of his conversation with Eban. FRUS 15: 278. These activities of the organized representatives of the special relationship paradigm were designed to change the administration's arms sale policy and thus to supply arms to Israel.

5. Dulles's telephone conversation of February 13, 1957, with Congressman John M. Vorys. *Dulles Papers*, Box 6, "Telephone Conversations" folder: 1. See also the Secretary's telephone conversation of February 19, 1957, with Dr. Rosewell Barnes, *Dulles Papers*, Box 6, "Telephone Conversations" folder: 1; Ben-Zvi, *The Limits of the Special Relationship*, p. 73. Note that this initial view was significantly modified during Eisenhower's second term. Thus, in July 1958, Dulles asked Eban to impress upon his friends at the top of the AZC the need to convince their allies in Congress to lend their support for the administration's posture of intervention in Lebanon. Whereas, during its first term the administration profoundly resented many of the lobbying activities of the AZC and other Jewish organizations and questioned their legitimacy, it now came around— under a revised regional setting—to openly request the backbone of the special relationship paradigm to use its leverage over Congress in order to promote its strategy in Lebanon. As Melman and Raviv note, this was "only the first of many occasions on which a U.S. administration would ask pro-Israel lobbyists— the only powerful group that cares about foreign aid and events abroad—to help with a non-Israel issue." Melman and Raviv, *Friends in Deed*, pp. 88–89.

6. Kenen, *Israel's Defense Line*, p. 109.

7. The article was written by Roscoe Drummond and was published on June 6, 1962, in *The Washington Post*.

8. Quoted from a memorandum of June 29, 1962, by the Department of State Executive Secretary, William H. Brubeck, and the President's Special Assistant for National Security Affairs, McGeorge Bundy. FRUS 17: *The Near East, 1961–1962* (Washington, DC.: United States Government Printing Office, 1994): 760.

9. Ibid., p. 760. After further consultations with the President's Special Assistant for National Security Affairs, McGeorge Bundy, the Department of State decided not to pursue the matter with Harman. See also Lee Riley Powell, *J. William Fulbright and his Time* (Memphis: Guild Binding Press, 1996), p. 372.

10. "Trends in Israel's Policy Toward the Arabs." Paper of November 10, 1953, from the Bureau of Near Eastern, South Asian, and African Affairs, in FRUS 9, pt. 1: 1407–1408.

11. Paper entitled "Conference Conclusions on the Danger of Arab-Israeli Tensions and Recommended Line of US Action," summarizing the conference of the U.S. Chiefs of Mission in the Middle East, held in Istanbul, May 11–May 14, 1954. The paper was drafted on May 14, 1954. FRUS 9, pt. 1: 1562. See also the memorandum of the conversation of July 16, 1954, between Byroade and Eban. FRUS 9, pt. 1: 1588–1590.

12. Memorandum of March 28, 1962, by Rusk, to Kennedy, entitled "Security Council Consideration of Syrian and Israeli Complaints." FRUS 17: 552.

13. Memorandum of April 11, 1962, from United Nations Adviser Ludlow to Talbot, entitled "Lake Tiberias." FRUS 17: 588. See also Little, "The Making of a Special Relationship," p. 568; Dean Rusk, As I Saw It (New York: Norton, 1990), p. 380.

14. Quoted from Rusk's March 28, 1962, memorandum to Kennedy. FRUS 17: 552. See also Spiegel, The Other Arab-Israeli Conflict, p. 380; Rusk, As I Saw It, pp. 380–381; Nadelmann, "American Policy Toward the Middle East, 1961–1966," p. 436; Little, "The Making of a Special Relationship," p. 568; Cheryl A. Rubenberg, Israel and the American National Interest: A Critical Examination (Urbana: University of Illinois, 1986), p. 92.

15. Alteras, Eisenhower and Israel, p. 86. See also Schoenbaum, The United States and the State of Israel, pp. 78, 94; Sharett, Personal Diary, 6 (1956): 1534–1536; Gazit, President Kennedy's Policy Toward the Arab States and Israel, p. 37.

16. FRUS 17: 42 (an editorial note). See also the memorandum of July 13, 1961, from Rusk to Kennedy. FRUS 17: 188, as well as the memorandum entitled "United States Position on Jerusalem," of May 31, 1962, from Lucius D. Battle, Special Assistant to Secretary of State Rusk, to McGeorge Bundy. FRUS 17: 688–691.

17. Byroade's remarks of November 7,1953. Memorandum of his conversation with Eban. FRUS 9, pt. 1: 1047.

18. Memorandum from Robert W. Komer, a senior staff member of the National Security Council, to Kennedy on January 15, 1962. FRUS 17: 402.

19. Ibid., p. 402. See also the memorandum of January 23, 1962, from Komer to Kennedy. FRUS 17: 438. See also Gazit, President Kennedy's Policy Toward the Arab States and Israel, pp. 16–17; Copeland, The Game of Nations, pp. 222–223.

20. See the memorandum of January 23, 1962, from Komer to Kennedy. FRUS 17: 438. See also the memorandum of January 10, 1962, from Rusk to Kennedy entitled "Action Program for the United Arab Republic." FRUS 17: 384–389; Komer's January 15, 1962, memorandum to Kennedy, in FRUS 17: 402; Spiegel, The Other Arab-Israeli Conflict, p. 102; Nadelmann, "American Policy Toward the Middle East, 1961–1966," p. 438; Little, "The Making of a Special Relationship," p. 568; Douglas Little, "The New Frontier on the Nile: JFK, Nasser, and Arab Nationalism," Journal of American History 75(1) (June 1988): 505–509; Schoenbaum, The United States and the State of Israel, pp. 132–133; Lenczowski, American Presidents and the Middle East, pp. 76–77. It should be emphasized

that in 1962, as much as one-third of the UAR's wheat consumption came from the PL-480 program.

21. Memorandum of December 8, 1961, from Komer to McGeorge Bundy entitled "A Shift in Policy Toward Nasser." FRUS 17: 360. See also the December 6, 1961, message from Rusk to American Ambassador in Cairo, John S. Badeau. FRUS 17: 356–359, and the memorandum of May 30, 1961, from Talbot to the Chairman of the Policy Planning Council in the Department of State, George C. McGee. FRUS 17: 142–145.

22. Byroade's remarks of May 11, 1953. Memorandum of his conversation with the Egyptian leadership FRUS 9, pt. 1: 14.

23. Memorandum of December 8, 1961, from Komer to McGeorge Bundy. FRUS 17: 362. See also Copeland, *The Game of Nations*, p. 223.

24. Memorandum of May 30, 1961, from Talbot to George C. McGee. FRUS 17: 143.

25. John S. Badeau, *The Middle East Remembered* (Washington, D.C., The Middle East Institute, 1983), p. 177; Kaufman, *The Arab Middle East and the United States*, p. 32. These overtures toward the UAR infuriated Saudi Arabia, which— in 1961—refused to renew the Pentagon's lease on the Dhahran airbase. Freiberger, *Dawn Over Suez*, p. 168. See also Komer's memorandum of May 28, 1962, to Kennedy. FRUS 17: 686. It is interesting to note that during the years 1946–1960, the total amount of U.S. aid to Egypt amounted to $254 million.

26. Memorandum of December 8, 1961 from Komer to McGeorge Bundy. FRUS 17: 362. See also Schoenbaum, *The United States and the State of Israel*, p. 134.

27. Memorandum of January 10, 1962, from Rusk to Kennedy. FRUS 17: 387.

28. Memorandum of May 30, 1961, from Talbot to George C. McGee. FRUS 17: 143.

29. Memorandum of December 8, 1961, from Komer to McGeorge Bundy. FRUS 17: 362. See also Rusk, *As I Saw It*, pp. 379–380; Gerges, *The Superpowers and the Middle East*, p. 155; Patchen, *Resolving Disputes Between Nations*, p. 133; Schoenbaum, *The United States and the State of Israel*, p. 134.

30. Quoted from Rusk's message of January 10, 1962, to Kennedy. FRUS 17: 386.

31. Quoted from Komer's message of June 30, 1961, to the President's Deputy Special Assistant for National Security Affairs, Walt W. Rostow. FRUS 17: 173. Italics added.

32. Quoted by Nadelmann, "American Policy Toward the Middle East, 1961–1966," p. 438. See also Lenczowski, *American Presidents and the Middle East*, p. 84. It should be emphasized that these accommodative premises remained essentially intact despite the bombardment of the Saudi border cities of Najran and Jizan by UAR's high-altitude bombers. The crisis itself unfolded after Colonel Abdellah al-Sallal and a group of Yemeni officers sympathetic to Nasser overthrew, on September 26, 1962, Imam Mohammad al-Badr and proclaimed a republic in Yemen. After Sallal had requested Nasser's support in combating al-Badr's insurgents (who were supported by Saudi Arabia), the UAR

sent to Yemen, in October 1962, an expedition force totaling 70,000 troops. See, on the Yemeni intervention, Freiberger, *Dawn Over Suez*, p. 170; Spiegel, *The Other Arab-Israeli Conflict*, pp. 102–106.

33. Lenczowski, *American Presidents and the Middle East*, p. 89.

34. Fawaz, A. Gerges, "The Kennedy Administration and the Egyptian-Saudi Conflict in Yemen: Co-Opting Arab Nationalism," *Middle East Journal* 49(2) (Spring 1995): 294.

35. Quoted from Senator Kennedy's address of March 23, 1960, at the Jewish Center in Milwaukee, Wisconsin. Papers of Kennedy (hereafter PPK), Pre-Presidential papers, Senate Files, Speeches and the Press, Box 907: Speeches Files, 1953–1960: 14. John F. Kennedy Presidential library, Boston (JFKL).

36. Ibid., pp. 14–15. See also Brown, *The Faces of Power*, p. 148; Burns, *Economic Aid and American Policy Toward Egypt*, p. 123; Brown, *The Faces of Power*, pp. 145–147; Lenczowski, *American Presidents and the Middle East*, pp. 69–70; Spiegel, *The Other Arab-Israeli Conflict*, p. 98; Gerges, *The Superpowers and the Middle East*, p. 155; Kaufman, *The Arab Middle East and the United States*, pp. 31–32; Little, "The New Frontier on the Nile," pp. 502–503. An early illustration of this accommodative attitude toward President Nasser and Arab nationalism was Senator Kennedy's support of Nasser's decision to nationalize the Suez Canal. Kennedy interpreted the decision as a "revolt in the Middle East against Western Colonialism;" Little, "From Even-Handed to Empty-Handed," p. 158.

37. Gerges, *The Superpowers and the Middle East*, p. 155. See also Kennedy's address at La Grande, Oregon, November 9, 1959, in John F. Kennedy, *The Strategy of Peace* (New York: Harper and Row, 1960), p. 107.

38. Memorandum of May 25, 1961, from Rusk to Kennedy. PPK, President's Office Files (hereafter POF), Box 119a: Ben-Gurion's visit of May 30, 1961: 1.

39. Komer's remarks of October 17, 1962. Memorandum of his conversation with the Minister of the Israeli Embassy in Washington, Mordechai Gazit. PPK, National Security Files (hereafter NSF), Box 119: Israel, General: 2. See also Schoenbaum, *The United States and Israel*, p. 133; Douglas Little, "A Fool's Errand: America and the Middle East, 1961–1969," in Diane Kunz, ed., *The Diplomacy of the Crucial Decade: American Foreign Relations During the 1960s* (New York: Columbia University Press, 1994), p. 288.

40. Anthony Rusonik, "Israeli Defense Doctrine and US Middle East Diplomacy: From Suez to the Loan Guarantees/Settlements Dispute," *The Jerusalem Journal of International Relations* 14(2) (September 1992): 52.

41. Kennedy's remarks of December 27, 1962. Memorandum of his conversation with Foreign Minister Meir. PPK, NSF, Box 118: Israel, General: 5. See also Komer's message of June 30, 1961, to Deputy Special Assistant Rostow. FRUS 17: 173; Walt, *The Origins of Alliances*, p. 96.

42. Lipson, "American Support for Israel," p. 135.

43. Quoted from Rusk's message of January 10, 1962, to Kennedy. FRUS 17: 386.

44. Quoted from Komer's message of January 15, 1962, to Kennedy. FRUS 17: 402.

45. Schoenbaum, *The United States and the State of Israel,* p. 137.

46. Kennedy's remarks of December 27, 1962. Memorandum of his conversation with Meir. PPK, NSF, Box 118 Israel, General: 6. Italics added. See also Little, "The Making of a Special Relationship," p. 568; Spiegel, *The Other Arab-Israeli Conflict,* p. 110; Walt, *The Origins of Alliances,* p. 95.

47. The assessment of the Defense Intelligence Agency was included in a memorandum of May 23, 1962, by Deputy Assistant Secretary of Defense for International Security Affairs, William P. Bundy, to Talbot. PPK, NSF, Box 118: Israel, General: 3. See also Gazit, *President Kennedy's Policy Toward the Arab States and Israel,* p. 41; Badeau, *The Middle East Remembered,* p. 176.

48. Memorandum of June 17, 1962, from Acting Assistant Secretary of State for Near Eastern and South Asian Affairs, James P. Grant, to Rusk. FRUS 17: 735. See also the paper entitled "Israel and United States Policy," drafted by the Director of the Office of Research and Analysis for Near East and South Asia in the Bureau of Intelligence and Research, Department of State. The paper was attached to the memorandum of June 7, 1962, from Assistant Secretary Talbot to Rusk. FRUS 17: 716. See also Gazit, "Israeli Military Procurement," p. 96.

49. Memorandum of June 17, 1962, from Grant to Rusk. FRUS 17: 736. See also Matti Golan, *Shimon Peres: A Biography* (London: Weidenfeld and Nicolson, 1982), p. 120.

50. Memorandum of June 10, 1962, from Rusk to Talbot. FRUS 17: 719.

51. On Nasser's July 21, 1962, proclamation, see Aluf Ben, "Missiles in the Nudist Beach," *Ha'aretz,* December 19, 1996, p. 2B. See also, on the UAR's missile program, Schoenbaum, *The Untied States and the State of Israel,* p. 138.

52. George, "Strategies for Facilitating Cooperation," p. 705. See also the remarks of Deputy Special Assistant for National Security Affairs, Carl Kaysen, which were made in his conversation of October 2, 1962, with Harman. PPK, NSF, Box 119: Israel, General: 3.

53. Quoted from Senator Kennedy's Cleveland address of February 24, 1957. *John F. Kennedy on Israel, Zionism and Jewish Issues* (New York: Herzl Press, 1965), p. 26.

54. Ibid. See also Senator Kennedy's Oregon address of November 9, 1959, in ibid., p. 49.

55. Quoted from Kennedy's letter of May 11, 1961, to President Nasser. FRUS 17: 112.

56. Memorandum entitled "Arab Refugees," of May 25, 1961, from Rusk to Kennedy. PPK, NSF, Box 119a: Israel, General: 1. For a comprehensive review of the traditional American position, on the basis of which the Johnson Plan was later delineated, see the memorandum of July 2, 1957, from Assistant Secretary of State for International Organization Affairs, Francis O. Wilcox, to Dulles, entitled "Detailed Review of the Palestine Refugee Problem." FRUS 17 (1955–1957): 661–677.

57. Memorandum entitled "Arab Refugees," of May 25, 1961, from Rusk to Kennedy. PPK, NSF, Box 119a: Israel, General: 2.

58. Kennedy's remarks of May 30, 1961. Memorandum of his May 30,

1961, conversation with Ben-Gurion. FRUS 17: 140. See also Gazit, *President Kennedy's Policy Toward the Arab States and Israel*, p. 18.

59. Ben-Gurion's remarks of May 30, 1961. Memorandum of his May 30, 1961, conversation with Kennedy. FRUS 17: 140. See also the memorandum of April 28, 1961, from Acting Secretary of State Chester B. Bowles to Kennedy. FRUS 17: 140, and the message of August 9, 1961, from Acting Secretary of State for Near Eastern and South Asian Affairs Armin H. Meyer, to Rusk. FRUS 17: 221.

60. Spiegel, *The Other Arab-Israeli Conflict*, p. 112.

61. Johnson's remarks of March 14, 1962. Memorandum of his conversation with William R. Crawford of the Bureau of Near Eastern and South Asian Affairs. FRUS 17: 526. See also Spiegel, *The Other Arab-Israeli Conflict*, p. 112.

62. Quoted from *The Johnson Plan: Considerations for the United States*. PPK, NSF, Box 118: Israel, General: 5.

63. Johnson's remarks of August 7, 1962. Memorandum of his conversation with Talbot. FRUS 17: 709. See also Spiegel, *The Other Arab-Israeli Conflict*, pp. 112–113; Gazit, *President Kennedy's Policy Toward the Arab States and Israel*, p. 40; Little, "From Even-Handed to Empty-Handed," p. 164.

64. Spiegel, *The Other Arab-Israeli Conflict*, p. 113.

65. See Johnson's remarks of August 7, 1962, to Talbot. FRUS 17: 708.

66. Ibid.

67. Quoted from Rusk's memorandum of May 25, 1961, to Kennedy. PPK, President's office Files, Box 119a: Israel's Security, Ben-Gurion's Visit: 1–2.

68. William Bundy's remarks. Memorandum of his May 23, 1962, conversation with Israeli Deputy Defense Minister Shimon Peres, which was sent to Talbot. PPK, NSF, Box 118: Israel, General: 3. See also Hersh, *The Samson Option*, p. 110.

69. Spiegel, *The Other Arab-Israeli Conflict*, pp. 114–115. See also Little, "America and the Middle East, 1961–1969," p. 288.

70. Quoted from Ben-Gurion's letter to Kennedy, of June 24, 1962. FRUS 17: 753–754. Italics added. See also the memorandum of June 17, 1962, from Grant to Rusk. FRUS 17: 734–736.

71. Quoted from Talbot's memorandum of August 9, 1962, to Deputy Special Counsel Feldman. FRUS 18: *The Near East, 1962–1963* (Washington DC.: United States Government Printing Office, 1995): 51–52. The Department of State's preference of a bargaining strategy consisting of a concurrent tradeoff between "an American gesture toward Israel," and "certain Israeli concessions" was not confined to the Hawk sale. For evidence concerning the Department's basic bargaining approach (from which the above citation was taken), see the memorandum of June 1, 1962, from Komer to McGeorge Bundy. FRUS 17: 691.

72. Quoted from Feldman's message of August 10, 1962, which was submitted to Kennedy. PPK, NSF, Box 118: Israel, General: 1.

73. Ibid. Italics added.

74. Quoted from Kennedy's letter of August 15, 1962, to Ben-Gurion. PPK, NSF, Box 118: Israel, General: 1–2.

75. Quoted from a White House Conference on the Johnson Plan, August 15, 1962. FRUS 18: 56–57. Italics added. See also Cockburn and Cockburn, *Dangerous Liaison*, p. 126.

76. Quoted from the report submitted from Deputy Special Counsel Feldman on August 19, 1962, to Kennedy. PPK, NSF, Box 118: Israel, General: 2. See also Feldman's report of his August 19, 1962, conversation with Ben-Gurion, in a message sent by the American Embassy in Israel to the Department of State on August 19, 162. FRUS 18: 64–66.

77. Quoted from the report submitted by Feldman on August 19, 1962, to Kennedy. PPK, NSF, Box 118: Israel, General: 2. Portions of this report were incorporated into Rusk's message of August 22, 1962, to Badeau in Cairo. See PPK, NSF, Box 118: Israel, General.

78. Harman's remarks of October 2, 1962. Memorandum of his conversation with Kaysen. PPK, NSF, Box 119: Israel, General. See also Herbert S. Parmet, *JFK: The Presidency of John F. Kennedy* (New York: Dial Press, 1983), pp. 225–226.

79. Kaysen's remarks of October 2, 1962. Quoted from ibid., p. 3. Italics added. See also Komer's memorandum of October 2, 1962, to Kennedy. FRUS 18: 152–154.

80. Komer's remarks of October 17, 1962. Memorandum of his conversation with Gazit. PPK, NSF, Box 119: Israel, General: 3. Earlier, on September 22, 1962, in a message to Deputy Special Assistant Kaysen, Komer stated: "As I see it, Israel—having gotten its Hawks—is making an all-out effort to sink the Johnson Plan." FRUS 18: 122. See also Schoenbaum, *The United States and the State of Israel*, p. 137.

81. Kennedy's remarks of December 27, 1962. Memorandum of his conversation with Meir. PPK, NSF, Box 118: Israel, General: 6. See also Shoenbaum, *The United States and the State of Israel*, p. 137. On the theoretical implications of the failure of this strategy of reciprocity (or tit-for-tat), see Patchen, *Resolving Disputes Between Nations*, p. 285.

82. Foreign Minister Meir's remarks of December 27, 1962, in PPK, NSF, Box 118: Israel, General: 4. Equally abortive was the administration's effort to mobilize such prominent representatives of the special relationship paradigm as Label Katz, President of B'nai B'rith, and Rabbi Irving Miller, President of the Conference of Presidents of Major American Jewish Organizations, in support of the Johnson Plan. For evidence on this initiative see the memorandum of the conversation of March 14, 1962, between Joseph Johnson and William R. Crawford, Jr. of the Bureau of Near Eastern and South Asian Affairs in the Department of State. FRUS 17: 526. See also Little, "From Even-Handed to Empty-Handed," pp. 169–177.

83. For evidence on the position of the Arab states concerning the Johnson Plan, see Rusk, *As I Saw It*, pp. 382–383. See also Gazit, *President Kennedy's Policy Toward the Arab States and Israel*, p. 40; Spiegel, *The Other Arab-Israeli Conflict*, pp. 115–116. For a review of the Israeli decision of September 16, 1962, to reject the Johnson Plan, see editorial note, FRUS 18: 118–119. For an equally irrec-

oncilable Israeli statement, see Rusk's report of his September 26, 1962, meeting with Meir. FRUS 18: 131–136.

84. George, "Strategies for Facilitating Cooperation," p. 703.

85. Quoted from Rusk's letter of January 29, 1963, to Ben-Gurion. PPK, NSF, Box 119: Israel, General: 1. See also Nadelmann, "American Policy Toward the Middle East, 1961–1966," p. 454.

86. Memorandum, "Arab Refugees," of March 28,1963, from Rusk to Kennedy. FRUS 18: 438–439.

87. Memorandum, "Israeli Opposition to the Johnson Plan," of September 20 1962, from Talbot to Rusk. FRUS 18: 114–115.

88. Ben-Gurion's remarks of June 2, 1961. Memorandum of his conversation with Adlai E. Stevenson, the US Representative to the United Nations. FRUS 17: 150. See also Johnson's remarks of September 29, 1961, to Talbot. FRUS 17: 264–265.

89. Quoted from Ben-Gurion's message of June 24, 1962, to Kennedy. FRUS 17: 753.

90. On November 6, 1961, the Israeli Knesset adopted "a refugee resolution," which ruled out the possibility that some of the Palestinian refugees would be permitted to return to Israeli territory. For a discussion of the resolution and its possible repercussions on the Johnson mission, see the memorandum of the conversation of November 14, 1961, between Harman and Talbot. FRUS 17: 327–329.

91. Memorandum, "The Johnson Plan," of September 30, 1962, from Talbot to Rusk. FRUS 18: 146–148. See also Walt, *The Origins of Alliances*, pp. 238–239.

92. Spiegel, *The Other Arab-Israeli Conflict*, p. 113. See also McGeorge Bundy, *Danger and Survival: Choices About the Bomb in the First Fifty Years* (New York: Random House, 1988), p. 510.

93. See Cohen, "Stumbling Into Opacity," pp. 218–219; Zaki Shalom, "Kennedy, Ben-Gurion and the Dimona Project, 1962–1963," *Israel Studies* 1(1) (Spring 1996): 9; Schoenbaum, *The United States and the State of Israel*, p. 137. For a somewhat different interpretation, see Hersh, *The Samson Option*, p. 110; Aronson, *The Politics and Strategy of Nuclear Weapons*, p. 72.

94. Kennedy's remarks of December 27, 1962. Memorandum of his conversation with Meir. PPK, NSF, Box 118: Israel, General: 8. See also Cohen, "Stumbling Into Opacity," pp. 196–197.

95. Avner Cohen, "Israel's Nuclear History: The Untold Kennedy-Eshkol Dimona Correspondence," *Journal of Israeli History* 12(2) (1995): 161; 172–173; Gazit, "Israeli Military Procurement," p. 96.

96. Kennedy's remarks of May 30, 1961. Memorandum of his conversation with Ben-Gurion. FRUS 17: 135. See also Zaki Shalom, "The Reaction of the Western Powers to Reports about the Construction of a Nuclear Reactor in Dimona," *Studies in Zionism, the Yishuv and the State of Israel* (Hebrew) 4 (1994): 170. See also Hersh, *The Samson Option*, p. 102.

97. Ben-Gurion's remarks of May 30, 1961. Memorandum of his conversa-

tion with Kennedy. FRUS 17: 135. See also Cohen, "Stumbling Into Opacity," *passim;* Shalom, "The Reaction of the Western Powers," p. 172.

98. Avner Cohen, "Most Favored Nation," *Bulletin of the Atomic Scientists* (January-February 1995): 52.

99. The British views were referred to in a memorandum of March 29, 1962, from Talbot to the First Secretary of the British Embassy in Washington, Denis Speares. Shalom, "The Reaction of the Western Powers," p. 169. See also Hersh, *The Samson Option,* pp. 110–111; Cockburn and Cockburn, *Dangerous Liaison,* pp. 88–89.

100. Memorandum, "Consequences of Israel's Acquisition of Nuclear Capability," of March 6, 1963, from Sherman Kent, Chairman of the Board of National Estimates in the Central Intelligence Agency (CIA), to the Director of Central Intelligence Agency, John A. McCone. FRUS 18: 399–40.

101. Shalom, "Kennedy, Ben-Gurion and the Dimona Project," p. 10. See also the message of July 7, 1963, from Rusk to Badeau. FRUS 18: 635; Little, "The Making of a Special Relationship," p. 570. Although this book is confined to the period 1953–1962, the discussion of the nuclear issue in American-Israeli relations covers certain developments that took place in 1963, and that were patterned on, or inextricably related to, earlier policies and actions.

102. Cohen, "Israel's Nuclear History," pp. 174–175. See also Zaki Shalom, "The Kennedy Administration and its Attitude Toward Israel's Nuclear Activity, 1962–1963," *Studies in Zionism, the Yishuv and the State of Israel* (Hebrew) 5 (1995): 133–134. In his letter of May 27, 1963, to Kennedy, Ben-Gurion proposed "annual visits to Dimona," which should be started in late 1963 or early 1964 (Cohen, "Israel's Nuclear History," p. 167).

103. Quoted from Kennedy's May 18, 1963, letter to Ben-Gurion. FRUS 18: 543–544. See also Shalom, "The Kennedy Administration," pp. 133–134. Earlier, in his unplanned meeting with Israeli Deputy Defense Minister Shimon Peres, of April 5, 1963, the President stated that the U.S. "was very, very concerned about any proliferation of nuclear weapons and that he, the President, would strongly hope that Israel would not develop or obtain this kind of weaponry." (Quoted from a memorandum of a telephone conversation between Feldman and Talbot, in which Feldman briefed Talbot of Peres's meeting with Kennedy. FRUS 18: 451). See also Rusk's message of May 10, 1963, to American Ambassador in Israel, Walworth Barbour, in which he defined the nuclear issue "as vital to peace and stability in the Middle East." FRUS 18: 525; Cohen, "Israel's Nuclear History," p. 166; Shalom, "Kennedy, Ben-Gurion and the Dimona Project," pp. 13–17.

104. Quoted from Kennedy's June 15, 1963, letter to Ben-Gurion. As a result of Ben-Gurion's resignation of the following day, the message was delivered to his successor, Levi Eshkol, three weeks later, on July 5, 1963, with minor modifications. FRUS 18: 592–593. See also Shalom, "The Kennedy Administration," pp. 140–141; Yitzhak Latz, "The Dimona Crisis," *Ma'ariv* (Hebrew), July 15, 1996, pp. 31–32. The article is based on an interview with Avner Cohen, who has studied the nuclear dimension in American-Israeli relations.

105. Quoted from Kennedy's June 15, 1963, letter to Ben-Gurion. FRUS 18: 592–593. See also Shalom, "Kennedy, Ben-Gurion and the Dimona Project," pp. 13–16; Latz, "The Dimona Crisis," p. 32.

106. In his May 14, 1963, meeting with Gazit, Komer acknowledged that "instead of continuing this kind of arm's length debate, with the risk of injured feelings on both sides, it might be better to begin some form of a quiet dialogue on the diplomatic level, which could encompass all issues of mutual concern. Among these were the possible repercussions of a change of regime in Jordan, the current Arab-Israeli arms balance and prospective changes, and the question of advanced weapons, as well as Ben-Gurion's request for a defense pact and further conventional arms." FRUS 18: 537. See also Latz, "The Dimona Crisis," p. 32.

107. Talbot's words. Quoted from his message of May 20, 1963, to Badeau. FRUS 18: 545.

108. Kennedy's words. Memorandum of his June 15, 1963, meeting with CIA Director McCone, Talbot and Komer. FRUS 18: 590. Italics added.

109. Komer's words of April 27, 1963. Memorandum of a meeting with the President, which was attended by Secretary of Defense Robert S. McNamara, and Special Assistant McGeorge Bundy. FRUS 18: 485.

110. Shalom, "Kennedy, Ben-Gurion and the Dimona Project," p. 20. In his message of September 10, 1963, to Kennedy, Rusk acknowledged that Prime Minister Eshkol had "gone at least part way to meet our request for adequate inspection of Dimona." FRUS 18: 700. See also Cohen, "Israel's Nuclear History," p. 181.

111. For an illustration of the administration's thinking on the matter, see an undated memorandum, prepared by the working group on arms limitation in the Middle East. FRUS 18: 563–568. See also Little, "The Making of a Special Relationship," p. 572; Yair Evron, *Israel's Nuclear Dilemma* (London: Routledge, 1994), p. 149; Shalom, "Kennedy, Ben-Gurion and the Dimona Project," p. 16.

112. Cohen, "Israel's Nuclear History," pp. 186–187. See also Gazit, *President Kennedy's Policy Toward the Arab States and Israel*, pp. 49–53.

113. Komer's words. Quoted from his message of July 23, 1963, to Kennedy, in which he acknowledged that "Nasser balked at the idea to sign on to a nuclear missile scheme." FRUS 18: 650. See also Komer's message of July 3, 1963, to Kennedy. FRUS 18: 623–624, and Kennedy's remarks of July 23, 1963. In the course of a White House conference which dealt with the issues of arms control and security guarantees to Israel, the President stated that had Nasser agreed to any kind of arms limitation arrangements, this would have "put pressure on the Israelis." FRUS 18: 660.

114. Aronson, *The Politics and Strategy of Nuclear Weapons*, p. 79; See also Latz, "The Dimona Crisis," p. 32; Evron, *Israel's Nuclear Dilemma*, p. 150.

115. Komer's words. Quoted from his message of July 23, 1963, to Kennedy. FRUS 18: 651.

116. Komer's words. Quoted from his memorandum of July 23, 1963, to

Kennedy, in which he summarized the position of the Department of State. FRUS 18: 650–651.

117. Quoted from a memorandum, of September 20, 1963, from Undersecretary of State George W. Ball, to McGeorge Bundy. FRUS 18: 706.

118. Quoted from a Department of State memorandum entitled "Israel's Security Guarantee," which was attached to Undersecretary Ball's memorandum of September 20, 1963, to McGeorge Bundy. FRUS 18: 707.

Chapter 5: Epilogue

1. Walt, *The Origins of Alliances*, p. 39. See also Rusonik, "Israeli Defense Doctrine and US Middle East Diplomacy," p. 47; Haas, "Epistemic Communities," p. 1.

2. See, on the Gruening Amendment, the memorandum of April 30, 1963, from Komer, to McGeorge Bundy. FRUS 18: 503–504. See also Walt, *The Origins of Alliances*, p. 38.

3. Kennedy's remarks. Quoted from the May 1, 1963, White House staff meeting. FRUS 18: 505.

4. Komer's words. Memorandum of his November 21, 1963, conversation with Gazit. FRUS 18: 798.

5. Walt, *The Origins of Alliances*, p. 254.

6. Ben-Zvi, *The Limits of the Special Relationship*, p. 81; Bard, *The Water's Edge and Beyond*, pp. 194–197.

7. Henry Kissinger, *White House Years* (Boston: Little, Brown, 1979), pp. 559–560.

8. Ibid., pp. 559–564. See also Reich, *Quest for Peace*, p. 374.

9. Kissinger, *White House Years*, pp. 550–551. See also Bard, *The Water's Edge and Beyond*, p. 300; David Pollock, *The Politics of Pressure: American Arms and Israeli Policy Since the Six Day War* (Westport: Greenwood Press, 1982), *passim*.

10. For an analysis of these crises, see Ben-Zvi, *The Limits of the Special Relationship*, chapters 4–5.

11. See, for example, Bard, *The Water's Edge and Beyond*, pp. 20–25; 267–287.

12. Organski, *The $36 Billion Bargain*, p. 27.

13. See Shibley Telhami and Jon Krasnick, "U.S. Public Attitudes Toward Israel: A Study of the Attentive and Issue Publics," *Israel Affairs* 2(3–4) (Spring/Summer 1996): 123–124; Thomas W. Lippman, "Clinton Steps Up Criticism of Israeli Housing Project," *The Washington Post*, March 11, 1997, p. A11; Duncan L. Clarke, "U.S. Security Assistance to Egypt and Israel: Politically Untouchable?" *The Middle East Journal* 51(2) (Spring 1997): 210.

Selected Bibliography

The following list includes the major works, which address or relate to various facets, theoretical or historical, of American-Israeli relations as they unfolded during the decade 1953–1962 as an integral part of the overall American posture in the Middle East.

Adams, Sherman. *Firsthand Report: The Story of the Eisenhower Administration.* New York: Harper and Row, 1961.

Agwani, M.S., ed. *The Lebanese Crisis, 1958.* New York: Asia Publishing House, 1965.

Alteras, Isaac. *Eisenhower and Israel: US-Israeli Relations, 1953–1960.* Gainesville: University Press of Florida, 1993.

Aronson, Geoffrey. *From Sideshow to Center Stage: US Policy Toward Egypt, 1946–1956.* Boulder: Westview Press, 1986.

Aronson, Shlomo. *Conflict and Bargaining in the Middle East.* Baltimore: Johns Hopkins University Press, 1978.

———. *The Politics and Strategy of Nuclear Weapons in the Middle East: Opacity, Theory, and Reality: 1960–1991.* Albany: State University of New York Press, 1992.

Axelrod, Robert. *The Evolution of Cooperation.* New York: Basic Books, 1984.

Badeau, John S. *The American Approach to the Arab World.* New York: Harper and Row, 1968.

———. *The Middle East Remembered.* Washington, D.C.: The Middle East Institute, 1983.

Badeeb, Saeed M. *The Saudi-Egyptian Conflict Over North Yemen, 1962–1970.* Boulder: Westview Press, 1986.

Baldwin, David A. *Economic Statecraft.* Princeton: Princeton University Press, 1984.

Ball, George W., and Ball, Douglas B. *The Passionate Attachment: America's Involvement with Israel, 1947 to the Present.* New York: Norton, 1992.

Bar-On, Mordechai. *The Gates of Gaza: Israel's Road to Suez and Back, 1955–1957.* New York: St. Martin's Griffin, 1994.

Bar-Siman-Tov, Yaacov. *Israel, The Superpowers, and the War in the Middle East.* New York: Praeger, 1987.

Bar-Yaacov, Nissim. *The Israeli-Syrian Armistice: Problems of Implementation, 1949–1966.* Jerusalem: The Magnes Press, 1967.

Bar-Zohar, Michael. *Ben-Gurion,* Vol. III (Hebrew). Tel-Aviv: Am-Oved, 1975.

Bard, Mitchell G. *The Water's Edge and Beyond: Defining the Limits to Domestic Influence on US Middle East Policy.* New Brunswick: Transaction, 1991.

Barnett, Michael N., ed. *Israel in Comparative Perspective: Challenging the Conventional Wisdom.* Albany: State University of New York Press, 1996.

Barzilai, Gad. *Wars, Internal Conflicts, and Political Order: A Jewish Democracy in the Middle East.* Albany: State University of New York Press, 1996.

Beling, Willard A. *The Middle East: Quest for an American Policy.* Albany: State University of New York Press, 1973.

Bell, Corall. *Negotiations from Strength: A Study in the Politics of Power.* New York: Knopf, 1963.

Ben-Gurion, David. *The Restored State of Israel* (Hebrew). Tel-Aviv: Am Oved, 1969.

———. *My Talks with Arab Leaders.* New York: Third Press, 1972.

Ben-Zvi, Abraham. *The American Approach to Superpower Collaboration in the Middle East, 1973–1986.* Boulder: Westview Press, 1986.

———. *The Illusion of Deterrence: The Roosevelt Presidency and the Origins of the Pacific War.* Boulder: Westview Press, 1987.

———. *The United States and Israel: The Limits of the Special Relationship.* New York: Columbia University Press, 1993.

Bercovitch, Jacob, and Jeffrey Z. Rubin, eds. *Mediation in International Relations: Multiple Approaches to Conflict Management.* London: Macmillan, 1992.

———, and Allison Houston, eds. *Resolving International Conflicts:The Theory and Practice of Mediation.* Boulder: Lynne Reinner Publishers, 1996.

Berman, Maureen R., and Joseph E. Johnson, eds. *Unofficial Diplomats.* New York: Columbia University Press, 1977.

Bialer, Uri. *Between East and West: Israel's Foreign Policy Orientation, 1948–1956.* Cambridge: Cambridge University Press, 1990.

Binder, Leonard, ed. *Politics in Lebanon.* New York: Wiley Books, 1966.

Blitzer, Wolf. *Between Washington and Jerusalem.* New York: Oxford University Press, 1985.

Brands, Henry William, Jr. *Into the Labyrinth: The United States and the Middle East, 1945–1993.* New York: McGraw-Hill, 1994.

Brecher, Michael. *The Foreign Policy System of Israel: Setting, Images, Process.* New Haven: Yale University Press, 1972.

———. *Decisions in Israel's Foreign Policy.* New Haven: Yale University Press, 1975.

Brown, L. Carl. *International Politics and the Middle East: Old Rules, Dangerous Game.* Princeton: Princeton University Press, 1984.

Brown, Seyom. *The Faces of Power: Constancy and Change in United States Foreign Policy from Truman to Clinton.* New York: Columbia University Press, 1994.

Bundy, McGeorge. *Danger and Survival: Choices About the Bomb in the First Fifty Years.* New York: Random House, 1988.

Burns, William J. *Economic Aid and American Policy Toward Egypt, 1955–1981.* Albany: State University of New York Press, 1985.

Campbell, John C. *Defense of the Middle East: Problems of American Policy*. New York: Praeger, 1960.

Carter, Barry E. *International Economic Sanctions*. Cambridge: Harvard University Press, 1988.

Clifford, Clark. *Counsel to the President: A Memoir*. New York: Random House, 1991.

Cockburn, Andrew, and Leslie Cockburn. *Dangerous Liaison: The Inside Story of the U.S.-Israeli Relationship*. London: Bodley Head, 1992.

Cohen, Michael J. *Truman and Israel*. Berkeley: University of California Press, 1990.

———. *Fighting World War Three from the Middle East: Allied Contingency Plans, 1945–1954*. London: Frank Cass, 1997.

Cohen, Raymond. *Culture and Conflict in Egyptian-Israeli Relations: A Dialogue of the Deaf*. Bloomington: Indiana University Press, 1990.

———. *Negotiating Across Cultures: Communication Obstacles in International Diplomacy*. Washington, DC.: United States Institute of Peace Press, 1991.

Cohen-Shany, Shmuel. *Paris Operation: Intelligence and Quiet Diplomacy in a New State*. Tel-Aviv: Ramot, 1994.

Copeland, Miles. *The Game of Nations: The Amorality of Power Politics*. London: Weidenfeld and Nicolson, 1969.

———. *Without Cloak or Dagger*. New York: Simon and Schuster, 1974.

Cottam, Richard. *Foreign Policy Motivation*. Pittsburgh: University of Pittsburgh Press, 1977.

Craig, Gordon A., and Alexander L. George. *Force and Statecraft: Diplomatic Problems of Our Time*. New York: Oxford University Press, 1994.

Dallek, Robert. *The American Style of Foreign Policy: Cultural Politics and Foreign Affairs*. New York: Oxford University Press, 1983.

Daudi, M.S., and M.S. Dajani, *Economic Sanctions: Ideals and Experience*. London: Routledge and Kegan Paul, 1983.

Dayan, Moshe. *Diary of the Sinai Campaign*. New York: Harper and Row, 1957.

———. *The Story of My Life*. New York: William Morrow, 1976.

Donovan, Robert J. *Eisenhower: The Inside Story*. New York: Harper and Row, 1956.

Dowty, Alan. *Middle East Crisis: U.S. Decision-Making in 1958, 1970, and 1973*. Berkeley: University of California Press, 1984.

Doxey, Margaret P. *Economic Sanctions and International Enforcement*. New York: Oxford University Press, 1980.

———. *Economic Sanctions in Contemporary Perspective*. New York: St. Martin's Press, 1987.

Draper, Theodore. *Israel and World Politics: The Roots of the Third Arab-Israeli War*. New York: Viking Press, 1968.

Drinan, Robert. *Honor the Promise: America's Commitment to Israel*. Garden City: Doubleday, 1977.

Eban, Abba. *An Autobiography*. Tel-Aviv: Steimatzky, 1977.

———. *Personal Witness: Israel Through My Eyes*. New York: Putnam's Sons, 1992.

Eisenhower, Dwight D. *The White House Years: Mandate for Change, 1953–1956.* New York: Doubleday, 1963.
————. *The White House Years: Waging Peace, 1956–1961.* New York: Doubleday, 1965.
Elath, Eliahu. *Through the Mist of Time: Reminiscences* (Hebrew). Jerusalem: Yad Izhak Ben-Zvi, 1989.
Evans, Peter B., Harold K. Jacobson, and Robert D. Putnam, eds. *Double-Edged Diplomacy: International Bargaining and Domestic Politics.* Berkeley: University of California Press, 1993.
Eveland, Wilbur Crane. *Ropes of Sand: America's Failure in the Middle East.* New York: Norton, 1980.
Evensen, Bruce J. *Truman, Palestine and the Press: Shaping the Conventional Wisdom at the Beginning of the Cold War.* Westport: Greenwood Press, 1992.
Evron, Yair. *War and Intervention in Lebanon: The Israeli-Syrian Deterrence Dialogue.* London: Croom Helm, 1987.
————. *Israel's Nuclear Dilemma.* London: Routledge, 1994.
Ewald, William Bragg, Jr. *Eisenhower the President: Crucial Days, 1951–1960.* Englewood Cliffs: Prentice-Hall, 1981.
Eytan, Walter. *The First Ten Years: A Diplomatic History of Israel.* New York; Simon and Schuster, 1987.
Falkowski, Lawrence S., ed. *Psychological Models in International Politics.* Boulder: Westview Press, 1979.
Feldman, Shai. *Israeli Nuclear Deterrence: A Strategy for the 1980s.* New York: Columbia University Press, 1982.
Ferrell, Robert H., ed. *The Eisenhower Diaries.* New York: Norton, 1981.
Finer, Herman. *Dulles Over Suez: The Theory and Practice of his Diplomacy.* Chicago: Quadrangle, 1964.
Fisher, Roger. *Basic Negotiating Strategy.* New York: Harper and Row, 1969.
Forsythe, David P. *United Nations Peacemaking: The Conciliation Commission for Palestine.* Baltimore: Johns Hopkins University Press, 1972.
Fraser, T.G. *The US and the Middle East Since World War 2.* New York: St. Martin's Press, 1991.
Freiberger, Steven Z. *Dawn Over Suez: The Rise of American Power in the Middle East.* Chicago: Ivan Dee, 1992.
Gaddis, John Lewis. *Strategies of Containment: A Critical Appraisal of Postwar American National Security Policy.* New York: Oxford University Press, 1982.
Garthoff, Raymond. *Detente and Confrontation: American-Soviet Relations from Nixon to Reagan.* Washington, DC.: The Brookings Institution, 1985.
Gazit, Mordechai. *President Kennedy's Policy Toward the Arab States and Israel: Analysis and Documents.* Tel-Aviv: The Shiloach Center, 1983.
Geldenhuys, Deon. *Isolated States: A Comparative Analysis.* Cambridge: Cambridge University Press, 1990.
George, Alexander L. and Richard Smoke. *Deterrence in American Foreign Policy: Theory and Practice.* New York: Columbia University Press, 1974.

_____, Philip J. Farley, and Alexander Dallin, eds. *U.S.-Soviet Security Cooperation: Achievements, Failures, Lessons.* New York: Oxford University Press, 1988.

_____, and William E. Simons, eds. *The Limits of Coercive Diplomacy.* Boulder: Westview Press, 1994.

Gerges, Fawaz A. *The Superpowers and the Middle East: Regional and International Politics, 1955–1967.* Boulder: Westview Press, 1994.

Gilboa, Eytan. *American Public Opinion Toward Israel and the Arab-Israeli Conflict.* Lexington: Lexington Books, 1987.

Glassman, Jon D. *Arms for the Arabs: The Soviet Union and War in the Middle East.* Baltimore: Johns Hopkins University Press, 1975.

Glick, Edward B. *The Triangular Connection: America, Israel, and American Jews.* London: Allen and Unwin, 1982.

Golan, Matti. *Shimon Peres: A Biography.* London: Weidenfeld and Nicolson, 1982.

Golden, Peter. *Quiet Diplomat: A Biography of Max M. Fisher.* New York: Cornwall Books, 1992.

Goldmann, Nahum. *The Autobiography of Nahum Goldmann: Sixty Years of Jewish Life.* New York: Holt, Rinehart and Winston, 1969.

Green, Stephen. *Taking Sides: America's Secret Relations with Militant Israel.* New York: William Morrow, 1984.

Greenstein, Fred I. *The Hidden-Hand Presidency: Eisenhower as Leader.* New York: Basic Books, 1982.

Grose, Peter. *Israel in the Mind of America.* New Hyork: Knopf, 1983.

Haas, Ernest B. *Beyond the Nation-State: Functionalism and International Organization.* Stanford: Stanford University Press, 1964.

Hahn, Peter L. *The United States, Great Britain, and Egypt, 1945–1956: Strategy and Diplomacy in the Early Cold War.* Chapel Hill: University of North Carolina Press, 1991.

Halperin, Samuel. *The Political World of American Zionism.* Detroit: Wayne State University Press, 1961.

Harder, Leon T. *Quagmire: America in the Middle East.* Washington, DC: Cato Institute, 1992.

Hersh, Seymour M. *The Samson Option: Israel's Nuclear Arsenal and American Foreign Policy.* New York: Random House, 1991.

Hertzberg, Arthur. *The Jews in America: Four Centuries of an Uneasy Encounter: A History.* New York: Simon and Schuster, 1989.

Herz, John H. *Political Realism and Political Idealism.* Chicago: The University of Chicago Press, 1951.

Hoffmann, Stanley. *Gulliver's Troubles, or the Setting of American Foreign Policy.* New York: McGraw-Hill, 1968.

Holland, Matthew F. *America and Egypt from Roosevelt to Eisenhower.* Westport: Praeger, 1996.

Hoopes, Townsend. *The Devil and John Foster Dulles.* Boston: Little, Brown, 1973.

Hufbauer, Gary Clyde, and Jeffrey J. Schott. *Economic Sanctions Reconsidered: His-*

tory and Current Policy. Washington, DC.: Institute for International Economics, 1990.

Huntington,, Samuel P. *American Politics: The Promise of Disharmony.* Cambridge: Harvard University Press, 1981.

Hutchison, Elmo H. *Violent Truce: A Military Observer Looks at the Arab-Israeli Conflict, 1951–1955.* New York: Davin-Adair, 1956.

Huth, Paul. *Extended Deterrence and the Prevention of War.* New Haven: Yale University Press, 1988.

Iklé, Fred Charles. *How Nations Negotiate.* New York: Praeger, 1963.

Immerman, Richard H., ed. *John Foster Dulles and the Diplomacy of the Cold War.* Princeton: Princeton University Press, 1990.

Inbar, Efraim, ed. *Regional Security Regimes: Israel and Its Neighbors.* Albany: State University of New York Press, 1995.

Issacs, Stephen D. *Jews in American Politics.* Garden City: Doubleday, 1974.

Janis, Irving L. *Groupthink: Psychological Studies of Policy Decisions and Fiascoes.* Boston: Houghton Mifflin, 1982 (2nd edition).

Jervis, Robert. *The Logic of Images in International Relations.* Princeton: Princeton University Press, 1970.

———. *Perception and Misperception in International Politics.* Princeton: Princeton University Press, 1976.

———, Richard Ned Lebow, and Janice Gross Stein. *Psychology and Deterrence.* Baltimore: The Johns Hopkins University Press, 1985.

———, and Jack Snyder, eds. *Dominos and Bandwagons: Strategic Beliefs and Great Power Competition in the Eurasian Rimland.* New York: Oxford University Press, 1991.

Kahneman, Daniel, Paul Slovak, and Amos Tversky. *Judgment Under Uncertainty: Heuristics and Biases.* New York: Cambridge University Press, 1982.

Kaplan, Robert D. *The Arabists: The Romance of an American Elite.* New York: The Free Press, 1993.

Kaufman, Burton I. *The Arab Middle East and the United States: Inter-Arab Rivalry and Superpower Diplomacy.* New York: Twayne Publishers, 1996.

Kaufman, Menachem, ed., *The American People and the Holy Land: Foundations of a Special Relationship.* Jerusalem: The Magnes Press, 1997.

Kaufmann, William W. *The Requirements of Deterrence.* Princeton: Center for International Studies, 1954.

Kenen, Isaiah L. *Israel's Defense Line: Her Friends and Foes in Washington.* Buffalo: Prometheus Books, 1981.

Kennedy, John F. *The Strategy of Peace.* New York: Harper and Row, 1960.

Kerr, Malcolm. *The Arab Cold War.* Oxford: Oxford University Press, 1971.

Kissinger, Henry. *White House Years.* Boston: Little, Brown, 1979.

———. *Diplomacy.* New York: Simon and Schuster, 1994.

Klieman, Aaron S. *Israel and the World After 40 Years.* New York: Pergamon-Brassey's, 1990.

Knorr, Klaus, ed. *Historical Dimensions of National Security Problems.* Laurence: University Press of Kansas, 1976.

_____, and Frank N. Trager, eds. *Economic Issues and National Security*. Lawrence: University of Kansas Press, 1977.

_____, and Patrick M. Morgan, eds. *Strategic Military Surprises: Incentives and Opportunities*. New Brunswick: Transaction Books, 1984.

Kollek, Teddy. *For Jerusalem: A Life*. London: Weidenfeld and Nicolson, 1978.

Korbani, Agnes G. *Intervention in Lebanon, 1958 and 1982: Presidential Decisionmaking*. New York: Praeger, 1991.

Krasner, Stephen D. *Defending the National Interest: Raw Materials Investments and U.S. Foreign Policy*. Princeton: Princeton University Press, 1978.

Kriesberg, Louis. *International Conflict Resolution: The U.S.-USSR and Middle East Cases*. New Haven: Yale University Press, 1992.

Kunz, Diane. *The Economic Diplomacy of the Suez Crisis*. Chapel Hill: The University of North Carolina Press, 1991.

_____, ed. *The Diplomacy of the Crucial Decade: American Foreign Policy in the 1960s*. New York: Columbia University Press, 1994.

Lauren, Paul Gordon, ed. *Diplomacy: New Approaches in History, Theory and Policy*. New York: The Free Press, 1979.

Lebow, Richard Ned, and Janice Gross Stein. *When Does Deterrence Succeed and How Do We Know*. Ottawa: Canadian Institute for International Peace, 1990.

_____. *We All Lost the Cold War*. Princeton: Princeton University Press, 1994.

Lenczowski, George. *The Middle East in World Affairs*. Ithaca: Cornell University Press, 1980.

_____. *American Presidents and the Middle East*. Durham: Duke University Press, 1990.

Lesch, David W. *Syria and the United States: Eisenhower's Cold War in the Middle East*. Boulder: Westview Press, 1992.

_____. *The Middle East and the United States: A Historical and Political Reassessment*. Boulder: Westview Press, 1996.

Levite, Ariel. *Offense and Defense in Israeli Military Doctrine*. Boulder: Westview Press, 1989.

Leyton-Brown, David. ed. *The Utility Of International Economic Sanctions*. New York: St. Martin's Press, 1987.

Lieber, Robert J. *No Common Power: Understanding International Relations*. New York: Harper Collins, 1995.

Lieberman, Elli. *Deterrence Theory: Success or Failure in Arab-Israeli Wars?* Washington, DC.: Institute for National strategic Studies, 1995.

Lloyd, Selwyn. *Suez 1956: A Personal Account*. London: Jonathan Cape, 1978.

Lockhart, Charles. *Bargaining in International Conflicts*. New York: Columbia University Press, 1979.

Losman, Donald L. *International Economic Sanctions: The Cases of Cuba, Israel, and Rhodesia*. Albuquerque: University of New Mexico Press, 1980.

Louis, Roger, and Roger Owen, eds. *Suez 1956: The Crisis and its Consequences*. Oxford: Clarendon Press, 1989.

Love, Kenneth. *Suez: The Twice-Fought War*. New York: McGraw-Hill, 1969.

Lucas, W. Scott. *Divided We Stand: Britain, the U.S., and the Suez Crisis.* London: Holder and Stoughton, 1991.

Macmillan, Harold. *Riding the Storm, 1956–1959.* London: Macmillan, 1971.

Maoz, Zeev. *Paradoxes of War: On the Art of National Self-Entrapment.* Boston: Unwin Hyman, 1990.

———. *National Choices and International Processes.* Cambridge: Cambridge University Press, 1990.

Marantz, Paul, and Blema S. Steinberg, eds. *Superpower Involvement in the Middle East: Dynamics of Foreign Policy.* Boulder: Westview Press, 1985.

Martin, Lawrence, ed. *Strategic Thought in the Nuclear Age.* London: Heinemann, 1979.

Martin, Lisa L. *Coercive Cooperation: Explaining Multilateral Economic Sanctions.* Princeton: Princeton University Press, 1992.

Maxwell, Stephen. *Rationality and Deterrence.* London: International Institute of Strategic Studies, 1968.

McMahon, Robert J. *The Cold War on the Periphery: The United States, India, and Pakistan.* New York: Columbia University Press, 1994.

Mearsheimer, John. *Conventional Deterrence.* Ithaca: Cornell University Press, 1983.

Melanson, Richard, and David Mayers, eds. *Reevaluating Eisenhower: American Foreign Policy in the 1950s.* Chicago: University of Illinois Press, 1987.

Melman, Yossi, and Dan Raviv. *Friends in Deed: Inside the U.S.-Israel Alliance.* New York: Hyperion, 1994.

Miller, Aaron David. *Search for Security: Saudi Arabian Oil and American Foreign Policy.* Chapel Hill: University of North Carolina Press, 1980.

Miller, Benjamin. *When Opponents Cooperate: Great Power Conflict and Collaboration in World Politics.* Ann Arbor: The University of Michigan Press, 1995.

Miscamble Wilson D. *George F. Kennan and the Making of American Foreign Policy, 1947–1950.* Princeton: Princeton University Press, 1992.

Morgan, Patrick M. *Deterrence: A Conceptual Analysis.* Beverly Hills: Sage Library of Social Science, 1983.

Morris, Benny. *Israel's Border War, 1949–1956.* Oxford: Clarendon Press, 1993.

Mosley, Leonard. *Power Play: Oil in the Middle East.* New York: Random House, 1973.

Neff, Donald. *Warriors at Suez: Eisenhower Takes America into the Middle East.* New York: Simon and Schuster, 1981.

Neustadt, Richard E. *Alliance Politics.* New York; Columbia University Press, 1970.

Nincic, Miroslav, and Peter Wallensteen, eds. *Dilemmas of Economic Coercion in World Politics.* New York: Praeger, 1983.

Nye, Joseph S. *The Making of America's Soviet Policy.* New Haven: Yale University Press, 1984.

Oren, Michael B. *Origins of the Second Arab-Israel War: Egypt, Israel and the Great Powers: 1952–1956.* London: Frank Cass, 1992.

Organski, A.F.K. *The $36 Billion Bargain: Strategy and Politics in U.S. Assistance to Israel.* New York: Columbia University Press, 1990.

Osgood, Charles E. *An Alternative to War or Surrender*. Urbana: University of Illinois Press, 1962.

Osgood, Robert Endicott. *Ideals and Self-Interest in America's Foreign Relations*. Chicago: The University of Chicago Press, 1953.

Oye, Kenneth A., Robert J. Lieber, and Donald Rothschild, eds. *Eagle Defiant: US Foreign Policy in the 1980s*. Boston: Little Brown, 1982.

————, ed. *Cooperation Under Anarchy*. Princeton: Princeton University Press, 1986.

Painter, David S. *Oil and the American Century: The Political Economy of U.S. Foreign Oil Policy, 1941–1954*. Baltimore: Johns Hopkins University Press, 1986.

Parker, Richard. *The Politics of Miscalculation in the Middle East*. Bloomington: Indiana University Press, 1993.

Parmet, Herbert S. *JFK: The Presidency of John F. Kennedy*. New York: Dial Press, 1983.

Patchen, Martin. *Resolving Disputes Between Nations: Coercion or Conciliation?* Durham: Duke University Press, 1988.

Paterson, Thomas, ed. *Kennedy's Quest for Victory: American Foreign Policy, 1961–1963*. New York: Oxford University Press, 1989.

Peres, Shimon. *David's Sling*. New York: Random House, 1970.

Princen, Thomas. *Intermediaries in International Conflict*. Princeton: Princeton University Press, 1992.

Polk, William R. *The United States and the Arab World*. Cambridge: Harvard University Press, 1975.

Pollock, David. *The Politics of Pressure: American Arms and Israeli Policy Since the Six Day War*. Westport: Greenwood Press, 1982.

Powell, Lee Reiley. *J. William Fulbright and his Time*. Memphis: Guild Binding Press, 1996.

Quandt, William B. *Decade of Decisions: American Policy Toward the Arab-Israeli Conflict, 1967–1976*. Berkeley: University of California Press, 1977.

————. *Camp David: Peacemaking and Politics*. Washington, DC.: The Brookings Institution, 1986.

————. *Peace Process: American Diplomacy and the Arab-Israeli Conflict Since 1967*. Washington, DC.: The Brookings Institution, 1993.

Qubain, Fahim I. *Crisis in Lebanon*. Washington, DC.: The Middle East Institute, 1961.

Rafael, Gideon. *Destination Peace: Three Decades of Israeli Foreign Policy*. New York: Stein and Day, 1981.

Ray, James Lee. *The Future of American-Israeli Relations: A Parting of the Way?* Lexington: The University Press of Kentucky, 1985.

Reich, Bernard. *Quest for Peace: United States-Israel Relations and the Arab-Israeli Conflict*. New Brunswick: Transaction Books, 1977.

————. *The United States and Israel: Influence in the Special Relationship*. New York: Praeger, 1984.

————. *Securing the Covenant: United States-Israel Relations After the Cold War*. Westport: Praeger, 1995.

Renwick, Robin. *Economic Sanctions*. Cambridge: Harvard Studies in International, 1981.

————. *Fighting With Allies: America and England at Peace and War*. New York: Times Books, 1996.

Rosenau, James N., ed. *International Politics and Foreign Policy*. New York: The Free Press, 1969.

————. *The Scientific Study of Foreign Policy*. New York: Nichols, 1980.

Rubenberg, Cheryl A. *Israel and the American National Interest: A Critical Examination*. Urbana: University of Illinois Press, 1986.

Rubin, Barry. *Secrets of State: The State Department and the Struggle Over U.S. Foreign Policy*. New York: Oxford University Press, 1985.

Rusk, Dean. *As I Saw It*. New York: Norton, 1990.

Russett, Bruce, ed. *Peace, War, and Numbers*. Beverly Hills: Sage, 1972.

Safran, Nadav. *From War to War: The Arab-Israeli Confrontation, 1948–1967*. New York: Pegasus, 1969.

————. *Israel: The Embattled Ally*. Cambridge: The Belknap Press of Harvard University Press, 1978.

Salomon, George, ed. *Jews in the Mind of America*. New York: Basic Books, 1966.

Saunders, Bonnie F. *The United States and Arab Nationalism: The Syrian Case, 1953–1960*. Westport: Praeger, 1996.

Schelling, Thomas C. *The Strategy of Conflict*. New York: Oxford University Press, 1963.

————. *Arms and Influence*. New Haven: Yale University Press, 1966.

Schlesinger, Arthur M. Jr. *The Cycles of American History*. Boston: Houghton Mifflin, 1986.

Schoenbaum, David. *The United States and the State of Israel*. New York: Oxford University Press, 1993.

Shaked, Haim, and Itamar Rabinovich, eds. *The Middle East and the United States: Perceptions and Policies*. New Brunswick: Transaction Books, 1980.

Shalev, Aryeh. *Cooperation Under the Shadow of Conflict: The Israeli-Syrian Armistice Regime, 1949–1955* (Hebrew). Tel-Aviv: Ma'arachot, 1989.

Shalom, Zaki. *David Ben-Gurion, the State of Israel, and the Arab World, 1949–1956* (Hebrew). Sede Boker: The Ben-Gurion Research Center, 1995.

Sharett, Moshe. *Personal Diary*, Vols. I-V, 1953–1956 (Hebrew). Tel-Aviv: Ma'ariv Book Guild, 1978.

Sheffer, Gabriel, ed. *Dynamics of Dependence: U.S.-Israeli Relations*. Boulder: Westview Press, 1987.

————. *Moshe Sharett: Biography of a Political Moderate*. Oxford: Clarendon Press, 1996.

Shimshoni, Jonathan. *Israel and Conventional Deterrence: Border Warfare from 1953 to 1970*. Ithaca: Cornell University Press, 1988.

Shoemaker, Christopher, and John Spanier. *Patron-Client State Relationships: Multilateral Crises in the Nuclear Age*. New York: Praeger, 1984.

Shuckburgh, Evelyn. *Descent to Suez Diaries, 1951–56*. New York: Norton, 1987.

Sigal, Leon V. *Fighting to a Finish: The Politics of War Termination in the United States and Japan, 1945.* Ithaca: Cornell University Press, 1988.

Silberstein, Laurence J., ed. *New Perspectives on Israeli History: The Early Years of the State.* New York: New York University Press, 1991.

Silverberg, Robert. *If I Forget Thee O Jerusalem: American Jews and the State of Israel.* New York: William Morrow, 1970.

Smoke, Richard. *War: Controlling Escalation.* Cambridge: Harvard University Press, 1977.

Snyder, Glenn H., and Paul Diesing. *Conflict Among Nations: Bargaining, Decision-Making and System Structure in International Crises.* Princeton: Princeton University Press, 1977.

Spiegel, Steven L. *The Other Arab-Israeli Conflict: Making America's Middle East Policy, from Truman to Reagan.* Chicago: The University of Chicago Press, 1985.

———, Mark H. Heller, and Jacob Goldberg, eds. *The Soviet-American Competition in the Middle East.* Lexington: Lexington Books, 1988.

Stein, Janice Gross, and David B. DeWitt, eds. *The Middle East at the Crossroads.* Oakville: Mosaic Press, 1983.

Stern, Paul C., Robert Axelrod, Robert Jervis, and Roy Radner, eds. *Perspectives on Deterrence.* New York: Oxford University Press, 1989.

Stevens, Georgiana, ed. *The United States and the Middle East.* New York: The American Assembly, 1964.

Stivers, William. *American Confrontation with Revolutionary Change in the Middle East, 1948–1983.* New York: St. Martin's Press, 1986.

Stock, Ernest. *Israel on the Road to Sinai, 1949–1956.* Ithaca: Cornell University Press, 1967.

Stookey, Robert W. *America and the Arab States: An Uneasy Encounter.* New York: John Wiley and Sons, 1975.

Telhami, Shibley. *Power and Bargaining in International Bargaining: The Path to the Camp David Accords.* New York: Columbia University Press, 1990.

Teveth, Shabtai. *Moshe Dayan.* London: Weidenfeld and Nicolson, 1972.

Thomas, Hugh. *The Suez Affair.* Harmondsworth: Penguin Books, 1970.

Tillman, Seth, P. *The United States in the Middle East: Interests and Obstacles.* Bloomington: Indiana University Press, 1982.

Tivnan, Edward. *The Lobby: Jewish Political Power and American Foreign Policy.* New York: Simon and Schuster, 1987.

Touval, Saadia. *Domestic Dynamics of Change from Confrontation to Accommodation Politics.* Princeton: Princeton University Press, 1973.

———. *The Peace Brokers: Mediators in the Arab-Israeli Conflict, 1948–1979.* Princeton: Princeton University Press, 1982.

Troen, Ilan Selwyn, and Moshe Shemesh, eds. *The Suez-Sinai Crisis, 1956: Retrospective and Reappraisal.* New York: Columbia University Press, 1990.

Walt, Stephen M. *The Origins of Alliances.* Ithaca: Cornell University Press, 1987.

Waltz, Kenneth. *Theory of International Politics.* Reading: Addison-Wesley, 1979.

Warren, Howe, and Sarah Hays Trott. *The Power Peddlers: How Lobbyists Mold America's Foreign Policy.* New York: Doubleday, 1977.

Waterbury, John. *The Egypt of Nasser and Sadat: Political Economy of Two Regimes.* Princeton: Princeton University Press, 1983.

Waxman, Chaim. *America's Jews in Transition.* Philadelphia: Temple University Press, 1983.

Weintraub, Sidney, ed. *Economic Coercion and U.S. Foreign Policy.* Boulder: Westview Press, 1982.

Wheelock, Keith. *Nasser's New Egypt: A Critical Analysis.* New York: Praeger, 1959.

Wittkopf, Eugene R. *Faces of Internationalism: Public Opinion and American Foreign Policy.* Durham: Duke University Press, 1990.

Wohlstetter, Robert. *Pearl Harbor: Warning and Decision.* Stanford: Stanford University Press, 1962.

Yaniv, Avner. *Deterrence Without the Bomb.* Lexington: Lexington Books, 1987.

Yergin, Daniel. *Shattered Peace: The Origins of the Cold War and the National Security State.* Boston: Houghton Mifflin, 1977.

Young, Oran. *The Politics of Force: Bargaining During International Crises.* Princeton: Princeton University Press, 1968.

———. *Bargaining: Formal Theories of Negotiation.* Urbana: University of Illinois Press, 1975.

Zagone, Frank C. *The Dynamics of Deterrence.* Chicago: The University of Chicago Press, 1992.

Zartman, I. William. *The Negotiation Process: Theories and Applications.* Beverly Hills: Sage Publications, 1977.

Zweig, Ronald W., ed. *David Ben-Gurion: Politics and Leadership in Israel.* London: Frank Cass, 1991.

Index

Abdullah, King of Jordan, 52
Abu Nuar, Ali, 67
Abu Sueir air base, 27
Adams, Sherman, 166–67n107
Adana, 69
AFL-CIO (American Federation of
  Labor–Congress of Industrial
  Organizations), 57
Africa, 19, 27, 35, 48, 63
Alpha Plan, 45, 48–51, 53, 61;
  concreteness of, 92; J. F. Dulles
  on, 23, 168n8; Gamma Plan
  and, 52; Sharett on, 23, 164n86,
  165n88
Alteras, Isaac, 56, 142n5
American-Israel Public Affairs
  Committee (AIPAC), 95, 96, 98
American Jews, see Jewish
  Americans
American Revolution, 11
American Zionist Committee for
  Public Affairs, 96
American Zionist Council, 98,
  181n5
Amman, 77
Anderson, Robert B., 51–52,
  158n47, 164n86, 166n94
Aqaba, 48
"Arab Cold War," 88
Arab countries: anti-Western, 36,
  88, 172n52; border disturbances
  and, 39; Byroade-Sharett discus-
  sion of, 152n6; defense role of,
  31; J. F. Dulles on, 33, 34, 36,

49; intelligence on, 83; Korean
  Peace Conference issue and,
  155n30; Lebanese intervention
  and, 172n52; military power of,
  84; proposed Negev concessions
  and, 23; pro-Western (see Pro-
  Western countries); repatriation
  to, 110, 112, 120; retaliation
  against (see Retaliatory raids);
  strategic importance of, 63;
  suspicions by, 52, 59–60, 98,
  124; sympathy with, 5; UAR
  founding and, 73, 171n43
Arab-Israeli relations: Alpha Plan
  and, 48, 51, 53; benign neglect
  of, 92; bipolar-confrontational
  strategy and, 28–29; Byroade
  on, 21–22, 33; Dimona issue
  and, 123–24; Egyptian/Syrian
  exploitation of, 70; Eisenhower
  on, 81; Hawk sale and, 15, 110,
  117, 121, 132; Israeli expansionism issue and, 45–46, 47;
  Johnson Plan and, 113, 114,
  116, 118, 119, 120; Jordanian
  Crisis and, 67, 78; Kennedy
  Administration and, 106, 107,
  111, 129; Komer on, 190n106;
  Nixon and, 135; NSC Planning
  Board on, 92; realist objectives
  for, 5; reassessment of, 61–62,
  63–64, 82, 89–91; Russell on,
  161n64; al-Said on, 72; security
  guarantees and, 20, 32, 50;